COLOR WHEELS
FOR THE HOME

COLOR WHEELS
FOR THE HOME

ThunderBay
P·R·E·S·S

San Diego, California

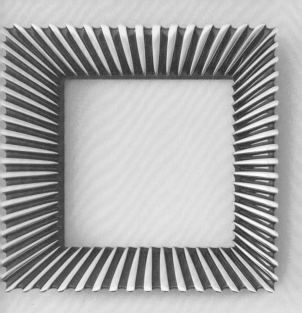

Thunder Bay Press
An imprint of the Baker & Taylor Publishing Group
10350 Barnes Canyon Road, San Diego, CA 92121
www.thunderbaybooks.com

All notations of errors or omissions should be addressed to Thunder Bay Press, Editorial Department, at the above address. All other correspondence (author inquiries, permissions) concerning the content of this book should be addressed to:

Axis Books Limited,
8c Accommodation Road
London NW11 8ED
United Kingdom

ISBN-13: 978-1-60710-300-4
ISBN-10: 1-60710-300-1

Printed in China
1 2 3 4 5 15 14 13 12 11

contents

Introduction

Color creates impact and atmosphere, and is one of the first things that people notice when entering a room. Color can make a home appear bright and fresh, or grand and formal; it can change the look and feel of a home almost instantly. Color also has mood-enhancing qualities, so it is essential that we surround ourselves with colors that we like and make us feel good inside our homes.

| 20 | 796 |

A bold combination of two complementary colors, orange and blue, creates an invigorating space that would suit a dynamic expressive type, but could overwhelm a more reclusive individual.

It is tempting when redesigning a home to choose colors that are in fashion at the present time. We are influenced by many factors; photographs in magazines, store displays, friend's homes, and television shows, for example, and it can be difficult to focus on what we actually like and respond to. It may be that you like a wide range of colors, and find it difficult to decide. The Home Color Selector can help you to refine your choices and understand how the choices you make will change the feel of your home. It can also help you to find ways to combine colors and work out which shades harmonize, and which will contrast. If you are trying to create a particular mood in your home, such as "tranquil," "elegant," or "fresh," you can turn to the relevant chapter and find the exact colors that will help you to achieve your aim.

Color schemes for lifestyles

When buying your home, you probably had an idea of the type of lifestyle you were hoping to create. A sophisticated, urban retreat to relax in at the end of the day, or a contemporary family home? An elegant country home or a fresh, light space where you can work? Choosing the right colors can help you to achieve the "feel" you desire. You may have a scheme already in your head, but want to check that it will work. Sometimes we want to repeat favorite colors that we have lived with before, or we want a complete change, or we may wish to try a scheme that we have seen elsewhere. Magazines and books are great for inspiration, but you also need to think about how they will work in your home and with your lifestyle.

For example, a minimalist scheme that uses neutral, tranquil colors may be ideal for a person who leads a hectic life, and longs for calm, but if you secretly crave a relaxing cocoon, you may need warmer colors in your home. A family with young children may find a neutral color scheme hard to maintain, but may want to capture that sense of calm as much as possible.

Strong, vibrant colors can bring energy and vitality to a home, especially in social areas, and may bring interest to a room that does not get good natural

175   4

The combination of deep red walls with the rich textures of the natural wood creates a warm cozy dining room, with a timeless elegance.

Introduction continued

82	815

Alternating areas of light and shade, and the cool color scheme of white walls with deep blue upholstery, combine to make a very contemporary room that is extremely tranquil.

light. Strong, rich colors create an atmosphere that we respond to immediately, while the effects of softer tones take longer for us to notice. However, it can be difficult to agree on strong colors, and in a shared home, they may be best restricted to accent colors.

If you yearn for bold colors, but your partner dislikes the idea, use the Home Color Selector to find colors that harmonize together, and use the bold colors in soft furnishings or art. Bear in mind that the colors in the rooms where we spend a long time will have a more profound and lasting effect on our moods than those in areas we just pass through. For example, a bold paint color on a feature wall in the hallway may lift your spirits when you enter your home, but may be overpowering in the main sitting room. A bold color in a child's room can be fun, but it may also stop them relaxing at bedtime.

In order to relax and feel comfortable, you need to find a color scheme that all the occupants of your home like. If a room is decorated in colors that make someone feel uncomfortable, they will instinctively avoid spending time there. This is the reason many of us walk into a new home and want to change everything. If you are constantly surrounded by colors you do not like, you will find it difficult to relax in your home. A strong color chosen by one person in the family may irritate others; for example, few men would feel comfortable in a pink room.

793   382

Light cool colors such as the blue of these kitchen cabinets in combination with the white walls and green plants help to reflect the maximum amount of light into the room, keeping it fresh and bright.

25   337

The deep firey orange of the color-washed walls could be overpowering, but here it is offset by the distressed timber paneling, and, with candles lit, makes for a sensual bathing experience.

how to use this book

This book is divided into three sections.

Chapter one:

Working with Color explains how to use the color wheel on the front of the book, along with an explanation of the basic principles of color theory. This includes how colors harmonize, together with an explanation of the key terms relating to working with color, such as hue, tone, and saturation.

Chapter two:

Color Personality contains an overview of how colors make us feel, and how we can use that to create the style of home we want. We introduce the moods that will be used in the Color Combinations section: tranquil, invigorating, elegant, sensual, and fresh.

Chapter three:

The Color Combinations section includes a comprehensive directory of color swatch combinations, so you can see at a glance which colors work together, and the effects combining colors will produce. The combinations are divided into moods and organized further into warm, cool, and neutral shades. Each color is from the Benjamin Moore paint range, so you can use the reference number to source the paint choice you have made.

main colors used in room sets enable instant access to unique color references

inspirational photographs demonstrate how color schemes and moods work in real homes and settings

each page features six color schemes based around the main mood color; all colors are selected from the Benjamin Moore Classic and Affinity ranges

choose the adjacent color swatch for monochrome schemes (see pages 22–23); these are easier to harmonize as all the hues are related

within elegant, tranquil, invigorating, sensual, and fresh, schemes are divided by warm, neutral, and cool

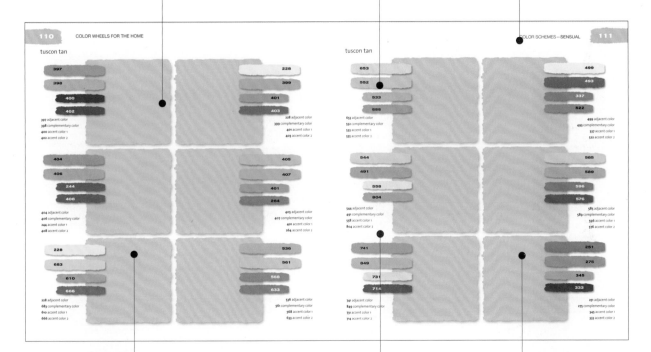

110 COLOR WHEELS FOR THE HOME

tuscon tan

397
398
400
402

397 adjacent color
398 complementary color
400 accent color 1
402 accent color 2

228
399
401
403

228 adjacent color
399 complementary color
401 accent color 1
403 accent color 2

404
406
244
408

404 adjacent color
406 complementary color
244 accent color 1
408 accent color 2

405
407
401
264

405 adjacent color
407 complementary color
401 accent color 1
264 accent color 2

228
683
610
666

228 adjacent color
683 complementary color
610 accent color 1
666 accent color 2

536
561
568
633

536 adjacent color
561 complementary color
568 accent color 1
633 accent color 2

COLOR SCHEMES—SENSUAL 111

tuscon tan

653
552
533
555

653 adjacent color
552 complementary color
533 accent color 1
555 accent color 2

499
493
337
522

499 adjacent color
493 complementary color
337 accent color 1
522 accent color 2

544
491
558
804

544 adjacent color
491 complementary color
558 accent color 1
804 accent color 2

585
589
596
576

585 adjacent color
589 complementary color
596 accent color 1
576 accent color 2

741
849
731
714

741 adjacent color
849 complementary color
731 accent color 1
714 accent color 2

251
275
345
333

251 adjacent color
275 complementary color
345 accent color 1
333 accent color 2

the color swatches are organized by adjacent and complementary color, then a choice of two accent colors; each color has a unique reference number so you can source the colors you have selected in the index to the Benjamin Moore color range

choose the complementary color if you like schemes that add vitality and energy into a room

select either accent swatch, or even both, to select a color suggestion for accessories and soft furnishing that will contrast and enliven your scheme

working
with color

When you walk into a room that has been designed by a professional interior designer, it usually feels "right." The room feels inviting, it has interest, and everything seems to work together. This is because a designer has learned how to bring color and texture together in ways that are harmonious and pleasing, without being safe or boring. Understanding some of the basic principals behind why some colors work together—and why some don't— will help you make choices you are happy with, and help create a professional look. It also helps to understand terms such as hue and saturation when working with design professionals. This chapter gives a brief overview of the basic ideas behind color theory, and how you can use it to your advantage.

the color wheel

Before you start choosing subtle shades, it is useful to understand how color works. Working out if colors go together, and whether they create harmony or contrast, is made easier by understanding how colors sit together on a color wheel.

A color wheel can help us to create color schemes that work. A color wheel is a visual way of showing how colors appear in the visible spectrum, as in a rainbow, from red to violet. The three primary colors are red, yellow, and blue, and most of us learn how to mix these at school, creating greens, purples, and oranges from these basic colors. Shown on a color wheel, the primary colors form the spokes of the color wheel. The greens, purples, and oranges are known as secondary colors, and these are also shown on the wheel. Tertiary colors are mixtures of primary and secondary hues, and form another triangle on the color wheel, each adding more complexity and variety.

Colors that are closest to each other on the color wheel are most harmonious. The colors on the opposite side of the wheel provide the greatest contrast; these are called complementary. For example, a harmonious scheme would include shades of blue and purple, while a contrasting scheme would include blue with orange. This color wheel shows bold colors but the same principle applies to more muted shades. Complementary colors balance and excite one another. You can use them to create lively contrasts and dramatic effects, for an invigorating scheme. Harmonious colors are a safer choice for an elegant or tranquil scheme.

ORANGE (SECONDARY COLOR)

Orange is a secondary color made up of red and yellow. It can be combined with its complementary color, blue, to create a warm and invigorating effect. When orange is combined with pale, neutral colors, such as cream, it creates a calm, warm, sensual effect.

YELLOW (PRIMARY COLOR)

Yellow is one of the three primary colors and works well with green shades. Imagine pale, crisp yellows and greens making a fresh, bright color scheme for a breakfast room. Yellow contrasts with purple and violet, which may look extreme in many adult rooms, but it would look fun in a child's bedroom. Pale shades of violet and yellow can work very well together, creating a lively contrast.

GREEN (SECONDARY COLOR)

Green is a versatile color. Dark, rich greens can work well in a formal, elegant room, especially when combined with harmonious blues and gold-yellows. Contrast with reds for eye-catching contrast that are perhaps best used in accessories. Pale greens are often teamed with pale yellows in wallpapers and soft furnishings, to create bright, fresh, but harmonious country schemes.

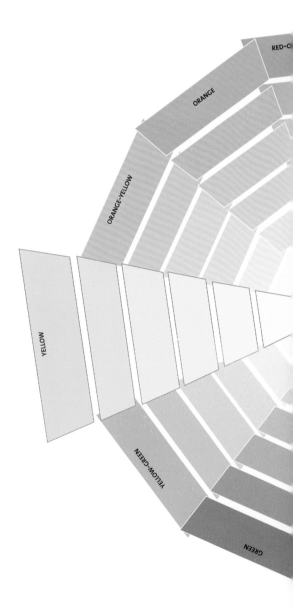

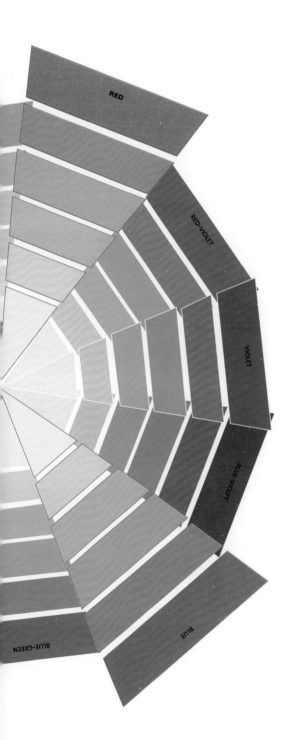

RED (PRIMARY COLOR)

The most powerful of the primary colors, red can be used to create a range of moods, from the comforting and cozy, to the dramatic and luxurious. It is harmonious with oranges and purples to create rich, sensual rooms. Using a small amount in a neutral room can add warmth and personality. Contrast red with blue or green for striking effects.

VIOLET (SECONDARY COLOR)

Purples and violets can be warm, rich, and luxurious. They are harmonious with blues and when used alongside warm neutrals, they can create very appealing room schemes. Purples contrast with oranges, which would be overpowering for many people, but used sparingly or for deliberate effect in art or soft furnishings, striking contrasts can add real impact to a room.

BLUE (PRIMARY COLOR)

A versatile color, blue can work well with its immediate neighbor, violet, both in pale pastel shades, and rich sensual shades. Blue and green are neighbors in nature, and also harmonize in many color schemes. Be aware that you need to choose shades from the same Color Personality section for harmony; a dark shade of blue would dominate a pale green, and vice versa.

HOW TO USE THE COLOR WHEEL

The color wheel on the cover of the book shows you some of the main colors from each color personality: tranquil, invigorating, elegant, sensual, and fresh. For example, if you want a blue scheme, you can turn the wheel to see which shades of blue will create each personality. If you want a bright, lively blue for a sunny kitchen room, turn the wheel to "fresh" to find a shade that will best suit your scheme. For an elegant evening room, turn the wheel to "elegant" to find a sophisticated shade. The wheel offers a small selection of shades to help you start your search; turn to the relevant chapters for more shades and combinations.

COMPLEMENTARY COLORS

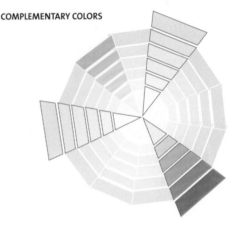

HARMONIOUS COLORS

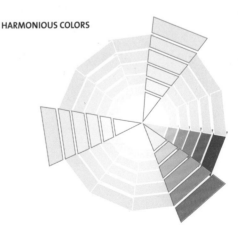

hues and saturation

Hue is another word for color. The colors on the spectrum color wheel are "pure" saturated hues. Saturation refers to the purity of a hue. When fully saturated, a hue is at its most intense.

We rarely choose colors for our homes that are strong and saturated, finding them too bold and rich. Most of us prefer more subtle, muted tones. Colors become less saturated when whites, creams, and grays are added. When we add white to pure hues they become lighter; this is known as a "tint." Tint shades appear more alive because they reflect more light than spectrum colors, and are often

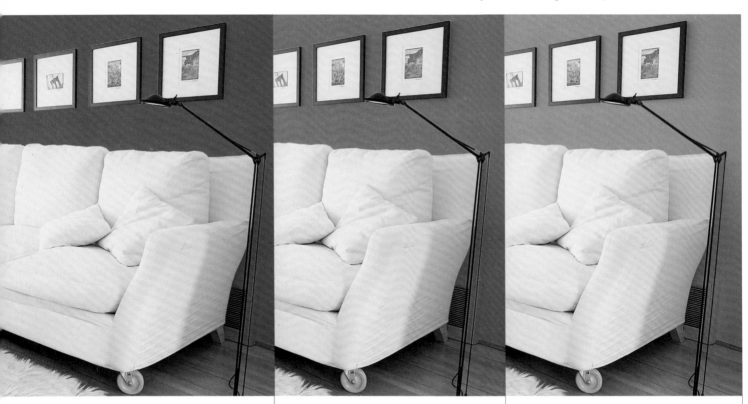

This is an example of using a fully saturated color, deep orange, to produce a rich effect, ideal for formal social events. Saturated hues can be combined with their complementary colors, such as orange with blue, to create a vibrant color scheme.

Here, a little white has been added to lighten the orange and create a warm, summery, and welcoming atmosphere, ideal for more informal social gatherings. The cream upholstery helps ensure that the overall effect is not too stimulating.

In this picture, much more white has been added to the orange to create a tint. By lightening the color of the background to this degree, the room now seems much more open and airy, suitable to be the main family room, and for general activities.

used to create fresh and invigorating schemes, as they help to bring light in to a space. Tints are often called pastels or powder colors; pink is a tint of red, while peach is a tint of orange. Tints are easy to live with. To create a harmonious scheme, you could use various tints from one color group. To create a contrasting scheme, choose tints from opposite sides of a color wheel. A "shade" is a hue to which black has been added, making it appear darker than the spectrum color from which it is derived. This can make a dramatic change. For example, adding black to red will turn it into maroon, while a shade of yellow will become brown. Decorating with a range of shades derived from the same color group can create an elegant, harmonious scheme, for example, creams with shades of chocolate brown.

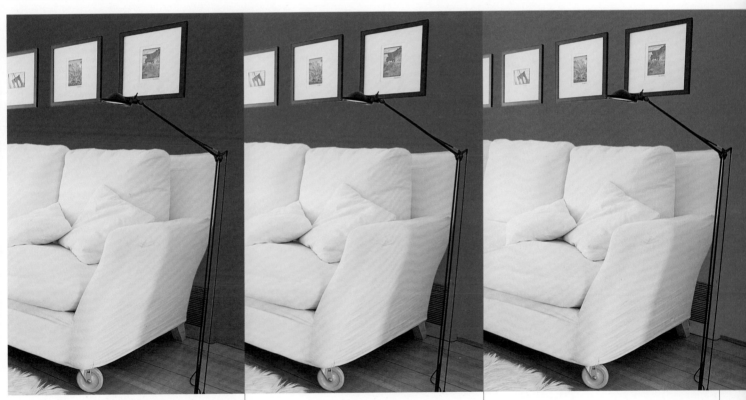

Deep saturation allows the hue's natural intensity and qualities to be used to maximum effect. Here, the deep indigo of the walls creates a cocooned space that feels warming, intimate, and secure—a haven on cold winter evenings.

Gray and white has been added to the pure hue to create a cooler, more subtle tone that is less vibrant and imposing. The room now seems more elegant, a suitable venue for activities such as light reading or study.

The more gray you add, the more muted and neutral the color becomes, creating a more subtle and less distinctive mood. The room appears both relaxing and inspiring, a place to recharge the batteries while planning the day ahead.

hues and tones

We talk about "tone" when talking about the lightness or darkness of one hue compared with another. A tone is light or dark depending on whether black, white, or gray has been added. The tone of a color can also indicate its brilliance and luminosity.

Tones are more muted and dusky colors, and they are less bright than the spectrum colors. A tone can be either light or dark depending on whether black has been added to a light color or white to a dark color. Tones are popular in decorating schemes, as the effect is matte and sophisticated, and creates a sophisticated, elegant look. They are ideal for social rooms such as sitting rooms, or dining rooms, and several tones of one color can be used together to create a harmonious scheme. Choosing the right tone for your room is therefore as im-portant as selecting the right hue. For example, if you want a blue room, but one that is elegant rather than invigorating, choose one of the blue tones from pages 50–85. A blue from another section would look too bright and jarring.

We tend to think of a color as just one tone, whereas a single color can often reflect more than one wavelength of light, giving it an iridescent quality like that of a peacock's feather or mother-of-pearl shell. The color showing through is known as an undertone.

These photographs show how different tones of yellow can create different schemes, from fresh to elegant.

RIGHT A pale tone of yellow creates a spacious and airy feel, ideal for a "fresh" scheme.

FAR RIGHT This yellow is slightly darker than the first but still has good saturation that creates an "invigorating" look.

Dark, fully saturated tones have
the most brilliance and intensity
and so make the most impact.
Use to create elegant, rich
schemes.

color temperature

When trying to achieve a certain feel in a room, think about whether you need a "hot" or "cold" temperature color. A room that does not get much natural light may need a "warm" color to add warmth and richness. Reds and oranges tend to have a warming effect, and blues tend to have a cooling effect on a room.

Generally, reds and oranges (the colors of fire) are warm, and blues and greens (the colors of sea, sky, and plants) are cool, with other colors on the wheel falling in between. However, it is not always that simple. Some blues are warmer than others, and some reds cooler than others. If a blue has a great deal of gray or white in it, it can look very cold. This would be a poor choice for a dark bathroom, which could look cold and uninviting. However, a blue that contains a lot of yellow can look warm and inviting. Similarly, a red that contains a lot of blue can appear cold; this can be a sophisticated color for an elegant scheme, but may be cold and uninviting in a dark room.

The temperature of a color is affected by its undertone and whether a hue has a warm or cool look. Every color can be regarded as either hot or cold depending on its undertone. So, for example, even though we think of red as being a hot color, it may well have a cool undertone. When you look through the Color Personality sections, you will see that there are "cool" colors in the fresh section, and "warm" colors in the elegant and sensual sections; although you may be looking for yellows, for example, each has its own distinct color temperature which can influence the final effect of your scheme.

This photograph enables you to see the effect of color temperature on a room. Generally, blue is the coolest color, relaxing and calming, and useful in quiet areas of the home. Greens are also cool.

Yellow is bright and cheerful, ideal for a sunny kitchen, for example. Orange and red are the warmest colors. Orange is cheery, while red is stimulating. You can make use of these qualities in your decorating schemes.

WARM AND COOL COLOR SCHEMES

When the walls of the room are a warm yellow, the effect is fresh yet inviting. If you have good natural light, this color would look bright. With poor natural light, this color would look darker and more formal. The same room shown in black and white.

When the walls of the room are a cool blue, the room looks colder, although still fresh. If your room had poor natural light, this blue may appear too cold. Although the rooms are different in feel and look, it is clear from comparing black-and-white photographs that the blue is similar to the yellow in terms of color value.

color harmonies and contrasts

Choosing colors that work well together is not always easy. For example, if you are cautious and choose whites and creams only, your scheme can look boring, cold, and unwelcoming. However, adding stark contrasting colors can make a room feel uncoordinated and cluttered. Successful color schemes use harmonious colors, with subtle contrast accent colors.

Knowing which colors work well together comes from trying colors alongside each other and really looking at the effect they create. Some people really know how to put colors together but it is always useful to check on the color wheel to see if you are right. The overall aim is to find the right balance so that the colors you use look harmonious and pleasing. Harmonious colors appear next to each other on the color wheel (see page 14), or use shades and tones of the same hue (see page 16). Choosing harmonious colors are essential if you are trying to create a sensual or relaxing scheme. You may want to introduce contrasting colors to liven up a fresh or invigorating scheme, but you can still aim for harmony.

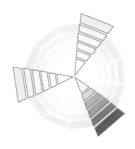

MONOCHROME HARMONY

A color scheme based on one color (monochrome) is an easy way to achieve harmony. Choose different shades and tones of a single color. You could choose the main color of your existing furniture and base your scheme on that. Turn to the Color Personality section that you want to achieve and vary the tones from very light to dark. In this picture, various shades of blue and white create a harmonious, interesting space. A dark shade has been used on the wall, and lighter colors have been used in the bed linen.

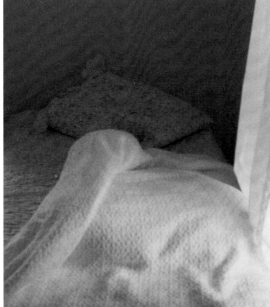

CONTRAST HARMONY

This form of harmony instills vitality and life into a basic color scheme by introducing touches of strong contrasting colors. Here for example, two contrasting accent colors, the red of the flowers and the blue-green of the vase, have been introduced into a monochromatic scheme so that they bring a much-needed excitement into an otherwise neutral, calm environment.

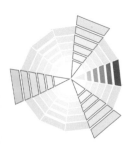

COMPLEMENTARY HARMONY

The purple and yellow work very well together, although from opposite sides of the color wheel. Subtle shades of the yellow and purple mean that this scheme is harmonious. Bright tones of purple and yellow would be too harsh and bright to live with in a bedroom. This effective scheme is elegant and sensual.

DECIDING ON A COLOR

One way of deciding whether colors are right for you is to consider carefully what your expectations are for your home. When choosing colors to suit your lifestyle, remember that the rules of color harmony still apply. For example, if you envisage that your home should be:

- a peaceful retreat: use soft tones, with greens, blues, and violets.

- a party house: use hot, bright, dramatic colors.

- a creative haven: use a mix of your favorite colors to stimulate the brain, or go cool and harmonious for a peaceful space.

- a place to relax: use neutral and light tones that create harmony and balance.

- a busy family home: use warm hues for living areas and cool colors for private spaces.

- a sensual, exotic space: use a combination of deep, rich colors, ideal for night time.

- an aesthetic masterpiece: use muted tones and a restricted palette.

ADJACENT HARMONY

This scheme uses colors that are next to each other on the color wheel. The blue-grays and the greens belong to the same family of colors, and naturally look good next to each other in a color scheme. The wooden cabinets would work well in most schemes. The silver of the range and hood adds light to the space and brings harmony to the scheme.

color
personality

The colors we use in our homes reflect our personalities, but they also have personalities of their own. These are based on their own qualities, but also on our personal associations. Associations may vary among cultures, but all colors trigger a personal, emotional response, based on memory and past experience. Colors remembered from childhood homes, for example, can evoke feelings of contentment that you may want to bring to your home, whether you know it or not.

The personality of a color can be a guide to where to use it in your home, as different colors can alter the way you respond to and use a room. Each section in this chapter will show you which colors will create a specific personality in a room. For example, if you want to create an elegant room, turn to the section on Elegant Colors (see pages 50–95) to find the colors that evoke that feeling. This is also useful if you are looking for a particular shade, and want to know what effect it will create. For example, if you are drawn to certain shades of blue, you may discover that you like fresh or invigorating shades, rather than warm sensual ones.

using color to change a room

The colors we choose for our home offer an important means of self-expression. They tell us who we are and reflect our attitudes, lifestyle, and what image we want to portray to the outside world. They also create a feeling in a home that anyone will pick up as soon as they enter.

A color's personality can transform a room. When choosing a room color, you need to take into account your personality and style preference, but you also need to consider the feeling you want to evoke and how you plan to use the room.

The personality of a color can be a guide to where to use it in your home, as different colors can alter the way you respond and use a room. If you want to feel more sociable, you might introduce red tones. If you prefer a qui-

eter life, introduce some calming colors, such as blues or greens. You may also choose colors because you want to create or convey a particular style or design idea. If you want to achieve a neutral, sophisticated look, turn to the elegant section (see pages 50–85) or the tranquil section (see pages 142–177). To create a warm, welcoming space, for example, in a family room, or an intimate dining area look at the section on invigorating colors (see pages 188–223).

PERSONALITY CHECKLIST

Outlines of the personalities of the main color groups are given below. As you select colors in the book, you may like to refer back to this list to see what your choices say about you, and what affect the colors will have in your home. Like everything in life, an excess can change a positive into negative, so it is wise not to use too much of any one color in your home.

RED
STRONG, VIBRANT

It is the color of blood, fire, and passion. At the same time, this eye-catching color is also the color of love and happiness. Red is warm, energetic, and vibrant. People who like red are dynamic and sociable. It would be a good choice for creating an invigorating or sensual space. Use red in family rooms or formal dining rooms, where activity counts over relaxation.

ORANGE
CREATIVE, FUN-LOVING

It is a striking color that we associate with the sun, ripe peaches, late-summer flowers, so orange has strong sensual connections and a built-in feel-good factor. Orange is as exciting as red, but less bold; it is ideal for brightening dull spaces. The orange personality is happy and favors companionship. Even lighter tones of orange are stimulating.

YELLOW
BRIGHT, ALERT

In daylight we feel safe, alert, and active, and so we think of yellow as a warm, friendly color. Yet we see green-yellow as decay in nature and so associate negative emotions with these hues. Yellow is bright and warming, and makes us feel optimistic, which is ideal for a room you use in the morning. A yellow household suggests a happy, healthy lifestyle, where the inhabitants are cheerful and full of ideas.

GREEN
HARMONIOUS, RESTFUL

Spring greens are linked to growth and youthfulness, and create a light, airy mood in a room, while darker greens are more lush and mysterious and make a much bolder statement. Soothing, fresh, and clean, green is the color of nature and growth, and is very relaxing. Dark, rich greens can be more formal, with elegant characteristics.

Consider also the function of the room. You may want your sitting room to be a sophisticated, tranquil space, ideal for evening entertaining. A bedroom will feel more relaxing if you choose colors for their sensual properties, rather than colors with stimulating properties. Yet you may need these spaces to link together, without clashing.

You may be choosing colors because you want to market your property and create a lifestyle that will appeal to specific buyers. An urban luxury apartment may suit elegant or tranquil colors, for example, and a tired property in need of updating may benefit from adding invigorating or fresh colors.

Before selecting your choice, remember to consider the size of the room and the amount of light it gets. A room that gets very little natural light may need fresh colors, or you may decide to go with the natural features, and make it a subdued, sensual room.

PINK

SECURITY AND TRUST

We are drawn to pink when we need reassurance. Loving and nurturing, the pink personality expresses the romantic nature of love so may be suitable for a bedroom. The inhabitants of a pink household are likely to be caring and compassionate to others.

PURPLE

DEEP, INTENSE, EMOTIONAL, EXOTIC

Purple stimulates the mind as well as the senses. People who favor purple like luxury and drama. People who live in purple homes are individuals. Time with them is unlikely to be forgotten. Purple can bring sensuality to a home.

NEUTRALS

FLEXIBLE AND RELAXING

Lovers of neutral shades value independence, and do not want to be pigeonholed. Tones of beige, gray, cream, and off-white are always popular and can provide a background to bolder color in soft furnishings and art. They can also be used alone to create a subtle, relaxing atmosphere.

VIOLET

DRAMATIC, MYSTERIOUS

This is reflected in the symbolism of this color in many religions and is reinforced by its appearance in nature. Sparkling minerals such as amethysts, and the patterns found in the iridescent plumage of some birds and on the wings of butterflies, make violet a color of surprise and wonder. It can be used to invigorate and freshen a room or add sensuality, depending on the tone.

BLUE

QUIET, SOOTHING

Dark blues have deeper and more mysterious associations, for example with the sky at midnight. It has a strong connection with sleep and dreaming, and can be ideal for creating an elegant evening room or a relaxing bedroom. Lighter blues can be calming and ideal for creating a tranquil space.

BLACK AND WHITE

SIMPLICITY AND PURITY

Shape and texture become more important in the absence of color. Black, white, and gray can be dramatic, but can be too severe to live with without using touches of accent colors. They can create an elegant, invigorating look.

tranquil colors

SPLENDOR

SAVANNAH CLAY

MEADOW PINK

NORTH CASCADES

WISPY GREEN

VIOLET MIST

IMPERIAL GRAY

DREAMCATCHER

VICTORIANA

Light neutrals help to maintain a feeling of space, and dark neutrals can be used to enlarge the appearance of a room by increasing its depth. Contrasting dark and light neutrals uses areas of shadow to create a room that is natural and tranquil.

To create a calm, peaceful, and tranquil space in your home, select colors in the Tranquil section. You can change the look and feel of a room by adding some cool, light colors. Light blues, greens, and neutrals are good choices. Faded tones are calming, but you can also introduce stronger accent colors to add warmth and comfort to a space. These stronger colors will also add personality to your space. Pastel shades of strong colors such as orange and purple can work (see pages 142–187), but choose the tones carefully.

Be careful when choosing colors with blue tones; they can feel cold. Test the color in your room throughout the day and see what effect light falling on the color has, and whether this creates the tranquil effect you are aiming for.

Shades of white on their own can be stark rather than tranquil. Think about choosing a harmonious or complementary color, perhaps for a feature wall, or in the soft furnishings. Try several shades of white, and experiment with paint finishes; matte and eggshell paints have a softer finish than many emulsions.

The natural coolness of a blue and white color scheme might not be an obvious choice for a bedroom, but contrasting it with the warm tones of the wooden bed has created a room that is a perfect place to seek tranquility.

LEFT Because of its calming effect and ties to water, blue is the most popular color for the bathroom. Combining blues and greens helps to emphasize that this as an area of relaxation and retreat.

RIGHT The basis of this calm bedroom is an adjacent harmony: palest yellow is the dominant color on the walls, with yellow-green in the alcoves.

invigorating colors

MOROCCAN SPICE

SUNRAYS

NOVA SCOTIA BLUE

WARM APPLE CRISP

LEMON GRASS

CHIC LIME

SOUNDS OF NATURE

TOOTY FRUITY

ROSE GARDEN

To create a lively, invigorating space use rich, warm hues. Using bright, hot harmonies will bring energy and vitality to your home—ideal for a breakfast room or bathroom. Warm reds, oranges, and yellows can bring richness and sunshine to a room. Very dark reds and oranges, however, can create a formal feel, so select the right tone for your lighting conditions.

Bright tones of most colors can create invigorating effects; lime greens, turquoise blues, and zesty lemons stimulate the mind and bring energy to a space. If a room has good natural lighting, these colors will enliven any room. Be careful that dark lighting conditions will dull these colors, and can create a murky effect.

If you are nervous to introduce large areas of an invigorating color, consider using it as an accent. Artwork, cushions, or a floor covering can introduce an invigorating color into a room, without overpowering.

TOP RIGHT Changing the color of, or adding cushions to a room is an easy and quick way of introducing strong color.

RIGHT The flowing curve of the mosaics, and the strong contrast between red and blue, bring an invigorating atmosphere to an otherwise neutral bathroom.

LEFT Yellow is a warm color without the heat of red or orange. Rather than stimulating the body, yellow energizes the mind, and when exposed to it, it can have a beneficial effect on our analytical capabilities.

LEFT Near opposites, such as blue and red, offer the benefit of contrast without being as dramatic as a pairing of true opposites. In this multi-function room, a blue/purple light has been used, which adds an intriguing bluish tinge to the white walls and sofa at night.

RIGHT Orange and red are great kitchen colors since they are known to stimulate the appetite; both are used in this funky scheme, top, which has plenty of white to lighten the mix.

LEFT The warm, natural woods used in this bathroom imbue it with a welcoming, earthy appeal. The deep blue sink provides a single block of color, which gives the scheme a modern twist.

elegant colors

BOTTLE OF BORDEAUX

PRINCESS

BALTIC GRAY

MAPLE SYRUP

WATERCOLOR BLUE

ICED GREEN

TREASURE TROVE

ALGONQUIN TRAIL

MARMALADE

When we think of elegance, we think of formal rooms, styled to make an impression. Elegant colors could be used in an entrance hall, a sitting room, or a dining room. Neutrals are ideal for creating elegant spaces; they are calm and sophisticated, and act as a backdrop to display items. Tones can be warm or cool, depending on the look you want to achieve. Taupes, whites, creams, and grays can evoke elegance, especially when teamed with textures in soft furnishings. Soft metallic colors can be elegant, if used as an occasional accent and can add warmth and glamour.

When thinking of elegance, also consider rich, luxurious colors, such as purples, reds, greens, and blues. Historically associated with wealth, rich color hues can add understated drama and opulence. Use sparingly as an accent to add warmth, especially to a formal evening room. Select tones that harmonize with your main neutral color to avoid garish clashing combinations.

The blue-gray kitchen cabinets against the soft cream of the walls provide a perfect setting for the rich plum island centerpiece, creating an elegant and timeless style.

Decorating your bathroom in colors that suggest water can really improve the way you use it. Using cool colors such as blues and greens make a bathroom look fresh, clean, and elegant, and can act as a reminder of revitalizing places by the sea, lakes, or rivers, that help create a positive frame of mind.

LEFT Neutral colors form the basis of this decorating scheme, enlarging the space and giving the room a relaxing feel. A golden-yellow statement wall makes an eye-catching feature and draws you toward the modern fireplace.

BELOW This is a modern take on the classic blue-and-white kitchen scheme; light blue walls are teamed with country-cream cupboards, and the stainless steel appliances bring the look right up to date.

sensual colors

ULTRA VIOLET

BURNT SIENNA

PARIS ROMANCE

TUCSON TAN

FREESIA

SECRET

DESERT VIEW

CROWNE HILL YELLOW

CORAL GLOW

To create an intimate space, perhaps in a bedroom or formal sitting room, sensual colors can be used to great effect. This group has two personalities: muted, soft and luxurious colors, and stimulating, rich colors. Select muted, warm creams, whites, and browns to provide a soft background to a scheme, and to suggest luxury and comfort. The sensual neutrals are subdued and subtle; nothing should be too bold or jarring; no bright whites or stark contrasts. Choose colors that are close in tone, and are adjacent on the color wheel; this will help to create harmony.

The second group is stimulating and rich, such as deep reds, burgundys, purples, and chocolate browns. Associated with passion and sensuality, these sensual colors evoke drama and excitement. Use sparingly to maintain subtlety; choose one bold color for a feature wall, or introduce to a neutral scheme with throws, cushions, and light fixtures.

RIGHT Using a purple will add a rich luxurious feel to a room, and when used with its complementaries, orange and yellow, it creates a warm and sensual space.

OPPOSITE The deep rich burgundy of the wall is enriched with the reflected light from the wood floor making for a dramatic entrance hall.

RIGHT Rich hues can be wonderfully opulent. The wine red used here is a powerful color, but the simplicity of the scheme and the use of plenty of pure white means it serves as a luxurious backdrop and does not overpower the room.

LEFT Subtle sea shades, such as this delicate blue-green, are perfect for the bathroom. Simple white paintwork and plenty of natural wood evoke the ambience of a beach-house retreat.

RIGHT Always consider the lighting when choosing the color for your living room. Dark shades work best when the windows are large and face west or south, to catch the strongest light in the early evening when the room comes into its own.

fresh colors

BUTTERED YAM

SAILOR'S DELIGHT

OLD STRAW HAT

HUSHED HUE

CRISP MORNING AIR

MINT JULEP

ORANGE FROTH

WISHING WELL

PINE FOREST

RIGHT The subtle orange tones in this breakfast room are ideal for stimulating the mind and gently invigorating the body for the start of a fresh day.

OPPOSITE Sky blue walls and natural wood are complemented perfectly by the foliage of the trees through the window, encapsulating all that is good on a fresh spring morning.

Bright, cheerful, and inspirational, fresh colors are ideal for family spaces, bathrooms, children's bedrooms, and morning rooms. Use to emphasize natural sunlight, or to inject brightness when a room lacks good natural daylight. Yellows, aquas, pale blues, and mint greens remind us of being outdoors, and being near the sea, and help to make a space feel fresh and bright.

For bathrooms, fresh blues and aquas are ideal colors, especially when teamed with bright whites. Clean and invigorating, these shades remind us of fresh water. Choose cool tones, rather than warm for freshness, especially in a sunny room. Be careful in darker rooms as these shades can appear cold. Bright and pale yellows are ideal for introducing freshness; choose a shade according to the light conditions in your room. Avoid mustard yellows. Bright, reflective whites can make any space feel fresh; avoid white with high gray content, as this can appear gloomy.

RIGHT There is strong visual contrast in this triadic scheme but it looks more balanced than a complementary harmony. It's a good way of creating a contemporary feel that is still restful and fresh. Here, green is the dominant color with accents of orange and violet.

LEFT White fixtures and tiles are always popular, because they look clean and crisp. A fresh color, like sunny yellow, on the walls and as a color accessory means the room looks anything but clinical.

RIGHT In a children's bedroom, plenty of brightly colored toys are likely to be on display. Choose a soft hue for the main color, to help create a relaxing ambience—and cast aside any thoughts of minimalism for the time being.

the color
combinations

The schemes in this chapter are created using a selection of colors from the Benjamin Moore Classic and Affinity ranges. Having decided on your scheme turn to the index on pages 280–288 to identify the unique BM number; this is all you need to take to the store and purchase your paint.

bottle of bordeaux

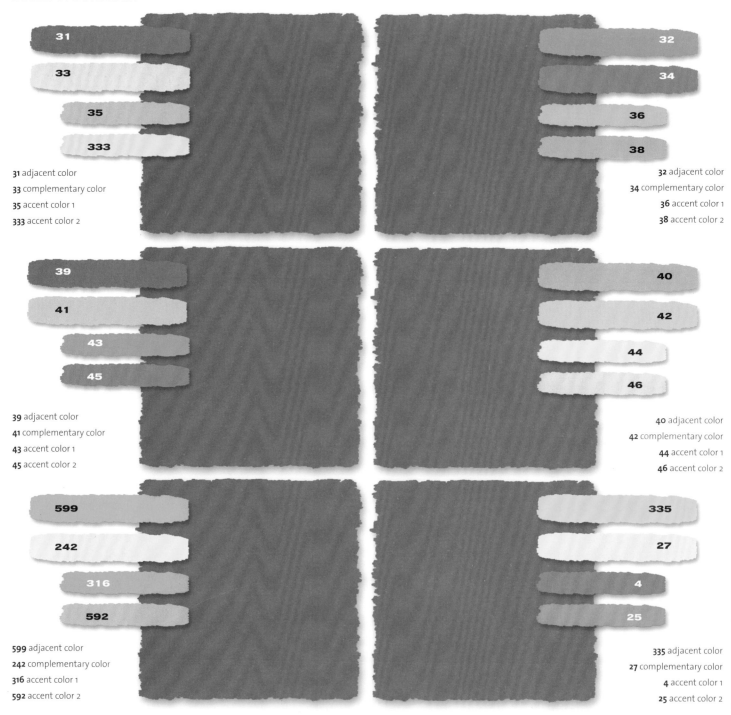

31 adjacent color
33 complementary color
35 accent color 1
333 accent color 2

32 adjacent color
34 complementary color
36 accent color 1
38 accent color 2

39 adjacent color
41 complementary color
43 accent color 1
45 accent color 2

40 adjacent color
42 complementary color
44 accent color 1
46 accent color 2

599 adjacent color
242 complementary color
316 accent color 1
592 accent color 2

335 adjacent color
27 complementary color
4 accent color 1
25 accent color 2

bottle of bordeaux

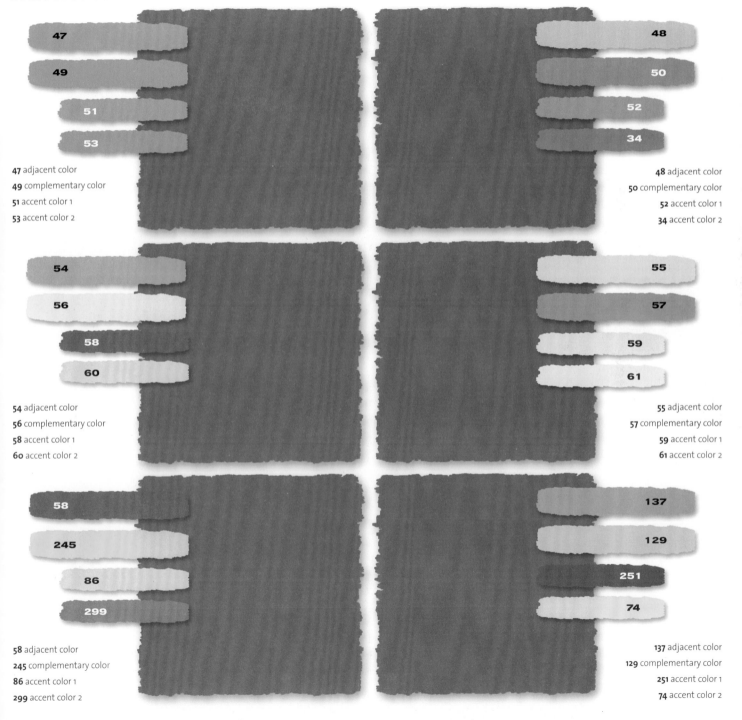

47 adjacent color
49 complementary color
51 accent color 1
53 accent color 2

48 adjacent color
50 complementary color
52 accent color 1
34 accent color 2

54 adjacent color
56 complementary color
58 accent color 1
60 accent color 2

55 adjacent color
57 complementary color
59 accent color 1
61 accent color 2

58 adjacent color
245 complementary color
86 accent color 1
299 accent color 2

137 adjacent color
129 complementary color
251 accent color 1
74 accent color 2

bottle of bordeaux

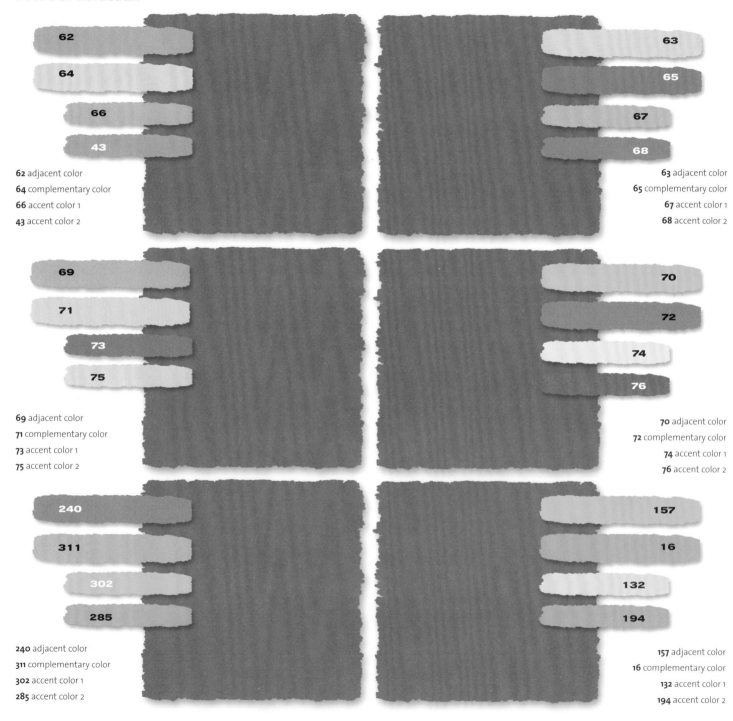

62 adjacent color
64 complementary color
66 accent color 1
43 accent color 2

63 adjacent color
65 complementary color
67 accent color 1
68 accent color 2

69 adjacent color
71 complementary color
73 accent color 1
75 accent color 2

70 adjacent color
72 complementary color
74 accent color 1
76 accent color 2

240 adjacent color
311 complementary color
302 accent color 1
285 accent color 2

157 adjacent color
16 complementary color
132 accent color 1
194 accent color 2

bottle of bordeaux

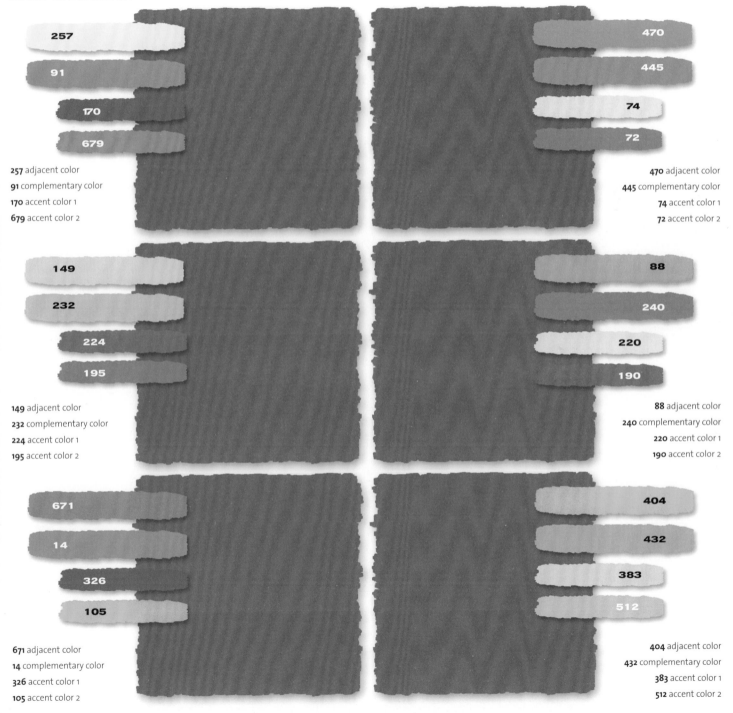

257
91
170
679

470
445
74
72

257 adjacent color
91 complementary color
170 accent color 1
679 accent color 2

470 adjacent color
445 complementary color
74 accent color 1
72 accent color 2

149
232
224
195

88
240
220
190

149 adjacent color
232 complementary color
224 accent color 1
195 accent color 2

88 adjacent color
240 complementary color
220 accent color 1
190 accent color 2

671
14
326
105

404
432
383
512

671 adjacent color
14 complementary color
326 accent color 1
105 accent color 2

404 adjacent color
432 complementary color
383 accent color 1
512 accent color 2

princess

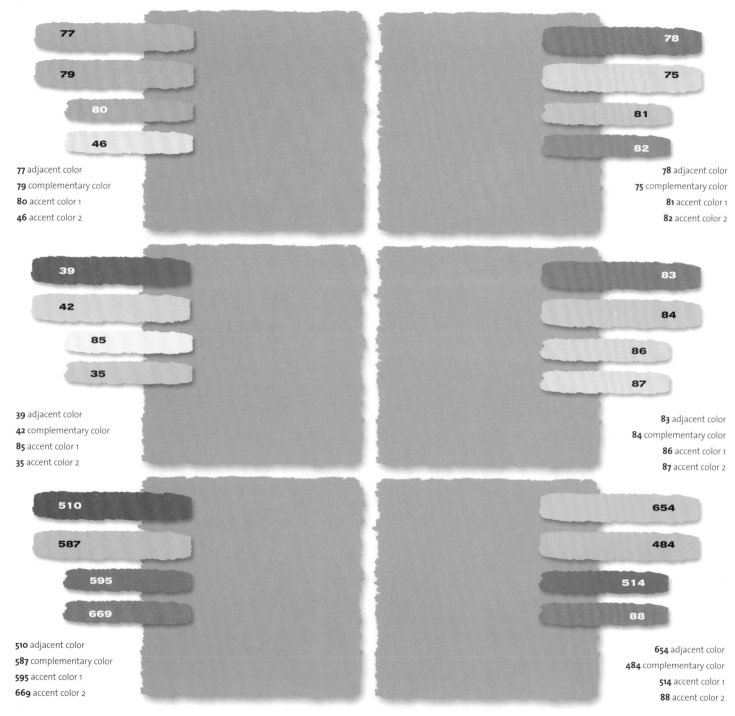

77
79
80
46

78
75
81
82

77 adjacent color
79 complementary color
80 accent color 1
46 accent color 2

78 adjacent color
75 complementary color
81 accent color 1
82 accent color 2

39
42
85
35

83
84
86
87

39 adjacent color
42 complementary color
85 accent color 1
35 accent color 2

83 adjacent color
84 complementary color
86 accent color 1
87 accent color 2

510
587
595
669

654
484
514
88

510 adjacent color
587 complementary color
595 accent color 1
669 accent color 2

654 adjacent color
484 complementary color
514 accent color 1
88 accent color 2

princess

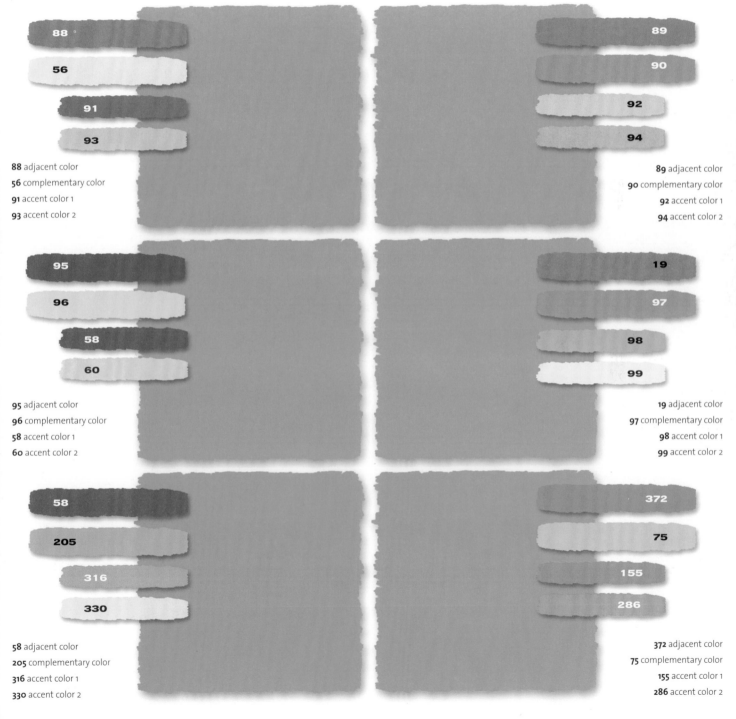

88 adjacent color
56 complementary color
91 accent color 1
93 accent color 2

89 adjacent color
90 complementary color
92 accent color 1
94 accent color 2

95 adjacent color
96 complementary color
58 accent color 1
60 accent color 2

19 adjacent color
97 complementary color
98 accent color 1
99 accent color 2

58 adjacent color
205 complementary color
316 accent color 1
330 accent color 2

372 adjacent color
75 complementary color
155 accent color 1
286 accent color 2

princess

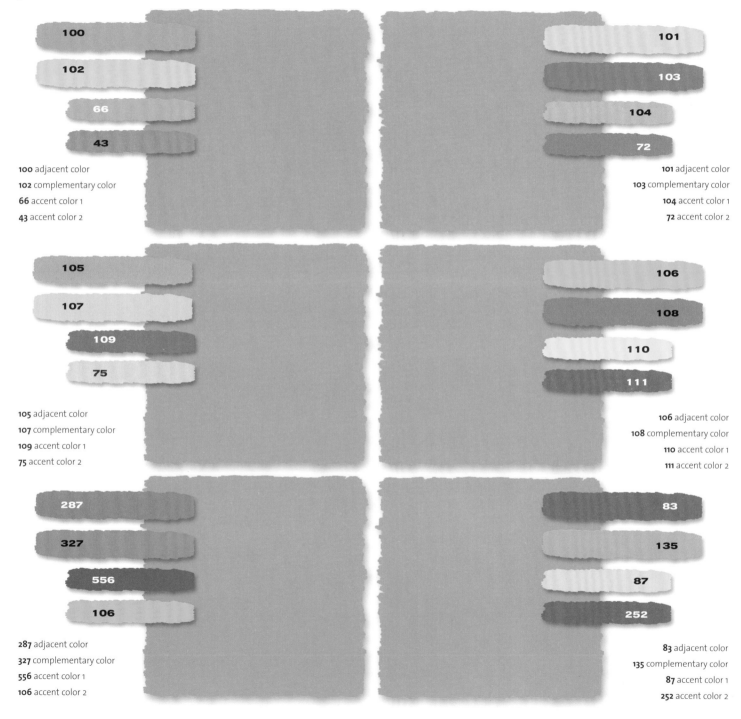

100

101

102

103

66

104

43

72

100 adjacent color
102 complementary color
66 accent color 1
43 accent color 2

101 adjacent color
103 complementary color
104 accent color 1
72 accent color 2

105

106

107

108

109

110

75

111

105 adjacent color
107 complementary color
109 accent color 1
75 accent color 2

106 adjacent color
108 complementary color
110 accent color 1
111 accent color 2

287

83

327

135

556

87

106

252

287 adjacent color
327 complementary color
556 accent color 1
106 accent color 2

83 adjacent color
135 complementary color
87 accent color 1
252 accent color 2

princess

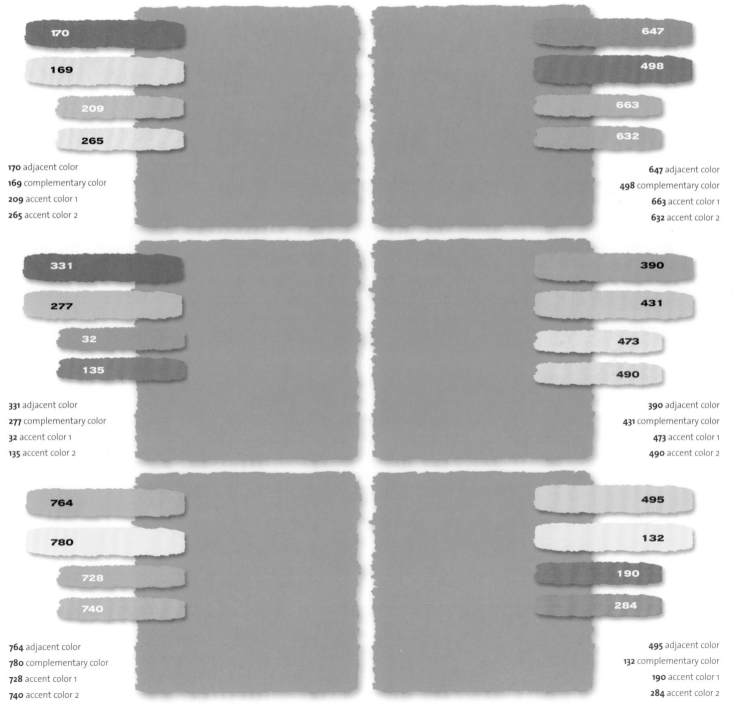

170 adjacent color
169 complementary color
209 accent color 1
265 accent color 2

647 adjacent color
498 complementary color
663 accent color 1
632 accent color 2

331 adjacent color
277 complementary color
32 accent color 1
135 accent color 2

390 adjacent color
431 complementary color
473 accent color 1
490 accent color 2

764 adjacent color
780 complementary color
728 accent color 1
740 accent color 2

495 adjacent color
132 complementary color
190 accent color 1
284 accent color 2

baltic gray

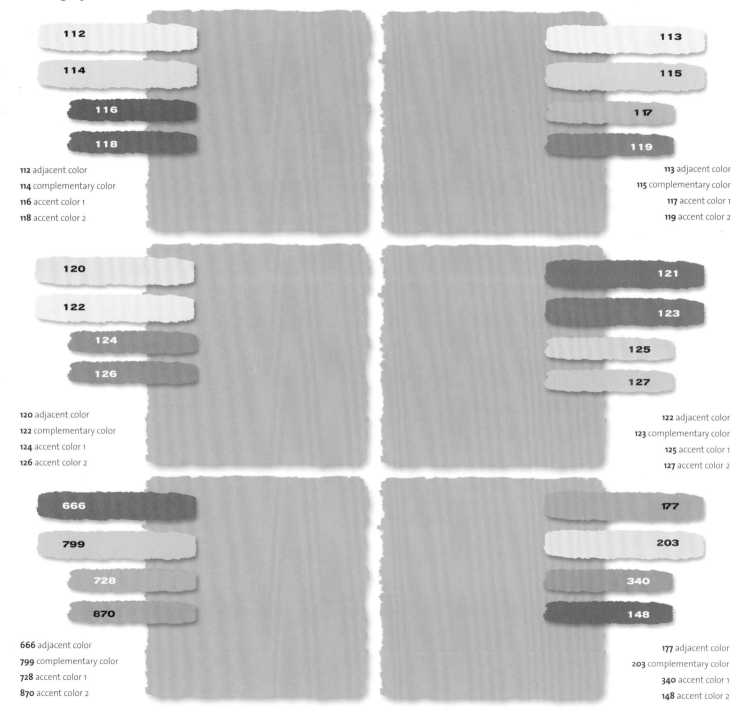

112
114
116
118

113
115
1 17
119

112 adjacent color
114 complementary color
116 accent color 1
118 accent color 2

113 adjacent color
115 complementary color
117 accent color 1
119 accent color 2

120
122
124
126

121
123
125
127

120 adjacent color
122 complementary color
124 accent color 1
126 accent color 2

122 adjacent color
123 complementary color
125 accent color 1
127 accent color 2

666
799
728
870

177
203
340
148

666 adjacent color
799 complementary color
728 accent color 1
870 accent color 2

177 adjacent color
203 complementary color
340 accent color 1
148 accent color 2

baltic gray

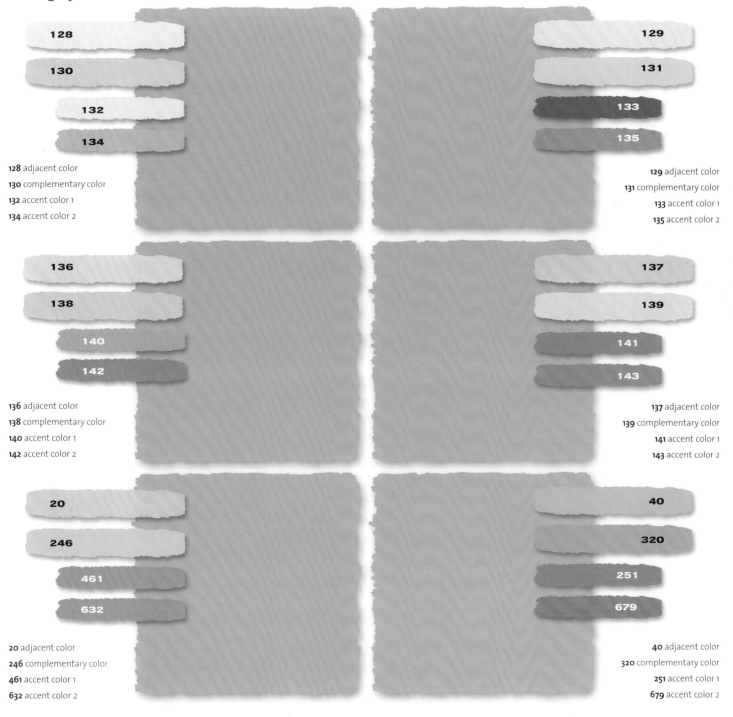

128

130

132

134

128 adjacent color
130 complementary color
132 accent color 1
134 accent color 2

129

131

133

135

129 adjacent color
131 complementary color
133 accent color 1
135 accent color 2

136

138

140

142

136 adjacent color
138 complementary color
140 accent color 1
142 accent color 2

137

139

141

143

137 adjacent color
139 complementary color
141 accent color 1
143 accent color 2

20

246

461

632

20 adjacent color
246 complementary color
461 accent color 1
632 accent color 2

40

320

251

679

40 adjacent color
320 complementary color
251 accent color 1
679 accent color 2

baltic gray

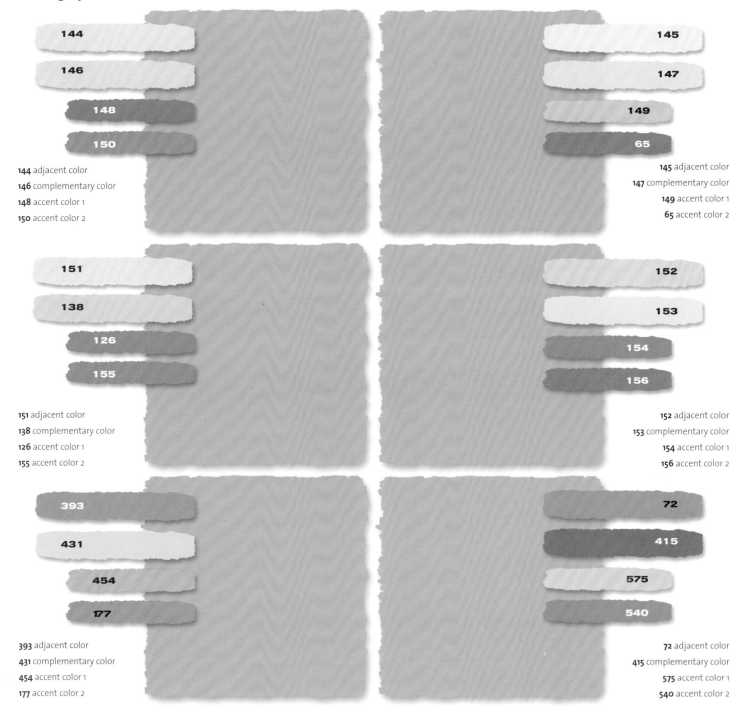

144

146

148

150

144 adjacent color
146 complementary color
148 accent color 1
150 accent color 2

145

147

149

65

145 adjacent color
147 complementary color
149 accent color 1
65 accent color 2

151

138

126

155

151 adjacent color
138 complementary color
126 accent color 1
155 accent color 2

152

153

154

156

152 adjacent color
153 complementary color
154 accent color 1
156 accent color 2

393

431

454

177

393 adjacent color
431 complementary color
454 accent color 1
177 accent color 2

72

415

575

540

72 adjacent color
415 complementary color
575 accent color 1
540 accent color 2

baltic gray

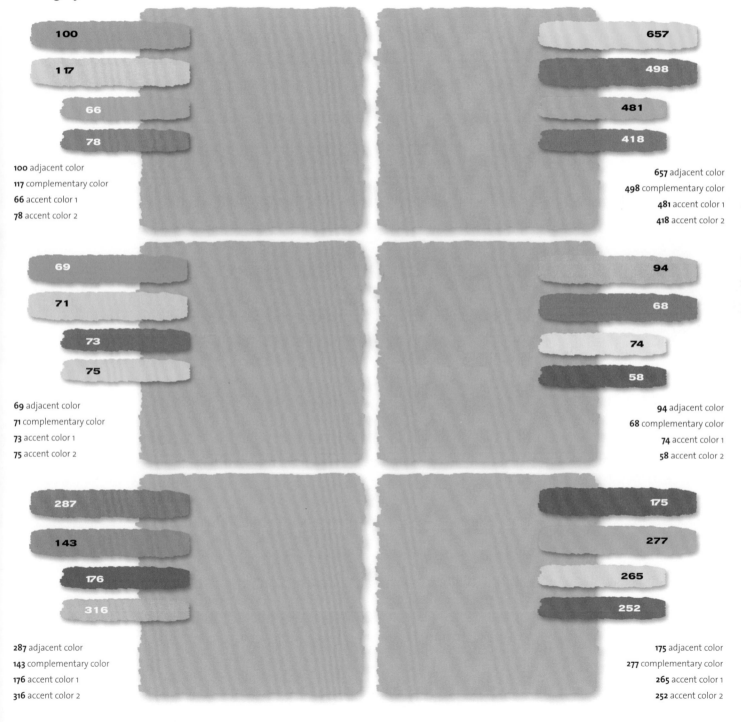

100 adjacent color
117 complementary color
66 accent color 1
78 accent color 2

657 adjacent color
498 complementary color
481 accent color 1
418 accent color 2

69 adjacent color
71 complementary color
73 accent color 1
75 accent color 2

94 adjacent color
68 complementary color
74 accent color 1
58 accent color 2

287 adjacent color
143 complementary color
176 accent color 1
316 accent color 2

175 adjacent color
277 complementary color
265 accent color 1
252 accent color 2

maple syrup

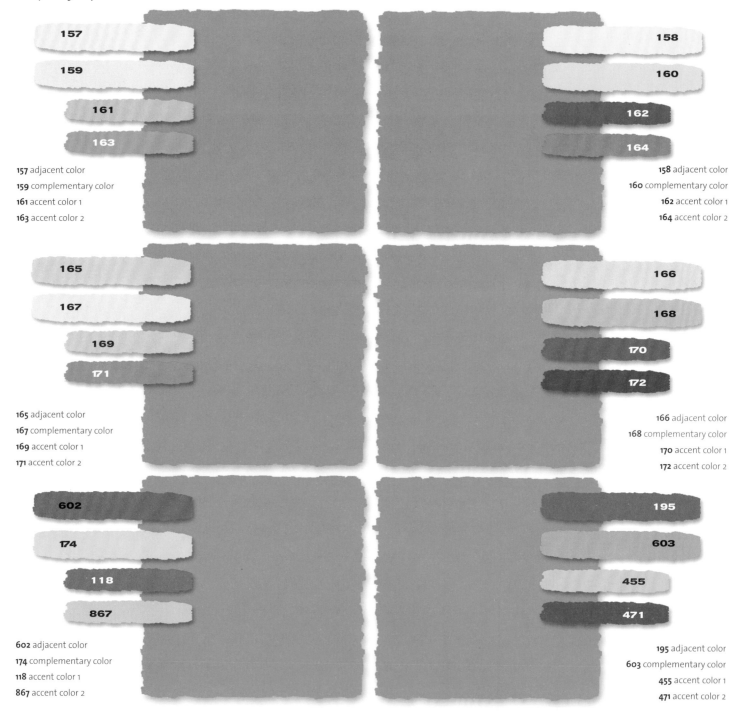

157 adjacent color
159 complementary color
161 accent color 1
163 accent color 2

158 adjacent color
160 complementary color
162 accent color 1
164 accent color 2

165 adjacent color
167 complementary color
169 accent color 1
171 accent color 2

166 adjacent color
168 complementary color
170 accent color 1
172 accent color 2

602 adjacent color
174 complementary color
118 accent color 1
867 accent color 2

195 adjacent color
603 complementary color
455 accent color 1
471 accent color 2

maple syrup

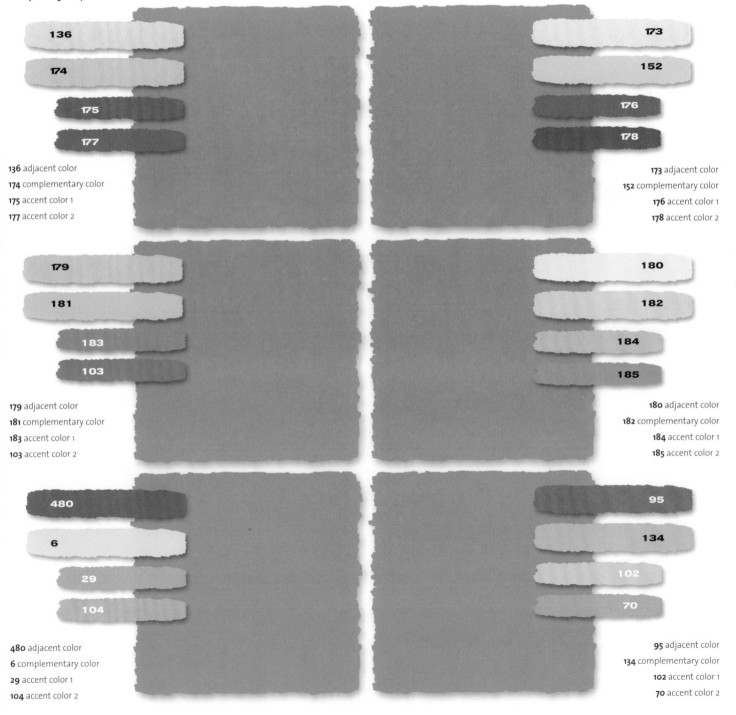

136 adjacent color
174 complementary color
175 accent color 1
177 accent color 2

173 adjacent color
152 complementary color
176 accent color 1
178 accent color 2

179 adjacent color
181 complementary color
183 accent color 1
103 accent color 2

180 adjacent color
182 complementary color
184 accent color 1
185 accent color 2

480 adjacent color
6 complementary color
29 accent color 1
104 accent color 2

95 adjacent color
134 complementary color
102 accent color 1
70 accent color 2

maple syrup

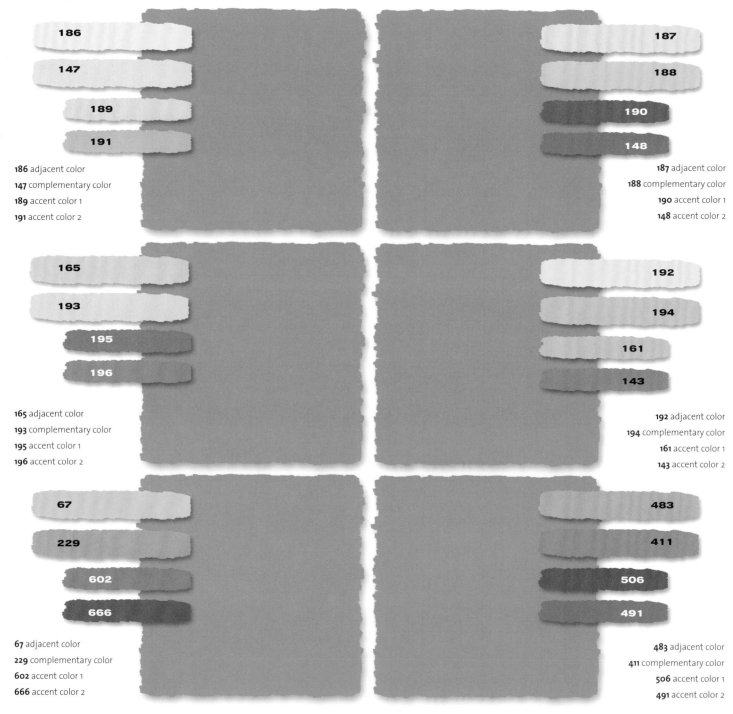

186
147
189
191

187
188
190
148

186 adjacent color
147 complementary color
189 accent color 1
191 accent color 2

187 adjacent color
188 complementary color
190 accent color 1
148 accent color 2

165
193
195
196

192
194
161
143

165 adjacent color
193 complementary color
195 accent color 1
196 accent color 2

192 adjacent color
194 complementary color
161 accent color 1
143 accent color 2

67
229
602
666

483
411
506
491

67 adjacent color
229 complementary color
602 accent color 1
666 accent color 2

483 adjacent color
411 complementary color
506 accent color 1
491 accent color 2

maple syrup

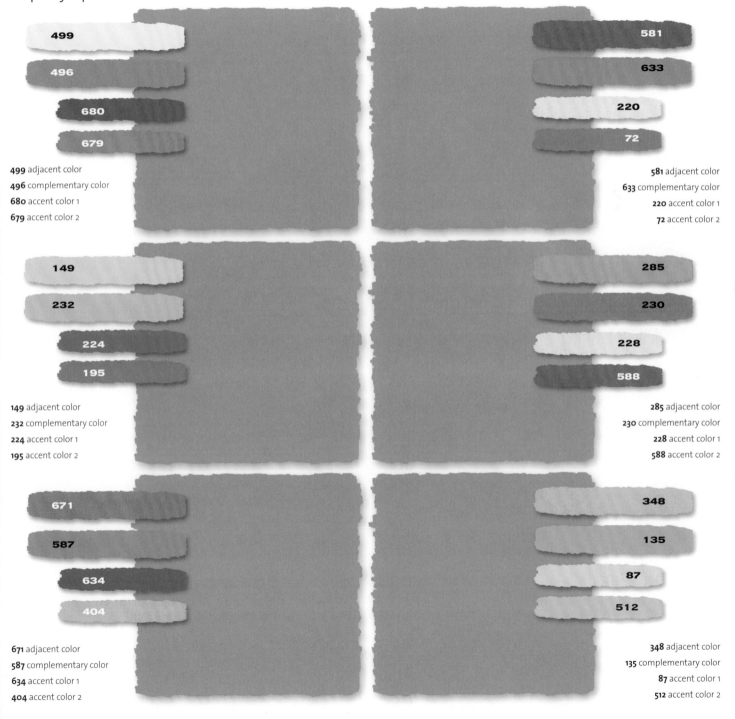

499
496
680
679

499 adjacent color
496 complementary color
680 accent color 1
679 accent color 2

581
633
220
72

581 adjacent color
633 complementary color
220 accent color 1
72 accent color 2

149
232
224
195

149 adjacent color
232 complementary color
224 accent color 1
195 accent color 2

285
230
228
588

285 adjacent color
230 complementary color
228 accent color 1
588 accent color 2

671
587
634
404

671 adjacent color
587 complementary color
634 accent color 1
404 accent color 2

348
135
87
512

348 adjacent color
135 complementary color
87 accent color 1
512 accent color 2

watercolor blue

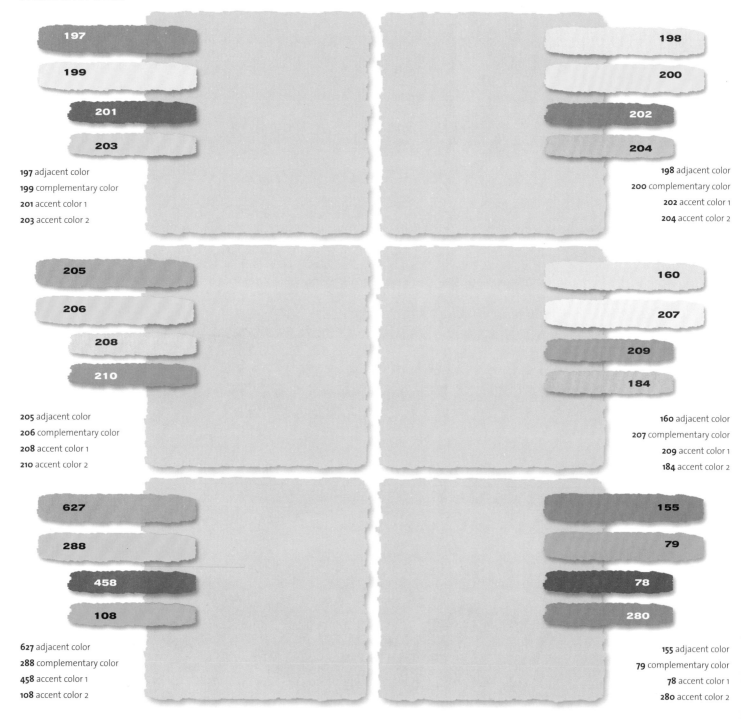

197

199

201

203

198

200

202

204

197 adjacent color
199 complementary color
201 accent color 1
203 accent color 2

198 adjacent color
200 complementary color
202 accent color 1
204 accent color 2

205

206

208

210

160

207

209

184

205 adjacent color
206 complementary color
208 accent color 1
210 accent color 2

160 adjacent color
207 complementary color
209 accent color 1
184 accent color 2

627

288

458

108

155

79

78

280

627 adjacent color
288 complementary color
458 accent color 1
108 accent color 2

155 adjacent color
79 complementary color
78 accent color 1
280 accent color 2

watercolor blue

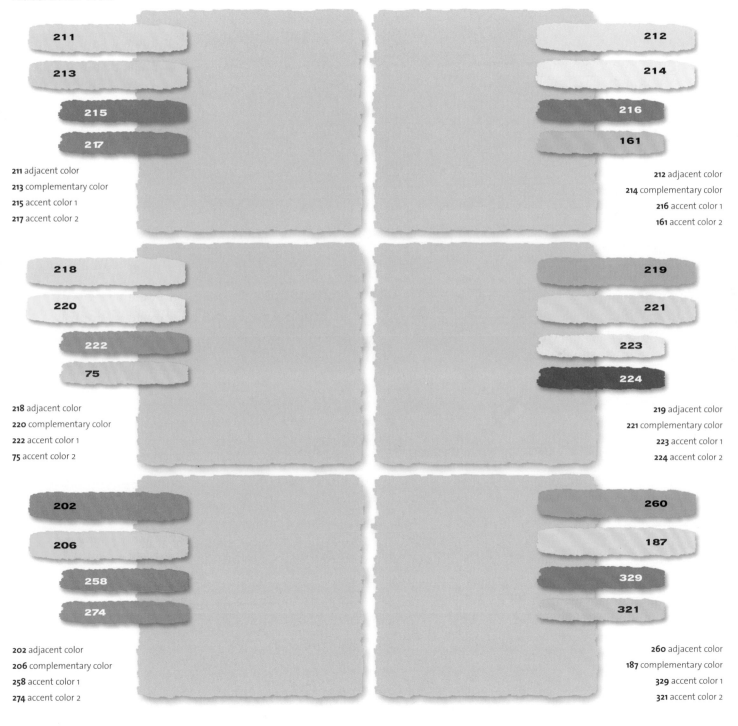

211 adjacent color
213 complementary color
215 accent color 1
217 accent color 2

212 adjacent color
214 complementary color
216 accent color 1
161 accent color 2

218 adjacent color
220 complementary color
222 accent color 1
75 accent color 2

219 adjacent color
221 complementary color
223 accent color 1
224 accent color 2

202 adjacent color
206 complementary color
258 accent color 1
274 accent color 2

260 adjacent color
187 complementary color
329 accent color 1
321 accent color 2

watercolor blue

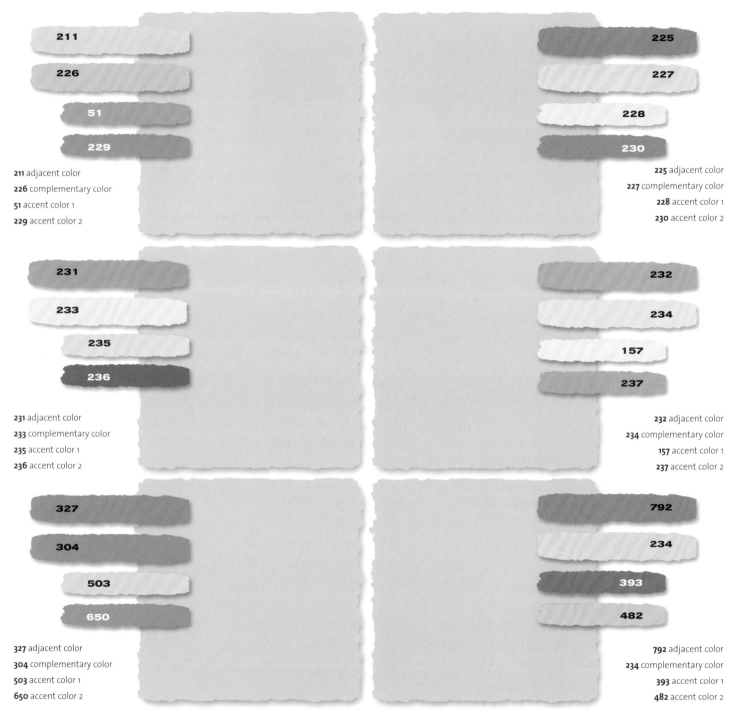

211
226
51
229

211 adjacent color
226 complementary color
51 accent color 1
229 accent color 2

225
227
228
230

225 adjacent color
227 complementary color
228 accent color 1
230 accent color 2

231
233
235
236

231 adjacent color
233 complementary color
235 accent color 1
236 accent color 2

232
234
157
237

232 adjacent color
234 complementary color
157 accent color 1
237 accent color 2

327
304
503
650

327 adjacent color
304 complementary color
503 accent color 1
650 accent color 2

792
234
393
482

792 adjacent color
234 complementary color
393 accent color 1
482 accent color 2

watercolor blue

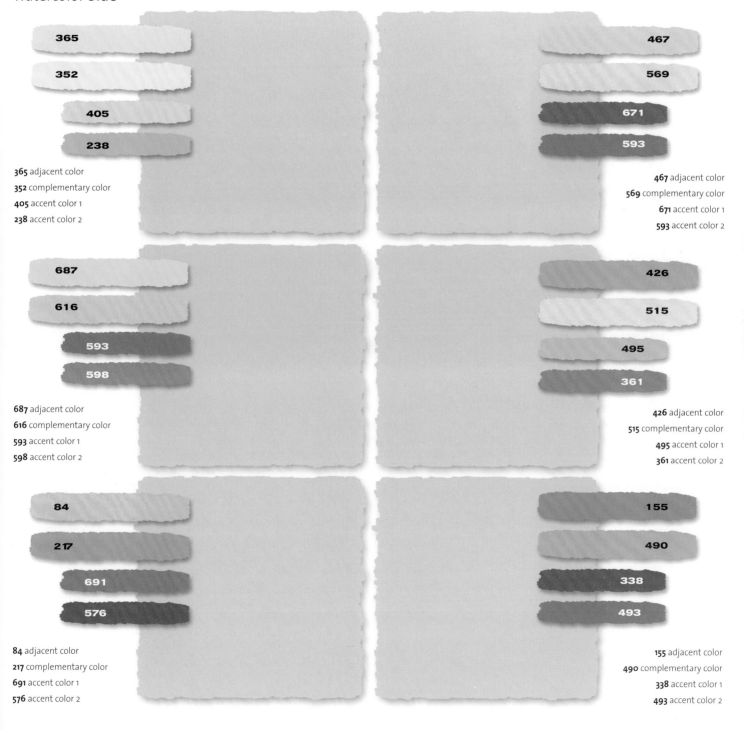

365

352

405

238

365 adjacent color
352 complementary color
405 accent color 1
238 accent color 2

467

569

671

593

467 adjacent color
569 complementary color
671 accent color 1
593 accent color 2

687

616

593

598

687 adjacent color
616 complementary color
593 accent color 1
598 accent color 2

426

515

495

361

426 adjacent color
515 complementary color
495 accent color 1
361 accent color 2

84

217

691

576

84 adjacent color
217 complementary color
691 accent color 1
576 accent color 2

155

490

338

493

155 adjacent color
490 complementary color
338 accent color 1
493 accent color 2

iced green

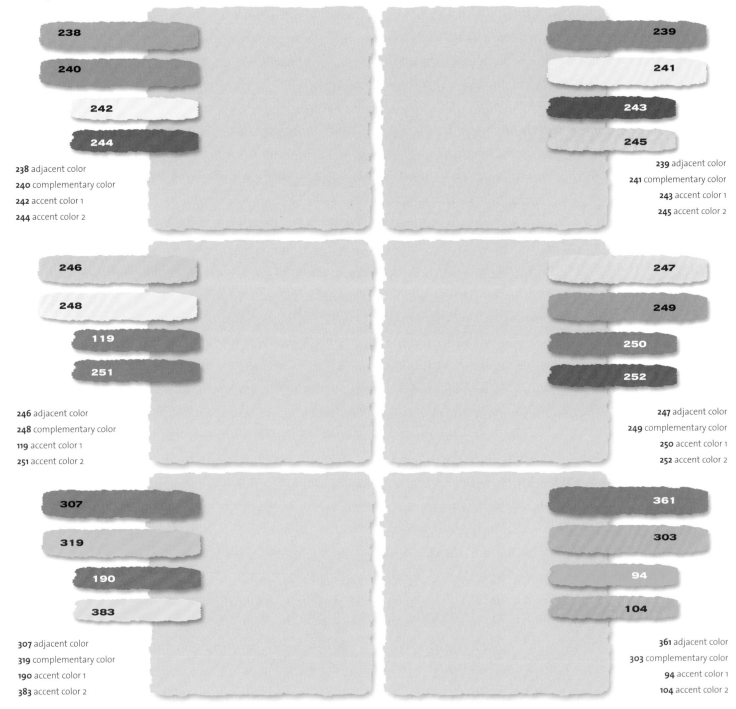

238

240

242

244

238 adjacent color
240 complementary color
242 accent color 1
244 accent color 2

239

241

243

245

239 adjacent color
241 complementary color
243 accent color 1
245 accent color 2

246

248

119

251

246 adjacent color
248 complementary color
119 accent color 1
251 accent color 2

247

249

250

252

247 adjacent color
249 complementary color
250 accent color 1
252 accent color 2

307

319

190

383

307 adjacent color
319 complementary color
190 accent color 1
383 accent color 2

361

303

94

104

361 adjacent color
303 complementary color
94 accent color 1
104 accent color 2

iced green

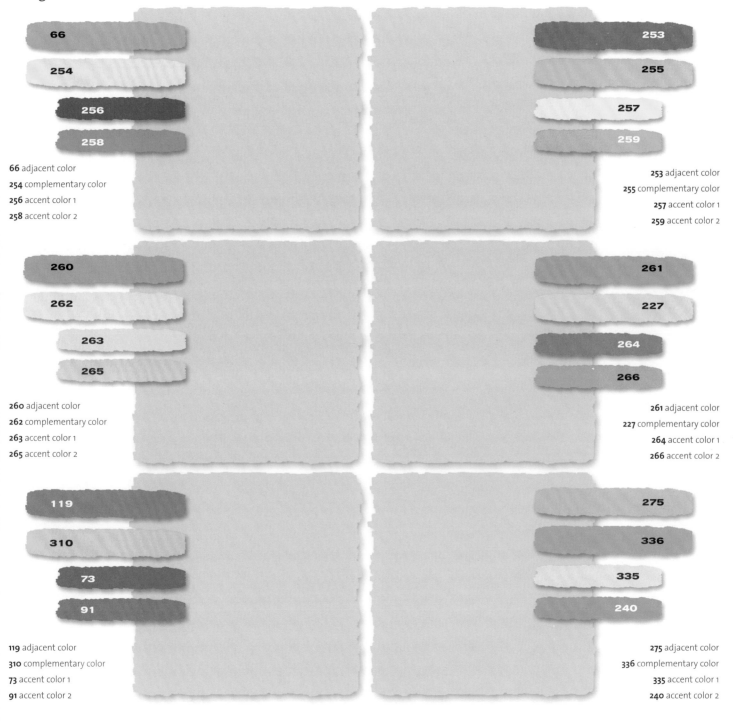

66 **66** adjacent color
254 complementary color
256 accent color 1
258 accent color 2

253 adjacent color
255 complementary color
257 accent color 1
259 accent color 2

260 adjacent color
262 complementary color
263 accent color 1
265 accent color 2

261 adjacent color
227 complementary color
264 accent color 1
266 accent color 2

119 adjacent color
310 complementary color
73 accent color 1
91 accent color 2

275 adjacent color
336 complementary color
335 accent color 1
240 accent color 2

iced green

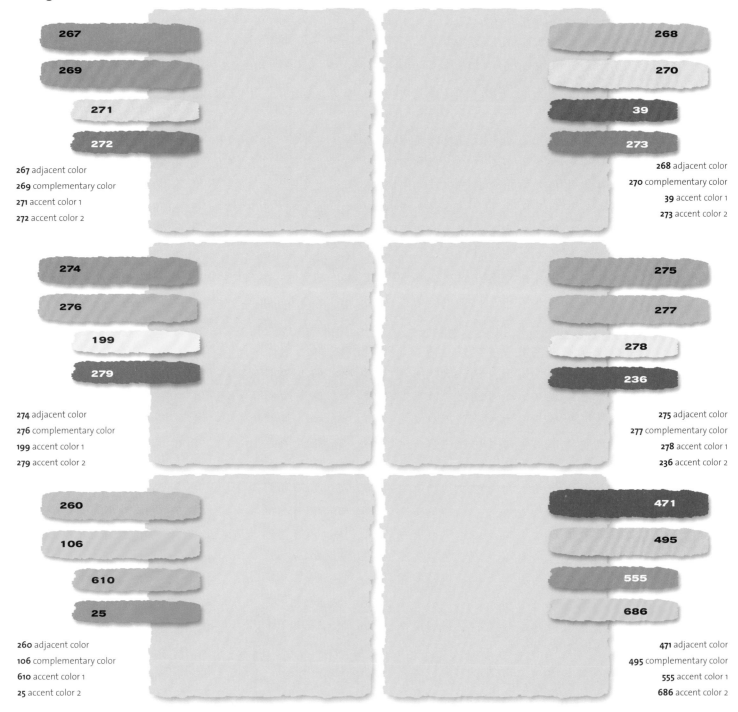

267

269

271

272

267 adjacent color
269 complementary color
271 accent color 1
272 accent color 2

268

270

39

273

268 adjacent color
270 complementary color
39 accent color 1
273 accent color 2

274

276

199

279

274 adjacent color
276 complementary color
199 accent color 1
279 accent color 2

275

277

278

236

275 adjacent color
277 complementary color
278 accent color 1
236 accent color 2

260

106

610

25

260 adjacent color
106 complementary color
610 accent color 1
25 accent color 2

471

495

555

686

471 adjacent color
495 complementary color
555 accent color 1
686 accent color 2

iced green

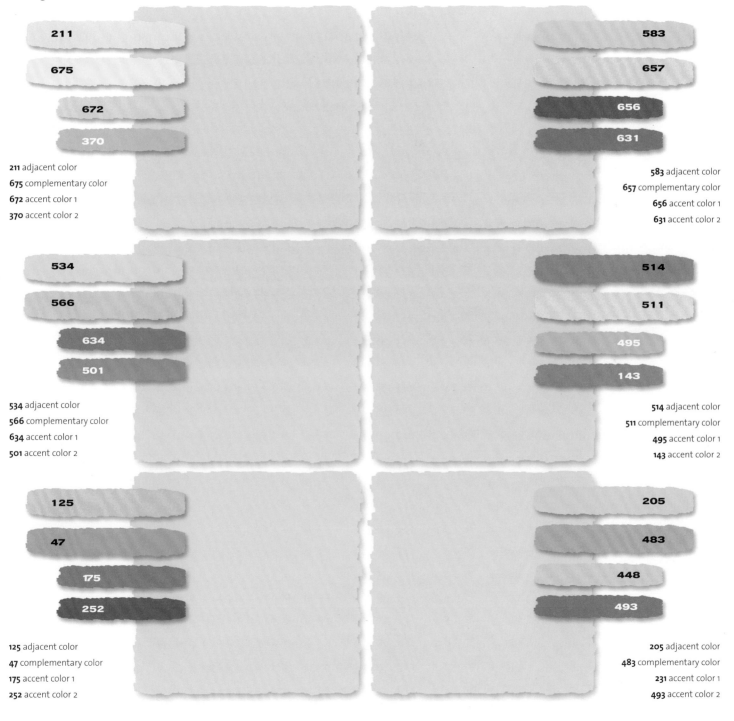

211
675
672
370

211 adjacent color
675 complementary color
672 accent color 1
370 accent color 2

583
657
656
631

583 adjacent color
657 complementary color
656 accent color 1
631 accent color 2

534
566
634
501

534 adjacent color
566 complementary color
634 accent color 1
501 accent color 2

514
511
495
143

514 adjacent color
511 complementary color
495 accent color 1
143 accent color 2

125
47
175
252

125 adjacent color
47 complementary color
175 accent color 1
252 accent color 2

205
483
448
493

205 adjacent color
483 complementary color
231 accent color 1
493 accent color 2

treasure trove

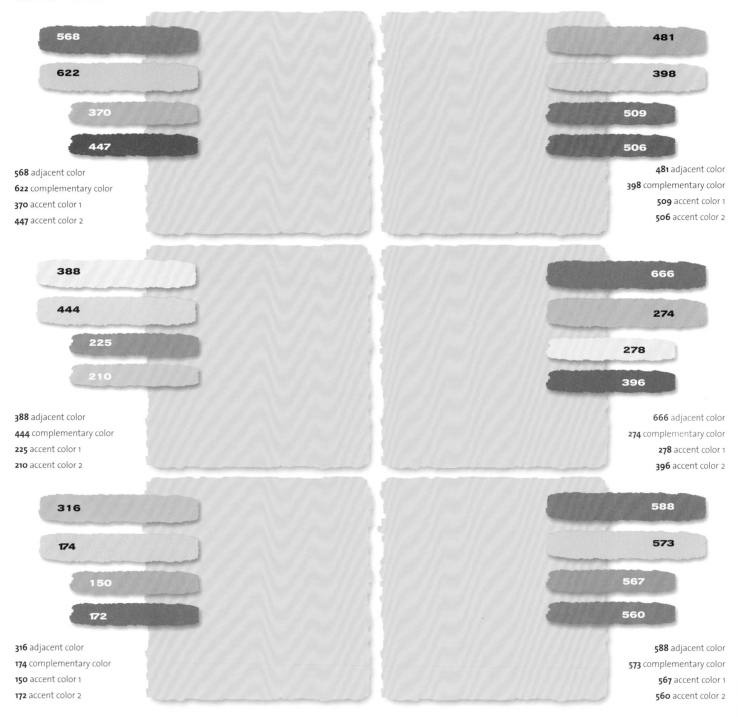

568
622
370
447

481
398
509
506

568 adjacent color
622 complementary color
370 accent color 1
447 accent color 2

481 adjacent color
398 complementary color
509 accent color 1
506 accent color 2

388
444
225
210

666
274
278
396

388 adjacent color
444 complementary color
225 accent color 1
210 accent color 2

666 adjacent color
274 complementary color
278 accent color 1
396 accent color 2

316
174
150
172

588
573
567
560

316 adjacent color
174 complementary color
150 accent color 1
172 accent color 2

588 adjacent color
573 complementary color
567 accent color 1
560 accent color 2

treasure trove

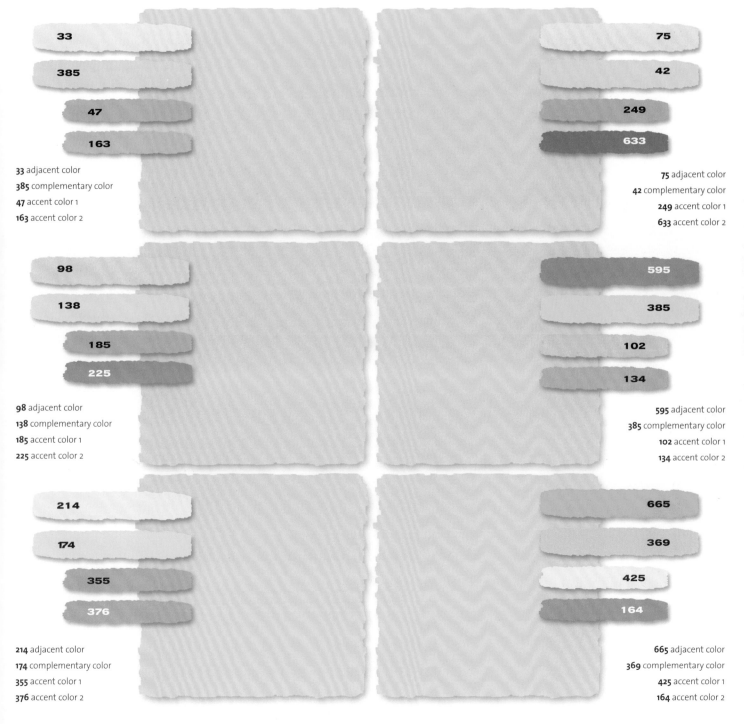

33

385

47

163

33 adjacent color
385 complementary color
47 accent color 1
163 accent color 2

75

42

249

633

75 adjacent color
42 complementary color
249 accent color 1
633 accent color 2

98

138

185

225

98 adjacent color
138 complementary color
185 accent color 1
225 accent color 2

595

385

102

134

595 adjacent color
385 complementary color
102 accent color 1
134 accent color 2

214

174

355

376

214 adjacent color
174 complementary color
355 accent color 1
376 accent color 2

665

369

425

164

665 adjacent color
369 complementary color
425 accent color 1
164 accent color 2

treasure trove

673

674

644

665

673 adjacent color
674 complementary color
644 accent color 1
665 accent color 2

69

664

669

666

69 adjacent color
664 complementary color
669 accent color 1
666 accent color 2

660

669

675

15

660 adjacent color
669 complementary color
675 accent color 1
15 accent color 2

668

665

693

675

668 adjacent color
665 complementary color
693 accent color 1
675 accent color 2

653

597

485

522

653 adjacent color
597 complementary color
485 accent color 1
522 accent color 2

679

549

563

625

679 adjacent color
549 complementary color
563 accent color 1
625 accent color 2

treasure trove

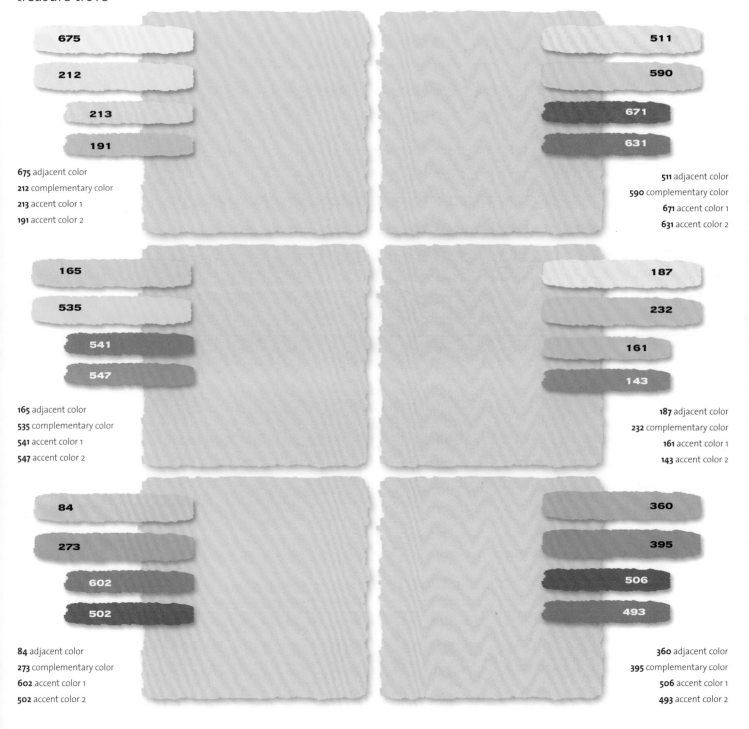

675

212

213

191

511

590

671

631

675 adjacent color
212 complementary color
213 accent color 1
191 accent color 2

511 adjacent color
590 complementary color
671 accent color 1
631 accent color 2

165

535

541

547

187

232

161

143

165 adjacent color
535 complementary color
541 accent color 1
547 accent color 2

187 adjacent color
232 complementary color
161 accent color 1
143 accent color 2

84

273

602

502

360

395

506

493

84 adjacent color
273 complementary color
602 accent color 1
502 accent color 2

360 adjacent color
395 complementary color
506 accent color 1
493 accent color 2

algonquin trail

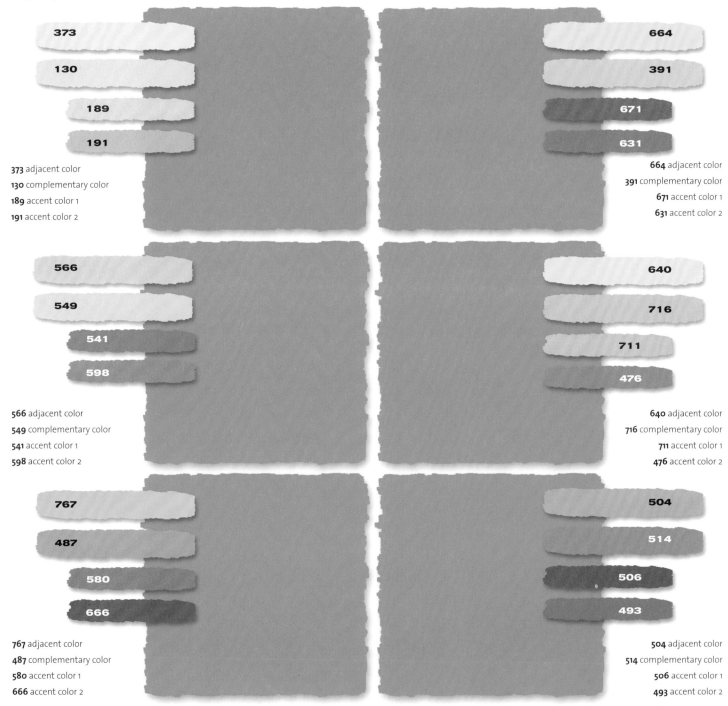

373 adjacent color
130 complementary color
189 accent color 1
191 accent color 2

664 adjacent color
391 complementary color
671 accent color 1
631 accent color 2

566 adjacent color
549 complementary color
541 accent color 1
598 accent color 2

640 adjacent color
716 complementary color
711 accent color 1
476 accent color 2

767 adjacent color
487 complementary color
580 accent color 1
666 accent color 2

504 adjacent color
514 complementary color
506 accent color 1
493 accent color 2

algonquin trail

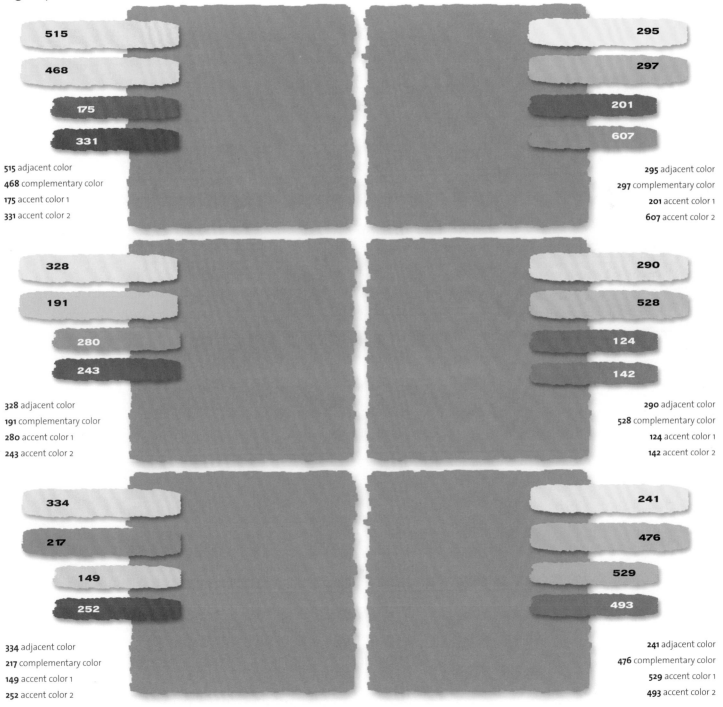

515 adjacent color
468 complementary color
175 accent color 1
331 accent color 2

295 adjacent color
297 complementary color
201 accent color 1
607 accent color 2

328 adjacent color
191 complementary color
280 accent color 1
243 accent color 2

290 adjacent color
528 complementary color
124 accent color 1
142 accent color 2

334 adjacent color
217 complementary color
149 accent color 1
252 accent color 2

241 adjacent color
476 complementary color
529 accent color 1
493 accent color 2

algonquin trail

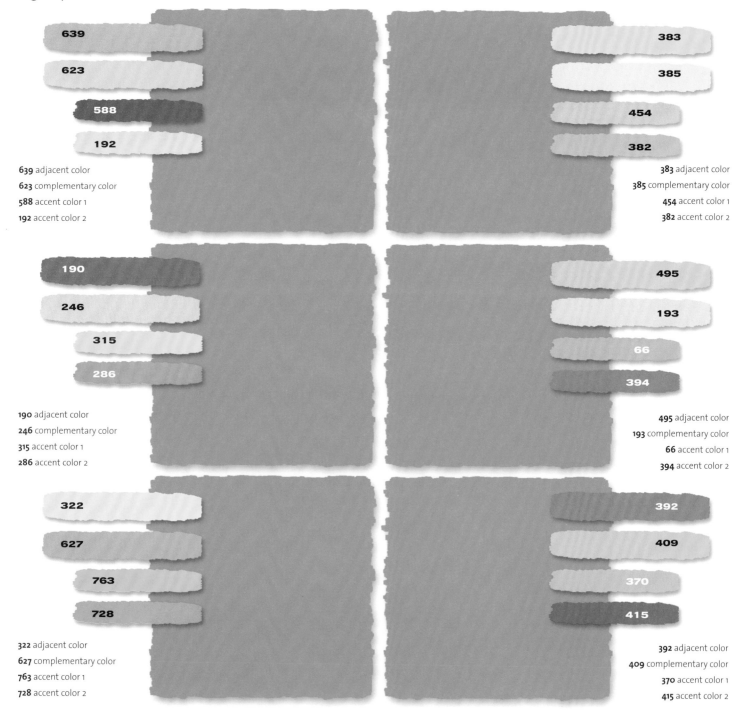

639
623
588
192

639 adjacent color
623 complementary color
588 accent color 1
192 accent color 2

383
385
454
382

383 adjacent color
385 complementary color
454 accent color 1
382 accent color 2

190
246
315
286

190 adjacent color
246 complementary color
315 accent color 1
286 accent color 2

495
193
66
394

495 adjacent color
193 complementary color
66 accent color 1
394 accent color 2

322
627
763
728

322 adjacent color
627 complementary color
763 accent color 1
728 accent color 2

392
409
370
415

392 adjacent color
409 complementary color
370 accent color 1
415 accent color 2

algonquin trail

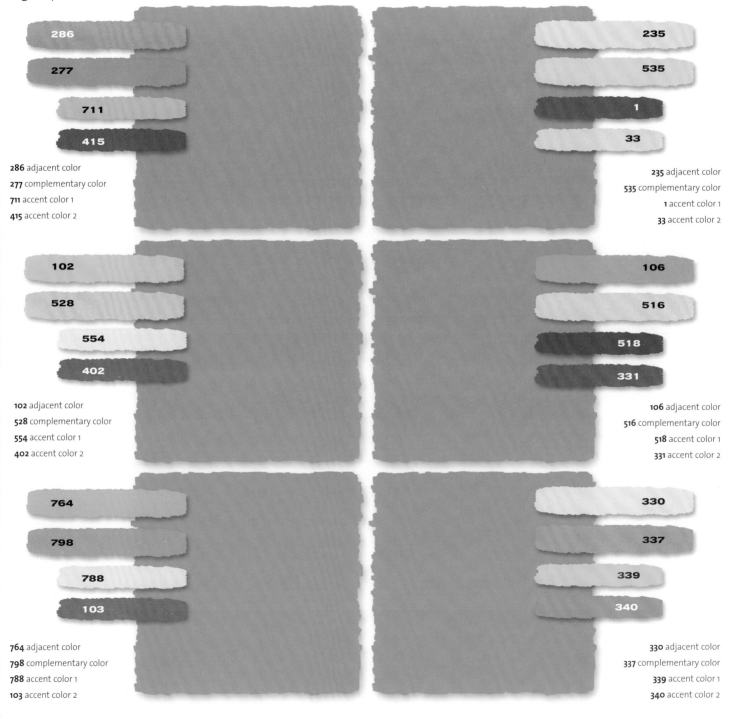

286
277
711
415

235
535
1
33

286 adjacent color
277 complementary color
711 accent color 1
415 accent color 2

235 adjacent color
535 complementary color
1 accent color 1
33 accent color 2

102
528
554
402

106
516
518
331

102 adjacent color
528 complementary color
554 accent color 1
402 accent color 2

106 adjacent color
516 complementary color
518 accent color 1
331 accent color 2

764
798
788
103

330
337
339
340

764 adjacent color
798 complementary color
788 accent color 1
103 accent color 2

330 adjacent color
337 complementary color
339 accent color 1
340 accent color 2

marmalade

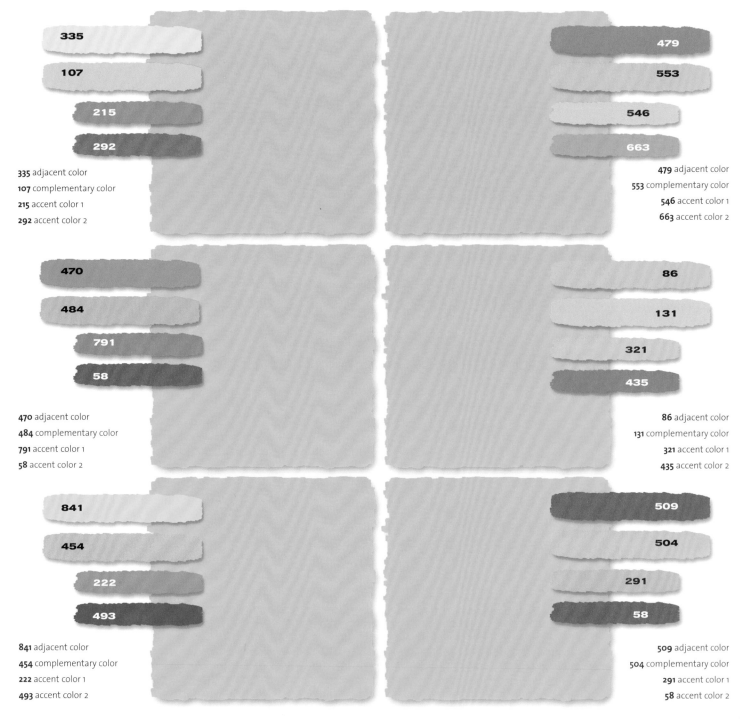

335
107
215
292

479
553
546
663

335 adjacent color
107 complementary color
215 accent color 1
292 accent color 2

479 adjacent color
553 complementary color
546 accent color 1
663 accent color 2

470
484
791
58

86
131
321
435

470 adjacent color
484 complementary color
791 accent color 1
58 accent color 2

86 adjacent color
131 complementary color
321 accent color 1
435 accent color 2

841
454
222
493

509
504
291
58

841 adjacent color
454 complementary color
222 accent color 1
493 accent color 2

509 adjacent color
504 complementary color
291 accent color 1
58 accent color 2

marmalade

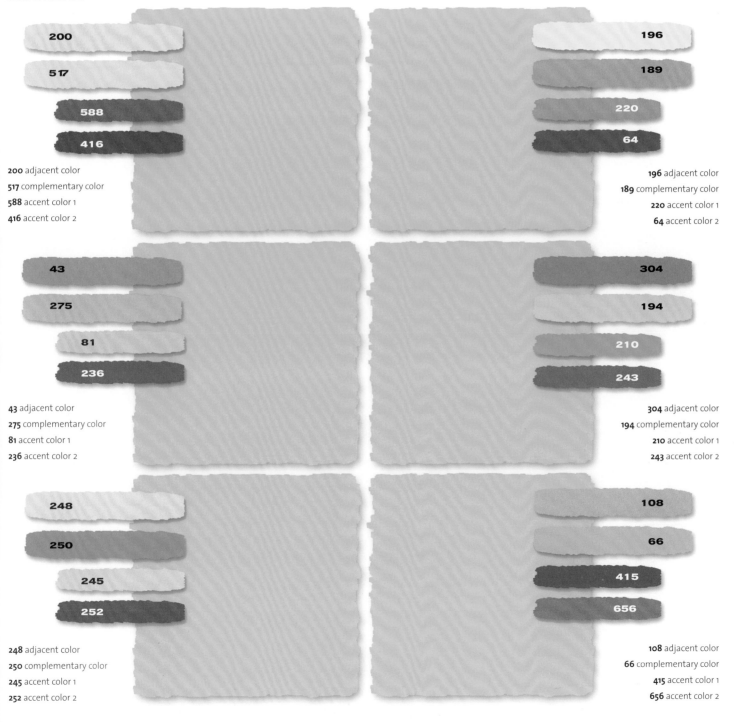

200
517
588
416

200 adjacent color
517 complementary color
588 accent color 1
416 accent color 2

196
189
220
64

196 adjacent color
189 complementary color
220 accent color 1
64 accent color 2

43
275
81
236

43 adjacent color
275 complementary color
81 accent color 1
236 accent color 2

304
194
210
243

304 adjacent color
194 complementary color
210 accent color 1
243 accent color 2

248
250
245
252

248 adjacent color
250 complementary color
245 accent color 1
252 accent color 2

108
66
415
656

108 adjacent color
66 complementary color
415 accent color 1
656 accent color 2

marmalade

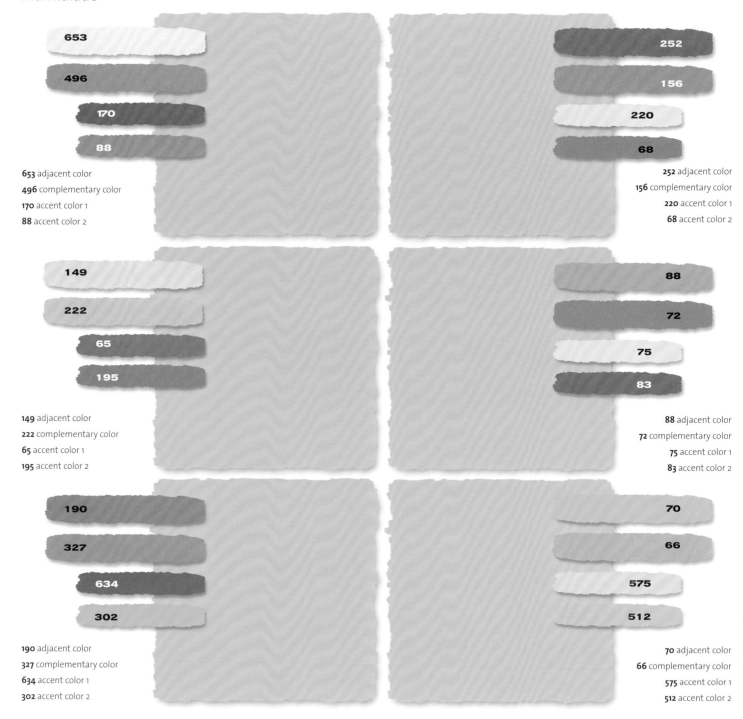

653
496
170
88

653 adjacent color
496 complementary color
170 accent color 1
88 accent color 2

252
156
220
68

252 adjacent color
156 complementary color
220 accent color 1
68 accent color 2

149
222
65
195

149 adjacent color
222 complementary color
65 accent color 1
195 accent color 2

88
72
75
83

88 adjacent color
72 complementary color
75 accent color 1
83 accent color 2

190
327
634
302

190 adjacent color
327 complementary color
634 accent color 1
302 accent color 2

70
66
575
512

70 adjacent color
66 complementary color
575 accent color 1
512 accent color 2

marmalade

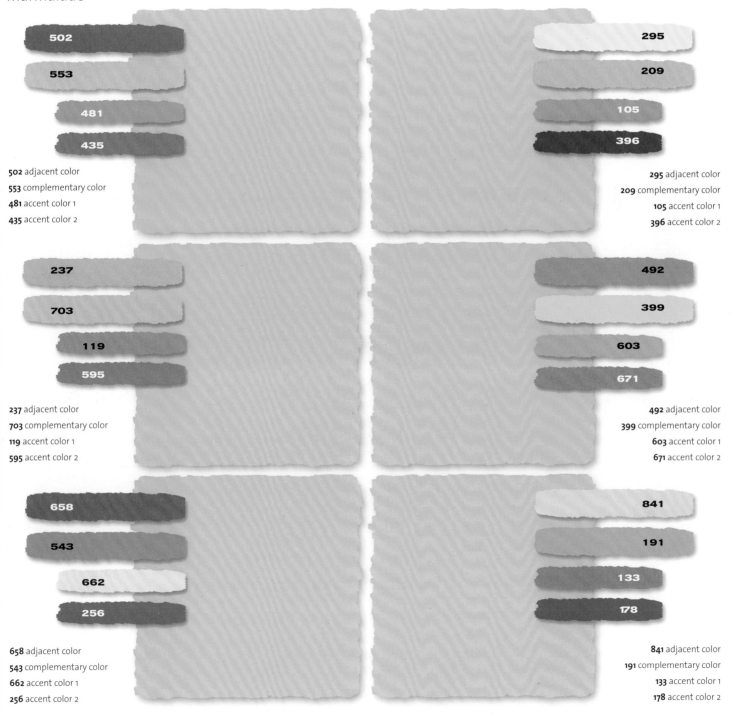

502

553

481

435

502 adjacent color
553 complementary color
481 accent color 1
435 accent color 2

295

209

105

396

295 adjacent color
209 complementary color
105 accent color 1
396 accent color 2

237

703

119

595

237 adjacent color
703 complementary color
119 accent color 1
595 accent color 2

492

399

603

671

492 adjacent color
399 complementary color
603 accent color 1
671 accent color 2

658

543

662

256

658 adjacent color
543 complementary color
662 accent color 1
256 accent color 2

841

191

133

178

841 adjacent color
191 complementary color
133 accent color 1
178 accent color 2

| 673 | 276 | 793 | 197 |
| 279 | 199 | 201 | 203 |

ABOVE Here, the color scheme is defined by soft furnishings, the combination of these subtle shades of gray, blue, pink, and brown creates a space that is elegant, cool, and extremely relaxing.

RIGHT These two contrasting blues are a perfect and time-lasting color scheme for a simple classic bathroom. Here, the scheme is further enhanced by the contrasting oranges and yellows of the fruit. Alternatively these contrasting colors could be introduced by means of bath towels, or decorative bottles of colored bath oils.

4	165
193	195

LEFT The rich terra-cotta of the walls create a cozy bathing environment. The crisp white of the basin and towel coupled with the steely blue opaque glass prevent the room becoming too dark and overpowering.

1	58
56	54

RIGHT Rich dark reds have a timeless quality, which—when combined with strong browns of the wood and the cushions, and set off by the neutral sofa covering—produce an elegant contemporary living space.

3	141		2	91
137	143		93	56

BELOW By using many neutral colors this scheme conveys an immediate impression of calm. The accent colors are provided by the thriving plants which also add to the ambience.

RIGHT Strong pinks can be overpowering but when combined with other rich colors, such as purple, create a feeling of opulence.

1	301
14	387

RIGHT The deep red wall is the main feature in this living room, bringing warmth and sensuality, cleverly contrasted by the green of the plant, and accented with a mixture of colored cushions.

6	185
137	461

87	243
231	292

LEFT Choosing a color scheme for the exterior of your home should take the surroundings into account. The subtle green of the building, with its contrasting white, sits perfectly among the well established planting.

RIGHT A mixture of matte and shiny surfaces creates an exciting interplay of finishes and colors in this traditional style kitchen. The golden glow of the tiles and cabinets helps to make this a cheerful and social place.

348	121	95	177
175	137	303	372

ABOVE Areas of strong color are used to great effect here. This otherwise neutral contemporary setting has been imbued with a warm and stimulating feel.

RIGHT Varying tones and textures of brown, warm tan, and rich chocolate bring a feeling of luxury and depth, energized by the bright orange bed linen.

ultra violet

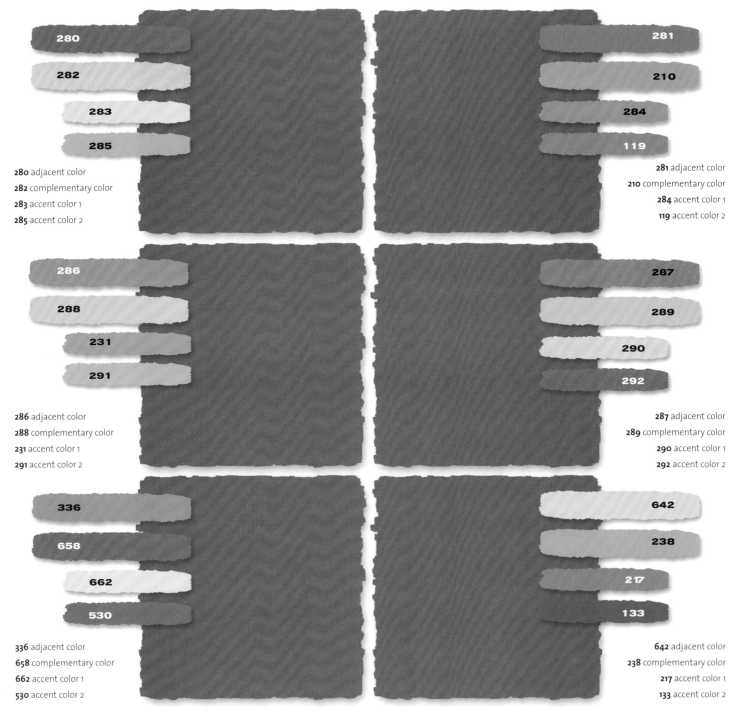

280
282
283
285

281
210
284
119

280 adjacent color
282 complementary color
283 accent color 1
285 accent color 2

281 adjacent color
210 complementary color
284 accent color 1
119 accent color 2

286
288
231
291

287
289
290
292

286 adjacent color
288 complementary color
231 accent color 1
291 accent color 2

287 adjacent color
289 complementary color
290 accent color 1
292 accent color 2

336
658
662
530

642
238
217
133

336 adjacent color
658 complementary color
662 accent color 1
530 accent color 2

642 adjacent color
238 complementary color
217 accent color 1
133 accent color 2

ultra violet

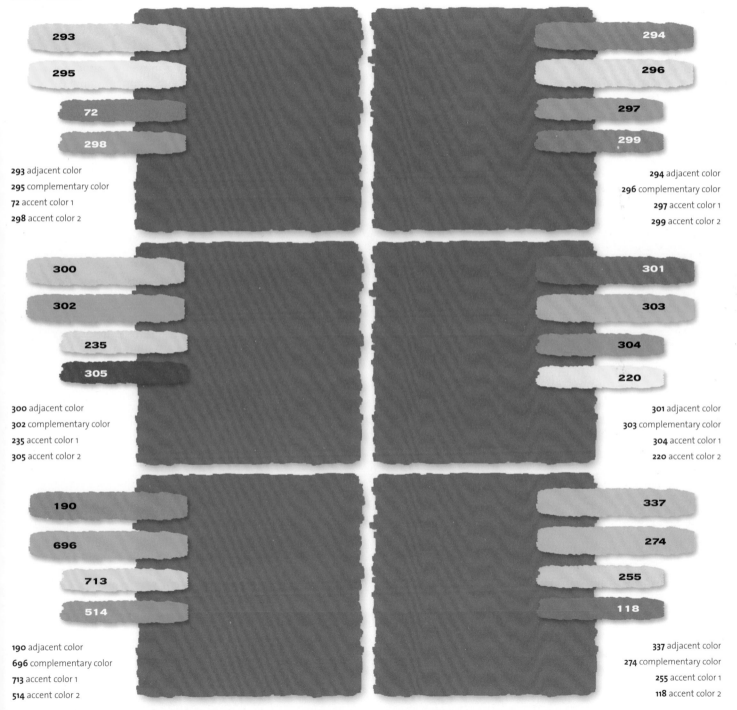

293
295
72
298

294
296
297
299

300
302
235
305

301
303
304
220

190
696
713
514

337
274
255
118

293 adjacent color
295 complementary color
72 accent color 1
298 accent color 2

294 adjacent color
296 complementary color
297 accent color 1
299 accent color 2

300 adjacent color
302 complementary color
235 accent color 1
305 accent color 2

301 adjacent color
303 complementary color
304 accent color 1
220 accent color 2

190 adjacent color
696 complementary color
713 accent color 1
514 accent color 2

337 adjacent color
274 complementary color
255 accent color 1
118 accent color 2

ultra violet

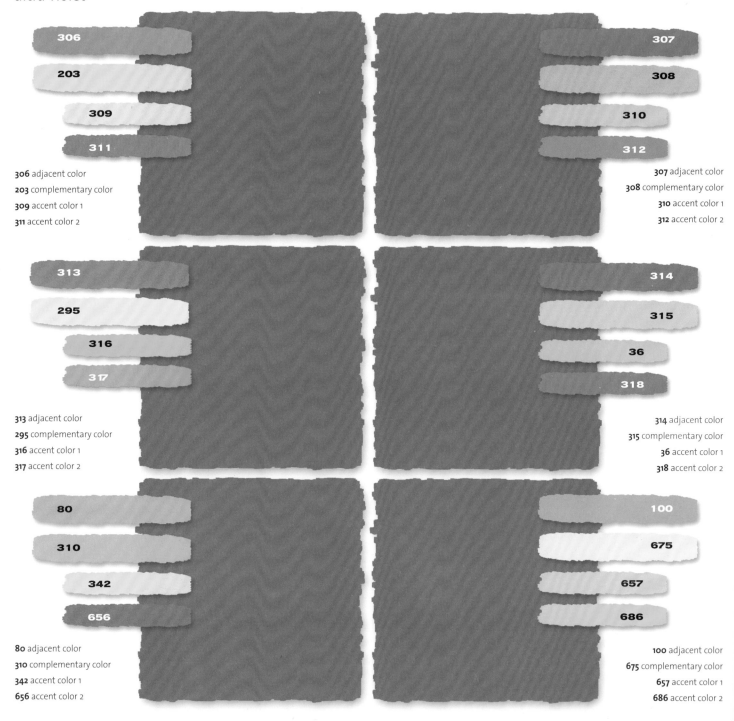

306 adjacent color
203 complementary color
309 accent color 1
311 accent color 2

307 adjacent color
308 complementary color
310 accent color 1
312 accent color 2

313 adjacent color
295 complementary color
316 accent color 1
317 accent color 2

314 adjacent color
315 complementary color
36 accent color 1
318 accent color 2

80 adjacent color
310 complementary color
342 accent color 1
656 accent color 2

100 adjacent color
675 complementary color
657 accent color 1
686 accent color 2

ultra violet

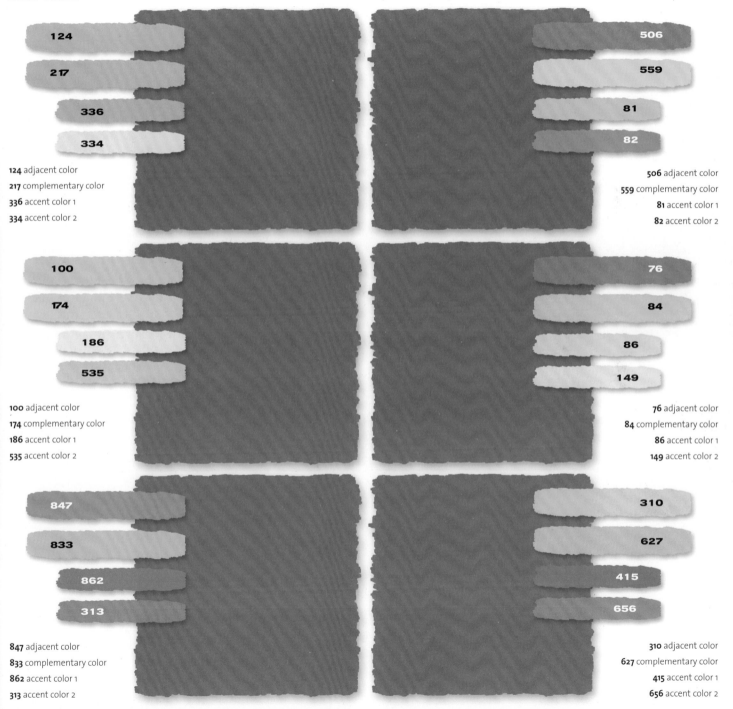

124
217
336
334

506
559
81
82

124 adjacent color
217 complementary color
336 accent color 1
334 accent color 2

506 adjacent color
559 complementary color
81 accent color 1
82 accent color 2

100
174
186
535

76
84
86
149

100 adjacent color
174 complementary color
186 accent color 1
535 accent color 2

76 adjacent color
84 complementary color
86 accent color 1
149 accent color 2

847
833
862
313

310
627
415
656

847 adjacent color
833 complementary color
862 accent color 1
313 accent color 2

310 adjacent color
627 complementary color
415 accent color 1
656 accent color 2

burnt sienna

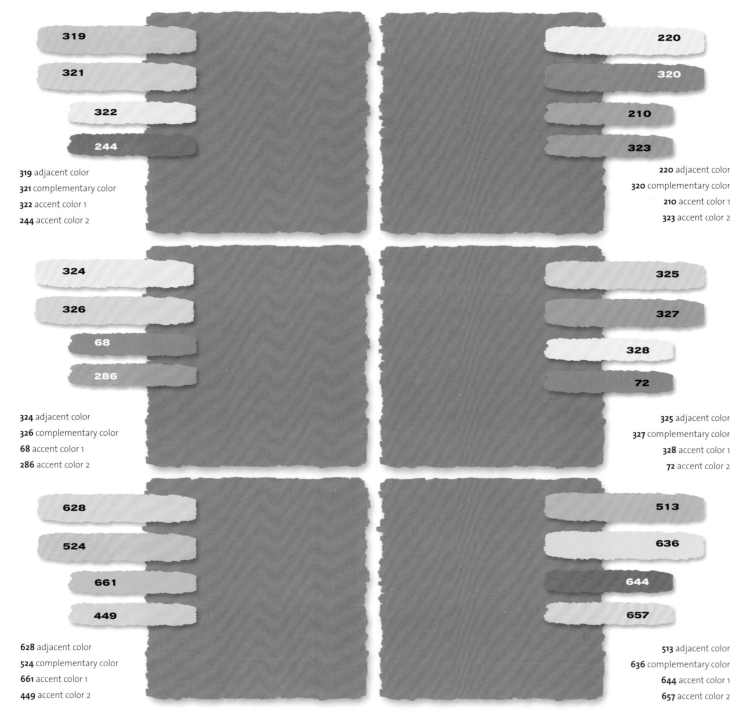

319
321
322
244

220
320
210
323

319 adjacent color
321 complementary color
322 accent color 1
244 accent color 2

220 adjacent color
320 complementary color
210 accent color 1
323 accent color 2

324
326
68
286

325
327
328
72

324 adjacent color
326 complementary color
68 accent color 1
286 accent color 2

325 adjacent color
327 complementary color
328 accent color 1
72 accent color 2

628
524
661
449

513
636
644
657

628 adjacent color
524 complementary color
661 accent color 1
449 accent color 2

513 adjacent color
636 complementary color
644 accent color 1
657 accent color 2

burnt sienna

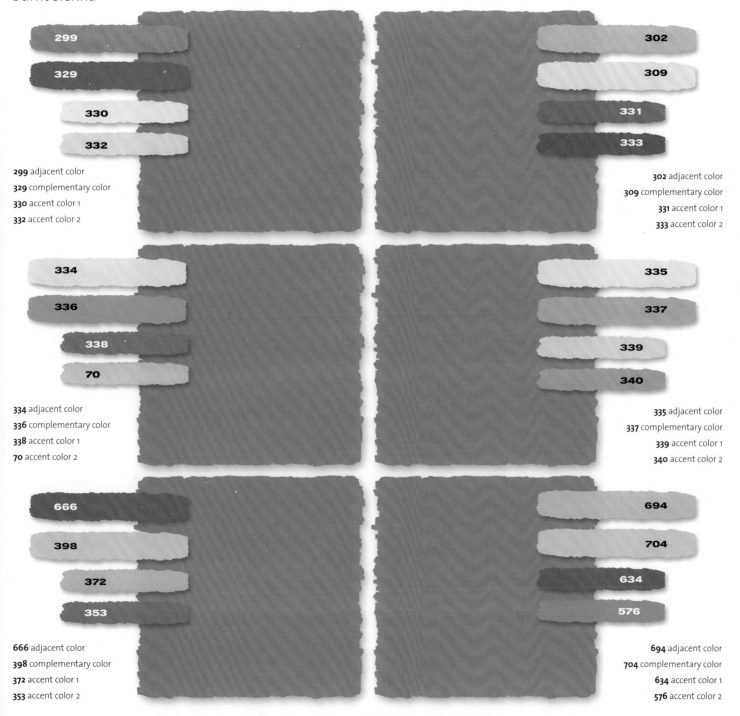

299
329
330
332

302
309
331
333

299 adjacent color
329 complementary color
330 accent color 1
332 accent color 2

302 adjacent color
309 complementary color
331 accent color 1
333 accent color 2

334
336
338
70

335
337
339
340

334 adjacent color
336 complementary color
338 accent color 1
70 accent color 2

335 adjacent color
337 complementary color
339 accent color 1
340 accent color 2

666
398
372
353

694
704
634
576

666 adjacent color
398 complementary color
372 accent color 1
353 accent color 2

694 adjacent color
704 complementary color
634 accent color 1
576 accent color 2

burnt sienna

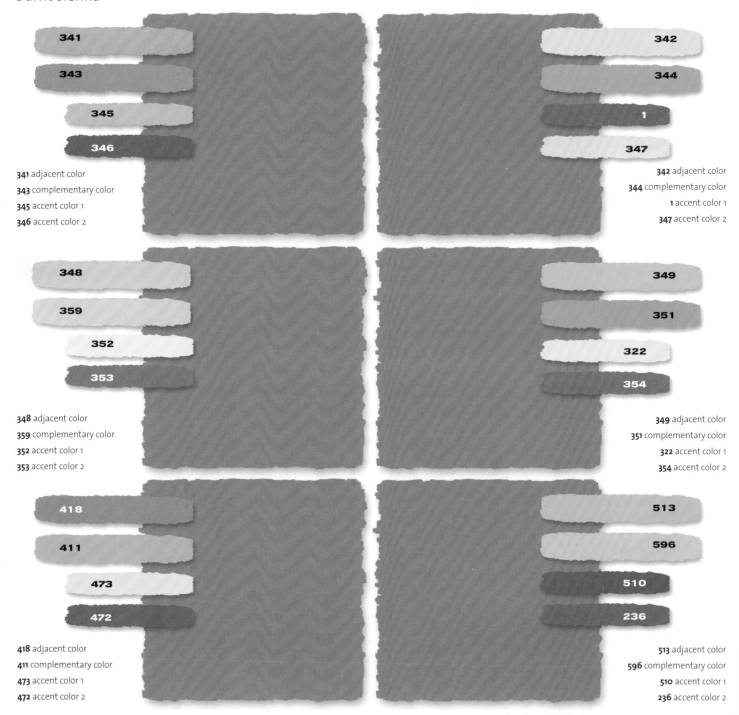

341

343

345

346

342

344

1

347

341 adjacent color
343 complementary color
345 accent color 1
346 accent color 2

342 adjacent color
344 complementary color
1 accent color 1
347 accent color 2

348

359

352

353

349

351

322

354

348 adjacent color
359 complementary color
352 accent color 1
353 accent color 2

349 adjacent color
351 complementary color
322 accent color 1
354 accent color 2

418

411

473

472

513

596

510

236

418 adjacent color
411 complementary color
473 accent color 1
472 accent color 2

513 adjacent color
596 complementary color
510 accent color 1
236 accent color 2

burnt sienna

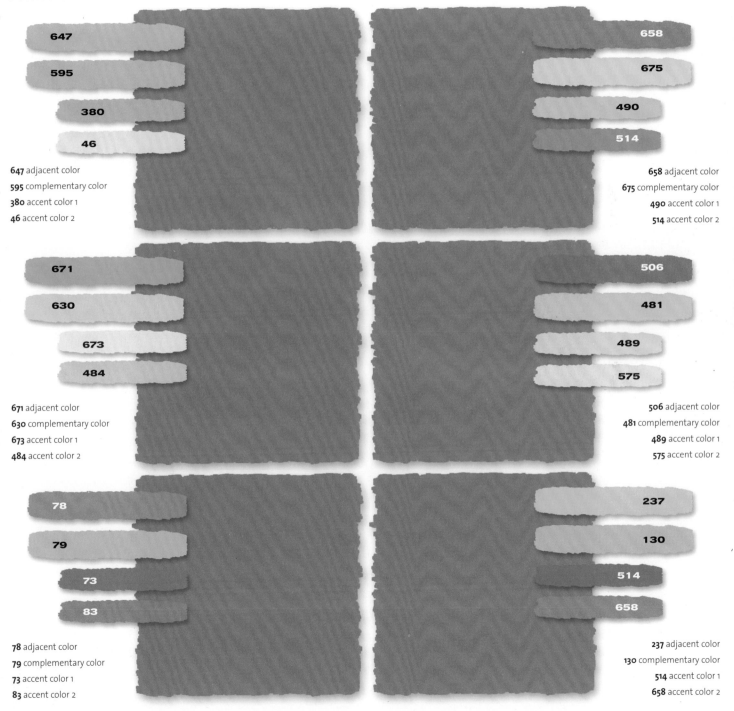

647
595
380
46

658
675
490
514

647 adjacent color
595 complementary color
380 accent color 1
46 accent color 2

658 adjacent color
675 complementary color
490 accent color 1
514 accent color 2

671
630
673
484

506
481
489
575

671 adjacent color
630 complementary color
673 accent color 1
484 accent color 2

506 adjacent color
481 complementary color
489 accent color 1
575 accent color 2

78
79
73
83

237
130
514
658

78 adjacent color
79 complementary color
73 accent color 1
83 accent color 2

237 adjacent color
130 complementary color
514 accent color 1
658 accent color 2

paris romance

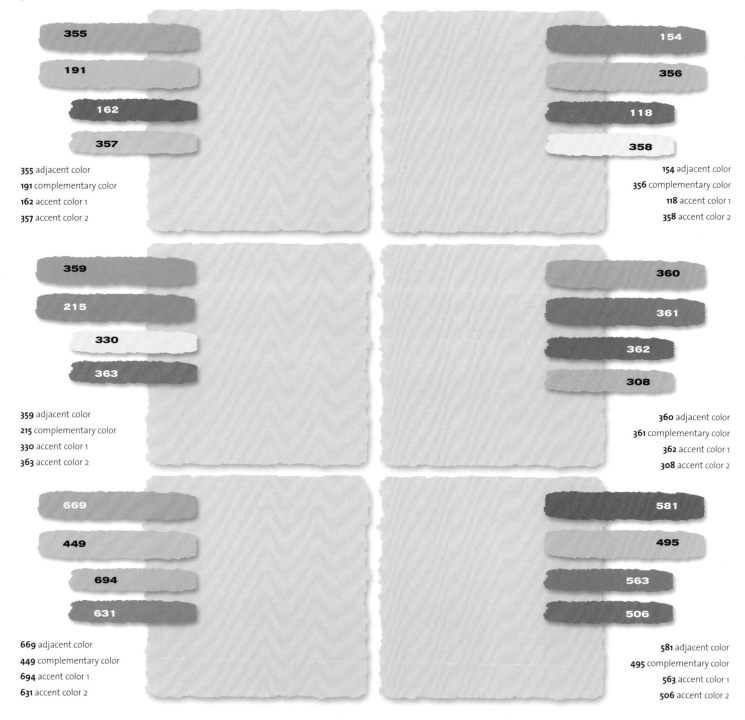

355

191

162

357

355 adjacent color
191 complementary color
162 accent color 1
357 accent color 2

154

356

118

358

154 adjacent color
356 complementary color
118 accent color 1
358 accent color 2

359

215

330

363

359 adjacent color
215 complementary color
330 accent color 1
363 accent color 2

360

361

362

308

360 adjacent color
361 complementary color
362 accent color 1
308 accent color 2

669

449

694

631

669 adjacent color
449 complementary color
694 accent color 1
631 accent color 2

581

495

563

506

581 adjacent color
495 complementary color
563 accent color 1
506 accent color 2

paris romance

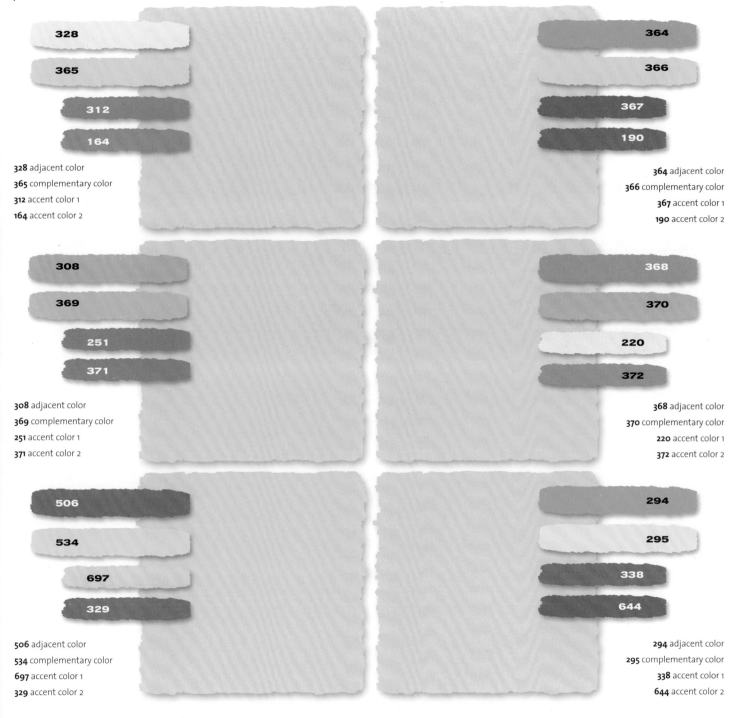

328
365
312
164

364
366
367
190

308
369
251
371

368
370
220
372

506
534
697
329

294
295
338
644

328 adjacent color
365 complementary color
312 accent color 1
164 accent color 2

364 adjacent color
366 complementary color
367 accent color 1
190 accent color 2

308 adjacent color
369 complementary color
251 accent color 1
371 accent color 2

368 adjacent color
370 complementary color
220 accent color 1
372 accent color 2

506 adjacent color
534 complementary color
697 accent color 1
329 accent color 2

294 adjacent color
295 complementary color
338 accent color 1
644 accent color 2

paris romance

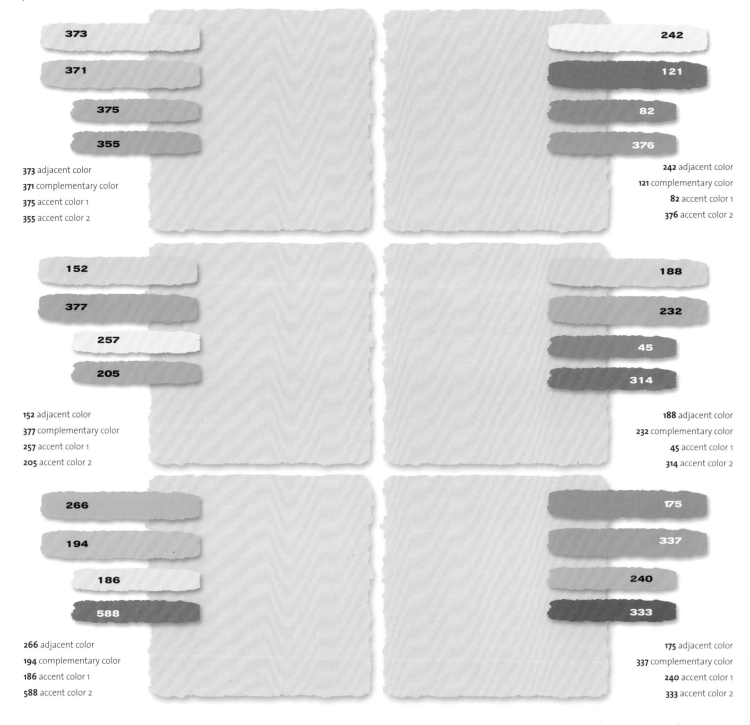

373

371

375

355

373 adjacent color
371 complementary color
375 accent color 1
355 accent color 2

242

121

82

376

242 adjacent color
121 complementary color
82 accent color 1
376 accent color 2

152

377

257

205

152 adjacent color
377 complementary color
257 accent color 1
205 accent color 2

188

232

45

314

188 adjacent color
232 complementary color
45 accent color 1
314 accent color 2

266

194

186

588

266 adjacent color
194 complementary color
186 accent color 1
588 accent color 2

175

337

240

333

175 adjacent color
337 complementary color
240 accent color 1
333 accent color 2

paris romance

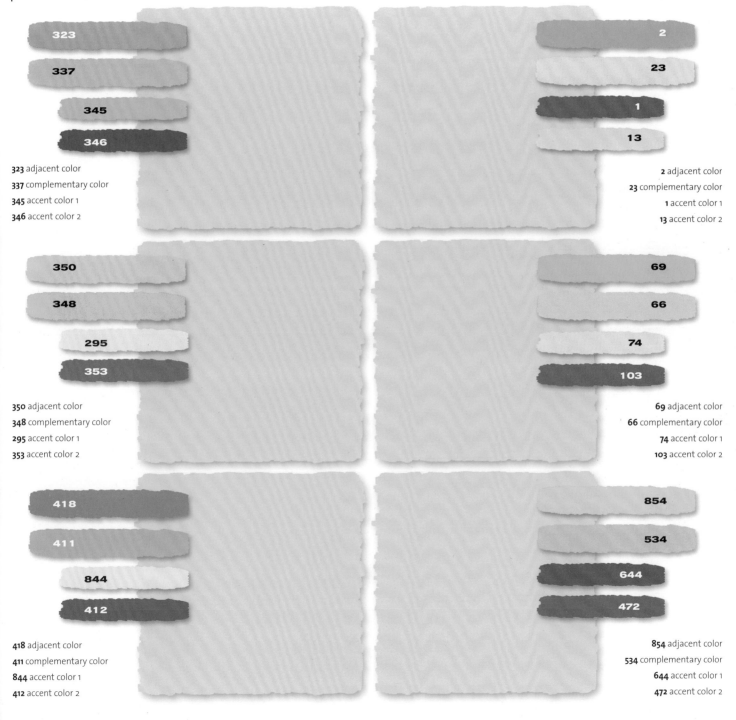

323 adjacent color
337 complementary color
345 accent color 1
346 accent color 2

2 adjacent color
23 complementary color
1 accent color 1
13 accent color 2

350 adjacent color
348 complementary color
295 accent color 1
353 accent color 2

69 adjacent color
66 complementary color
74 accent color 1
103 accent color 2

418 adjacent color
411 complementary color
844 accent color 1
412 accent color 2

854 adjacent color
534 complementary color
644 accent color 1
472 accent color 2

tuscon tan

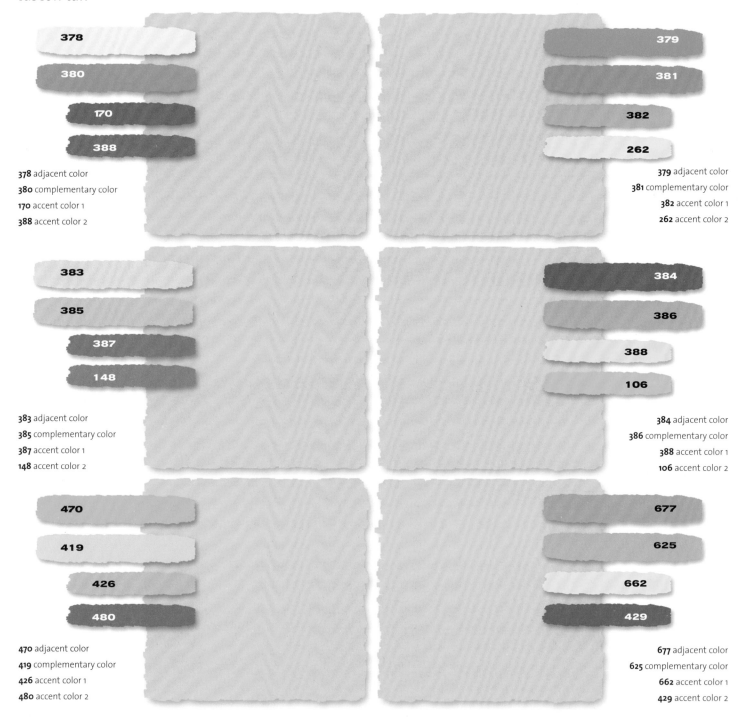

378
380
170
388

379
381
382
262

378 adjacent color
380 complementary color
170 accent color 1
388 accent color 2

379 adjacent color
381 complementary color
382 accent color 1
262 accent color 2

383
385
387
148

384
386
388
106

383 adjacent color
385 complementary color
387 accent color 1
148 accent color 2

384 adjacent color
386 complementary color
388 accent color 1
106 accent color 2

470
419
426
480

677
625
662
429

470 adjacent color
419 complementary color
426 accent color 1
480 accent color 2

677 adjacent color
625 complementary color
662 accent color 1
429 accent color 2

tuscon tan

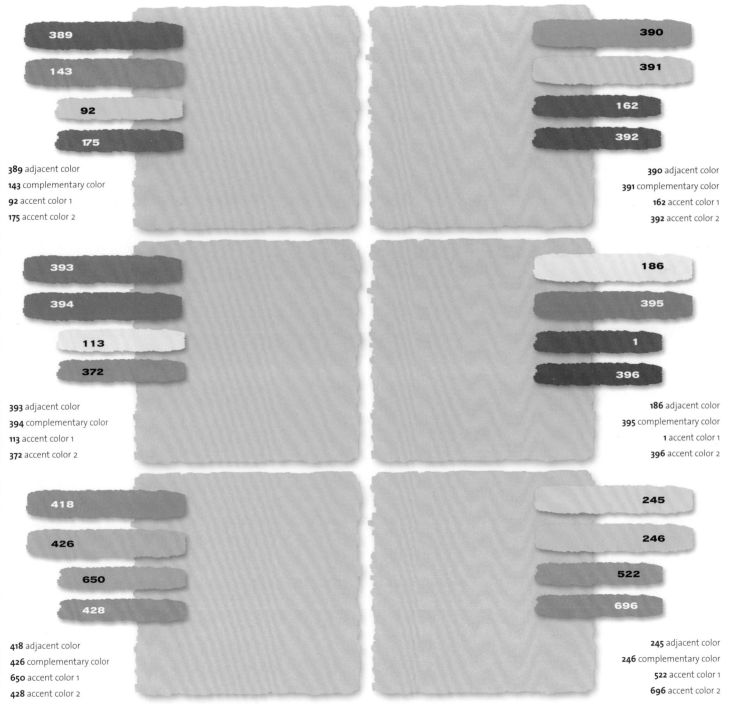

389
143
92
175

390
391
162
392

389 adjacent color
143 complementary color
92 accent color 1
175 accent color 2

390 adjacent color
391 complementary color
162 accent color 1
392 accent color 2

393
394
113
372

186
395
1
396

393 adjacent color
394 complementary color
113 accent color 1
372 accent color 2

186 adjacent color
395 complementary color
1 accent color 1
396 accent color 2

418
426
650
428

245
246
522
696

418 adjacent color
426 complementary color
650 accent color 1
428 accent color 2

245 adjacent color
246 complementary color
522 accent color 1
696 accent color 2

tuscon tan

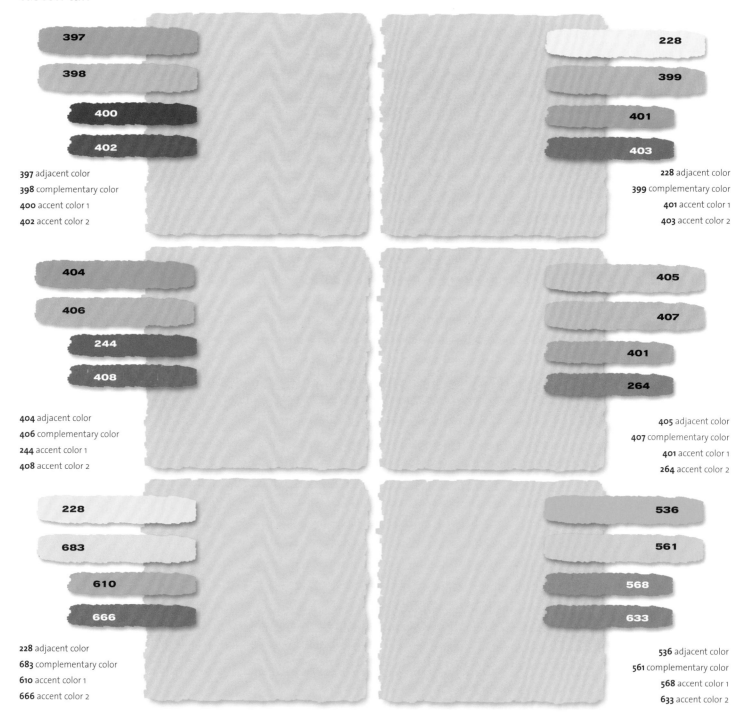

397

398

400

402

397 adjacent color
398 complementary color
400 accent color 1
402 accent color 2

228

399

401

403

228 adjacent color
399 complementary color
401 accent color 1
403 accent color 2

404

406

244

408

404 adjacent color
406 complementary color
244 accent color 1
408 accent color 2

405

407

401

264

405 adjacent color
407 complementary color
401 accent color 1
264 accent color 2

228

683

610

666

228 adjacent color
683 complementary color
610 accent color 1
666 accent color 2

536

561

568

633

536 adjacent color
561 complementary color
568 accent color 1
633 accent color 2

tuscon tan

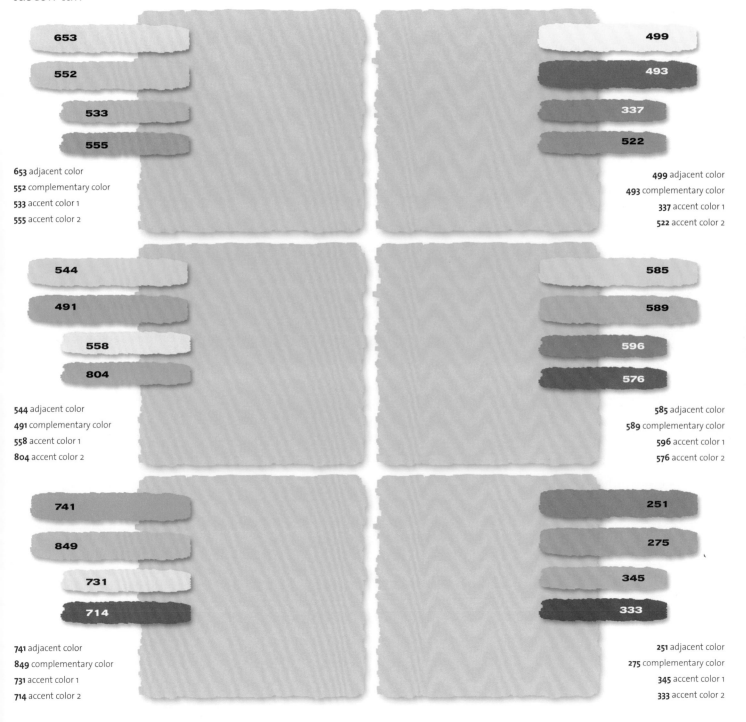

653
552
533
555

653 adjacent color
552 complementary color
533 accent color 1
555 accent color 2

499
493
337
522

499 adjacent color
493 complementary color
337 accent color 1
522 accent color 2

544
491
558
804

544 adjacent color
491 complementary color
558 accent color 1
804 accent color 2

585
589
596
576

585 adjacent color
589 complementary color
596 accent color 1
576 accent color 2

741
849
731
714

741 adjacent color
849 complementary color
731 accent color 1
714 accent color 2

251
275
345
333

251 adjacent color
275 complementary color
345 accent color 1
333 accent color 2

freesia

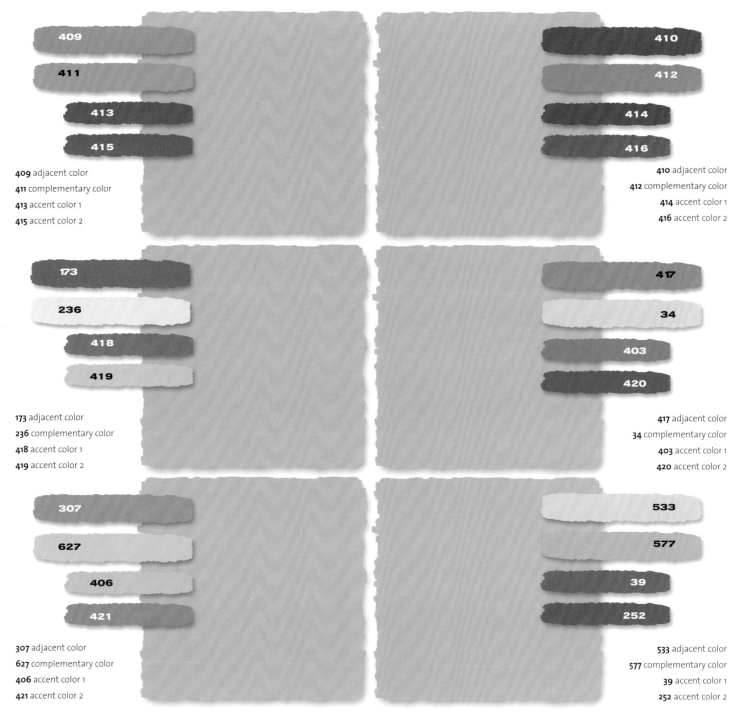

409 adjacent color
411 complementary color
413 accent color 1
415 accent color 2

410 adjacent color
412 complementary color
414 accent color 1
416 accent color 2

173 adjacent color
236 complementary color
418 accent color 1
419 accent color 2

417 adjacent color
34 complementary color
403 accent color 1
420 accent color 2

307 adjacent color
627 complementary color
406 accent color 1
421 accent color 2

533 adjacent color
577 complementary color
39 accent color 1
252 accent color 2

freesia

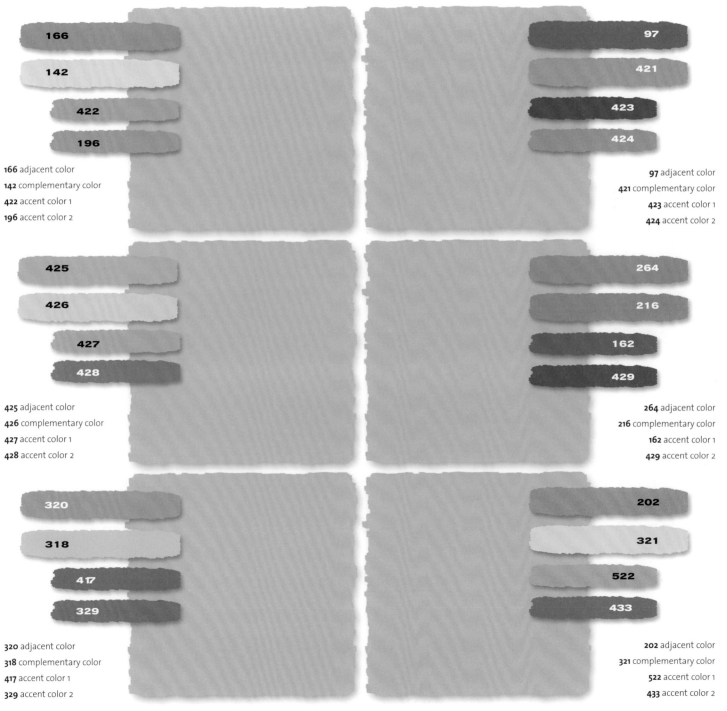

166 | 97

142 | 421

422 | 423

196 | 424

166 adjacent color
142 complementary color
422 accent color 1
196 accent color 2

97 adjacent color
421 complementary color
423 accent color 1
424 accent color 2

425 | 264

426 | 216

427 | 162

428 | 429

425 adjacent color
426 complementary color
427 accent color 1
428 accent color 2

264 adjacent color
216 complementary color
162 accent color 1
429 accent color 2

320 | 202

318 | 321

417 | 522

329 | 433

320 adjacent color
318 complementary color
417 accent color 1
329 accent color 2

202 adjacent color
321 complementary color
522 accent color 1
433 accent color 2

freesia

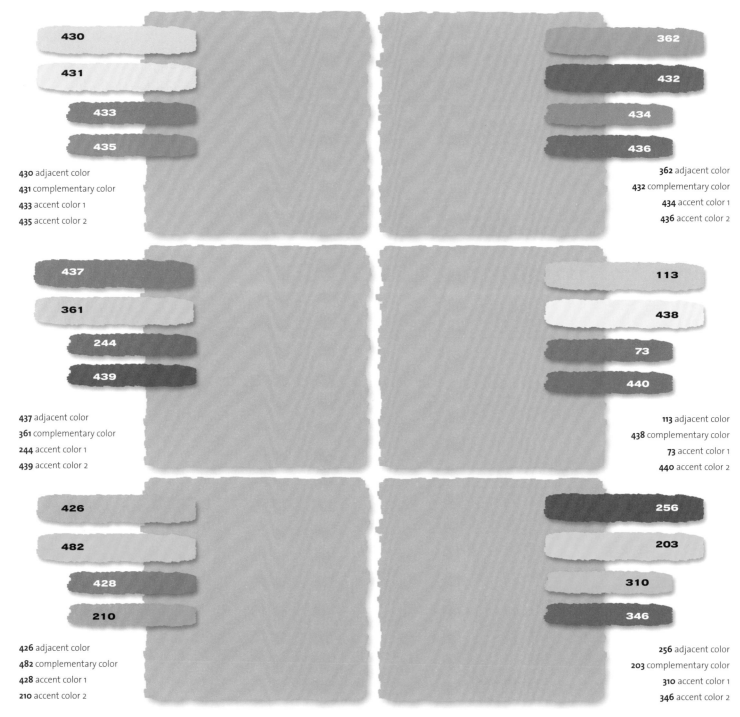

430
431
433
435

362
432
434
436

430 adjacent color
431 complementary color
433 accent color 1
435 accent color 2

362 adjacent color
432 complementary color
434 accent color 1
436 accent color 2

437
361
244
439

113
438
73
440

437 adjacent color
361 complementary color
244 accent color 1
439 accent color 2

113 adjacent color
438 complementary color
73 accent color 1
440 accent color 2

426
482
428
210

256
203
310
346

426 adjacent color
482 complementary color
428 accent color 1
210 accent color 2

256 adjacent color
203 complementary color
310 accent color 1
346 accent color 2

freesia

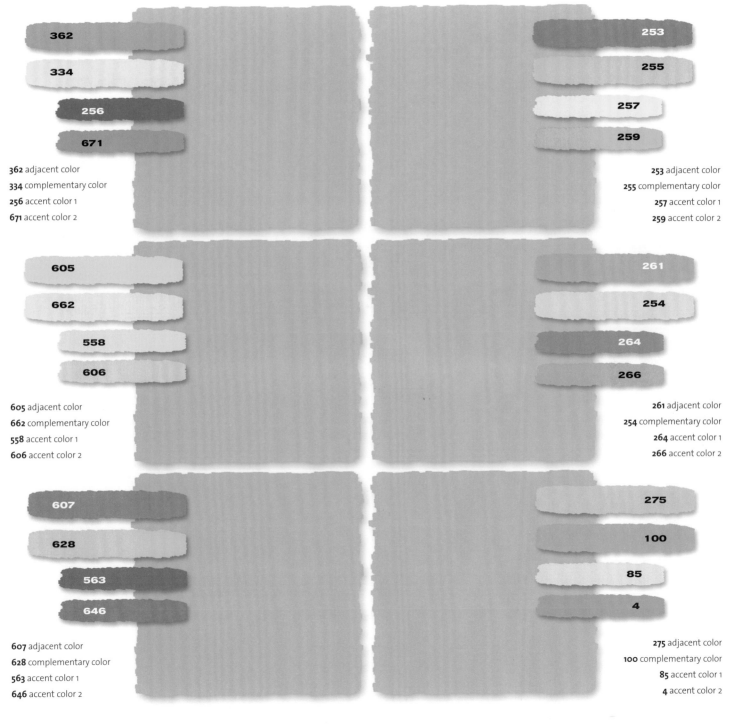

362

334

256

671

253

255

257

259

605

662

558

606

261

254

264

266

607

628

563

646

275

100

85

4

362 adjacent color
334 complementary color
256 accent color 1
671 accent color 2

253 adjacent color
255 complementary color
257 accent color 1
259 accent color 2

605 adjacent color
662 complementary color
558 accent color 1
606 accent color 2

261 adjacent color
254 complementary color
264 accent color 1
266 accent color 2

607 adjacent color
628 complementary color
563 accent color 1
646 accent color 2

275 adjacent color
100 complementary color
85 accent color 1
4 accent color 2

secret

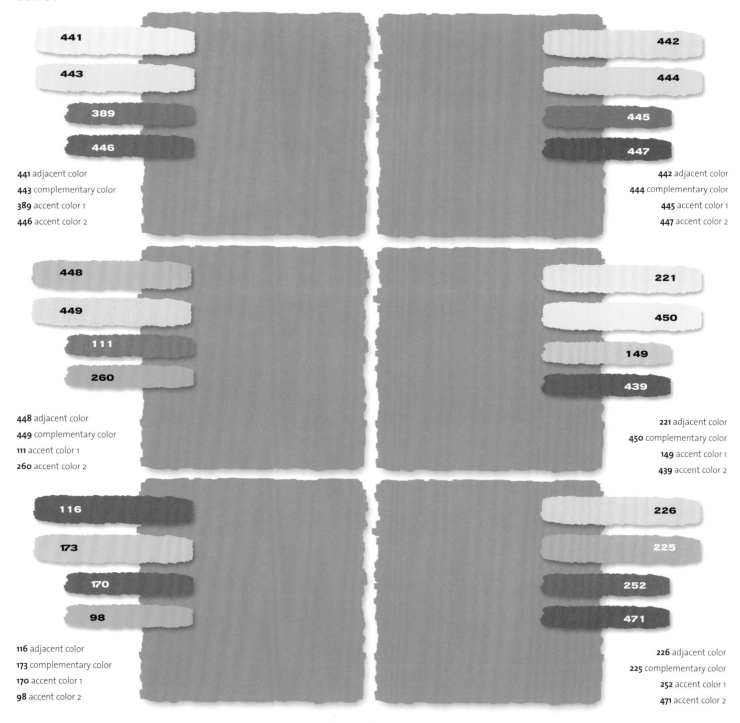

441
443
389
446

442
444
445
447

441 adjacent color
443 complementary color
389 accent color 1
446 accent color 2

442 adjacent color
444 complementary color
445 accent color 1
447 accent color 2

448
449
111
260

221
450
149
439

448 adjacent color
449 complementary color
111 accent color 1
260 accent color 2

221 adjacent color
450 complementary color
149 accent color 1
439 accent color 2

116
173
170
98

226
225
252
471

116 adjacent color
173 complementary color
170 accent color 1
98 accent color 2

226 adjacent color
225 complementary color
252 accent color 1
471 accent color 2

secret

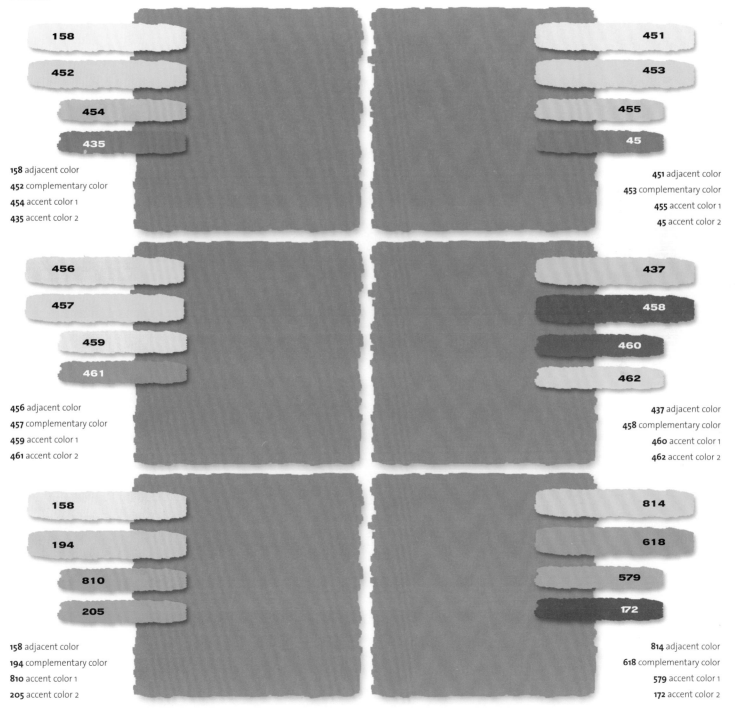

158 adjacent color
452 complementary color
454 accent color 1
435 accent color 2

451 adjacent color
453 complementary color
455 accent color 1
45 accent color 2

456 adjacent color
457 complementary color
459 accent color 1
461 accent color 2

437 adjacent color
458 complementary color
460 accent color 1
462 accent color 2

158 adjacent color
194 complementary color
810 accent color 1
205 accent color 2

814 adjacent color
618 complementary color
579 accent color 1
172 accent color 2

secret

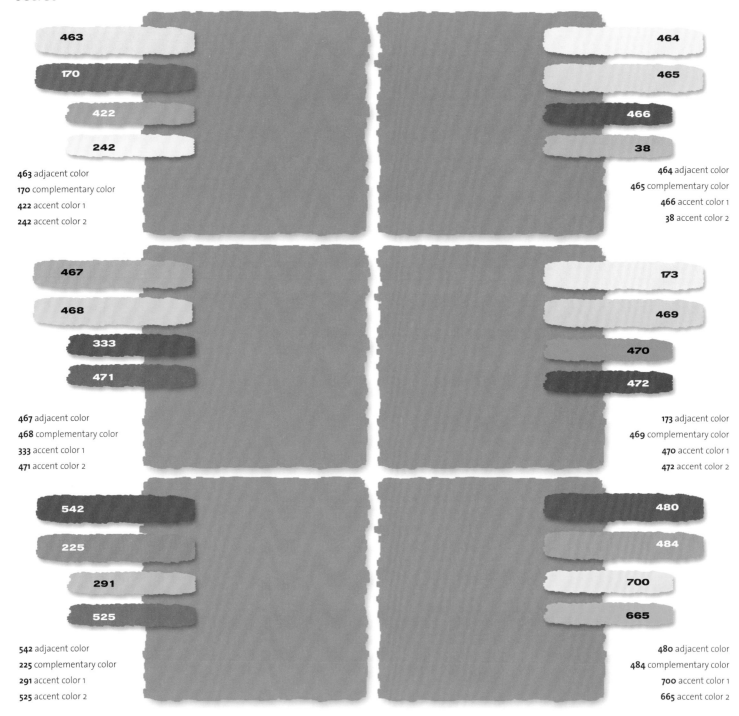

463
170
422
242

464
465
466
38

463 adjacent color
170 complementary color
422 accent color 1
242 accent color 2

464 adjacent color
465 complementary color
466 accent color 1
38 accent color 2

467
468
333
471

173
469
470
472

467 adjacent color
468 complementary color
333 accent color 1
471 accent color 2

173 adjacent color
469 complementary color
470 accent color 1
472 accent color 2

542
225
291
525

480
484
700
665

542 adjacent color
225 complementary color
291 accent color 1
525 accent color 2

480 adjacent color
484 complementary color
700 accent color 1
665 accent color 2

secret

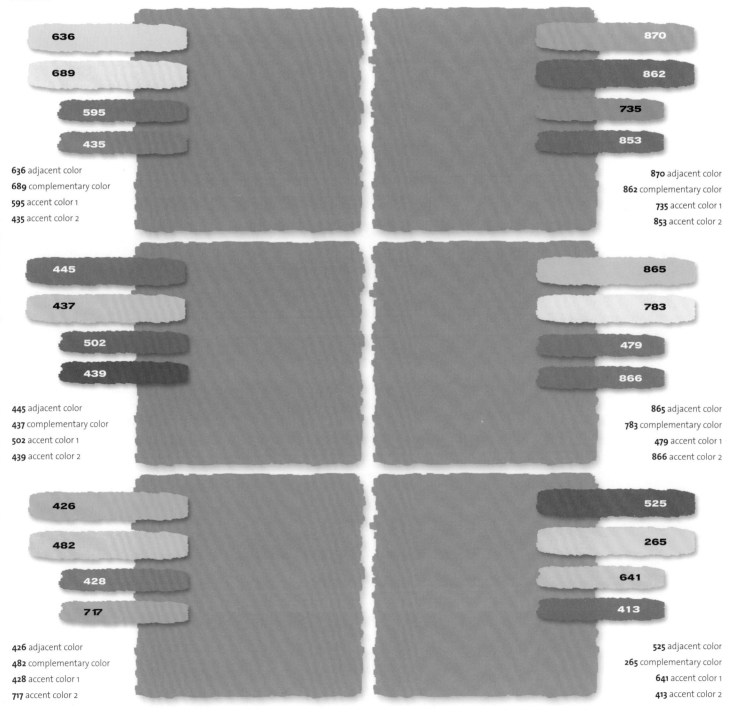

636 adjacent color
689 complementary color
595 accent color 1
435 accent color 2

870 adjacent color
862 complementary color
735 accent color 1
853 accent color 2

445 adjacent color
437 complementary color
502 accent color 1
439 accent color 2

865 adjacent color
783 complementary color
479 accent color 1
866 accent color 2

426 adjacent color
482 complementary color
428 accent color 1
717 accent color 2

525 adjacent color
265 complementary color
641 accent color 1
413 accent color 2

desert view

653

483

480

671

653 adjacent color
483 complementary color
480 accent color 1
671 accent color 2

563

505

473

607

563 adjacent color
505 complementary color
473 accent color 1
607 accent color 2

425

385

476

433

425 adjacent color
385 complementary color
476 accent color 1
433 accent color 2

671

433

437

666

671 adjacent color
433 complementary color
437 accent color 1
666 accent color 2

509

587

634

697

509 adjacent color
587 complementary color
634 accent color 1
697 accent color 2

697

704

662

490

697 adjacent color
704 complementary color
662 accent color 1
490 accent color 2

desert view

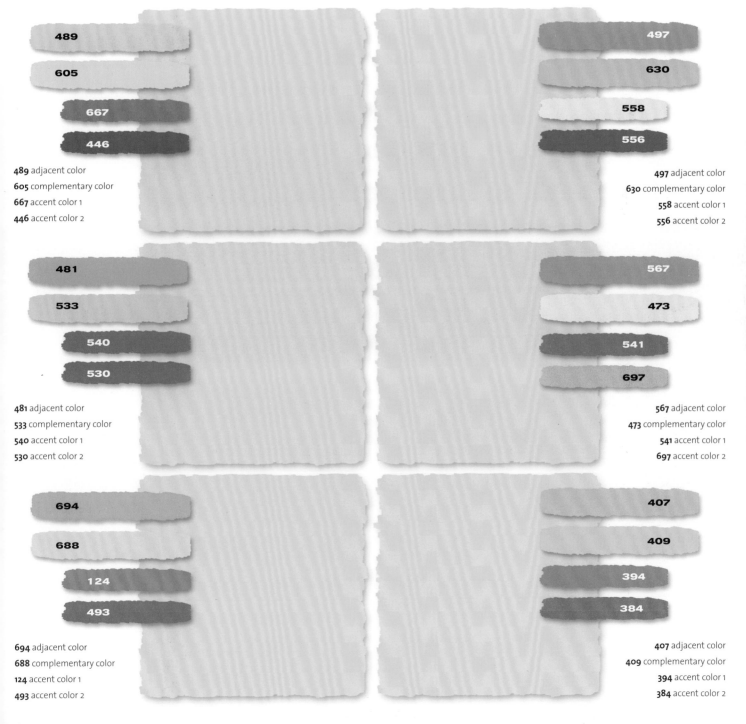

489

605

667

446

489 adjacent color
605 complementary color
667 accent color 1
446 accent color 2

497

630

558

556

497 adjacent color
630 complementary color
558 accent color 1
556 accent color 2

481

533

540

530

481 adjacent color
533 complementary color
540 accent color 1
530 accent color 2

567

473

541

697

567 adjacent color
473 complementary color
541 accent color 1
697 accent color 2

694

688

124

493

694 adjacent color
688 complementary color
124 accent color 1
493 accent color 2

407

409

394

384

407 adjacent color
409 complementary color
394 accent color 1
384 accent color 2

desert view

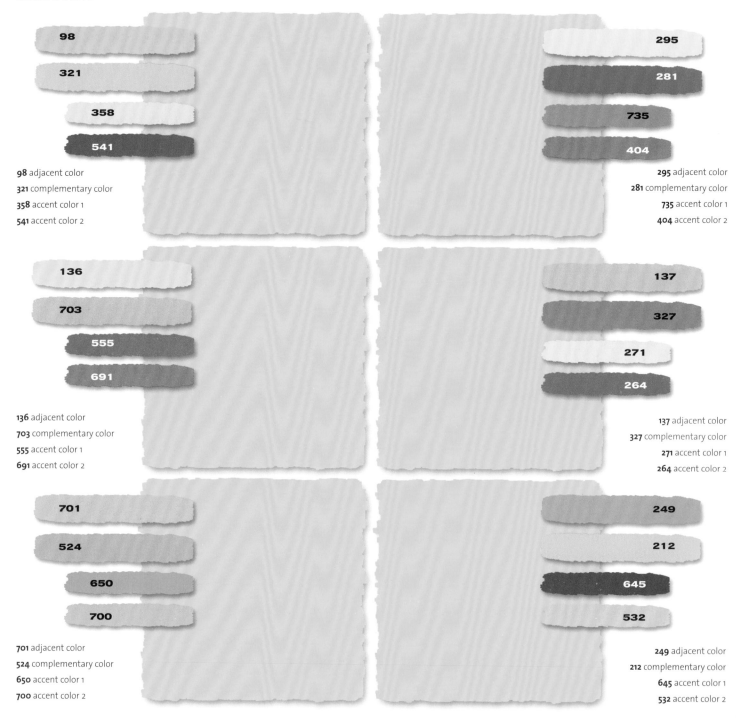

98

321

358

541

98 adjacent color
321 complementary color
358 accent color 1
541 accent color 2

295

281

735

404

295 adjacent color
281 complementary color
735 accent color 1
404 accent color 2

136

703

555

691

136 adjacent color
703 complementary color
555 accent color 1
691 accent color 2

137

327

271

264

137 adjacent color
327 complementary color
271 accent color 1
264 accent color 2

701

524

650

700

701 adjacent color
524 complementary color
650 accent color 1
700 accent color 2

249

212

645

532

249 adjacent color
212 complementary color
645 accent color 1
532 accent color 2

desert view

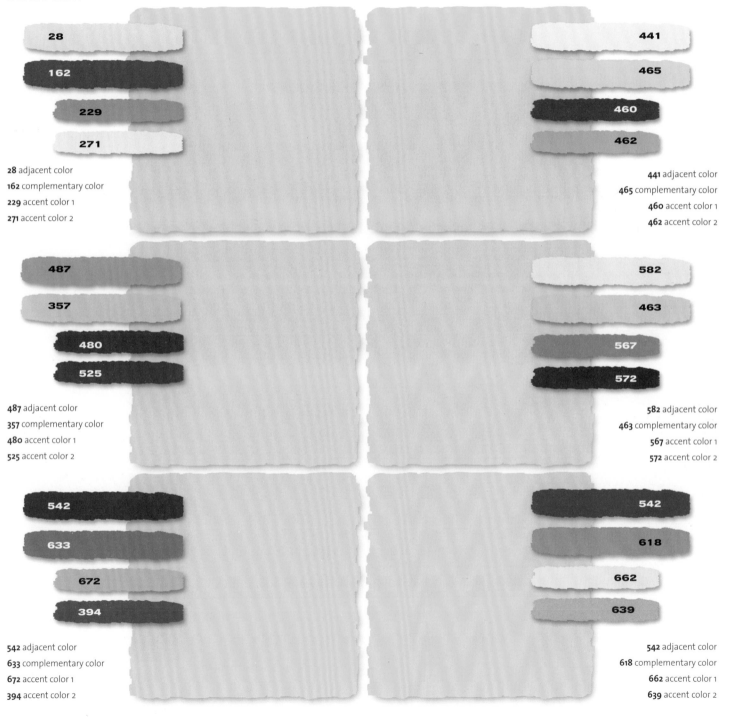

28

162

229

271

28 adjacent color
162 complementary color
229 accent color 1
271 accent color 2

441

465

460

462

441 adjacent color
465 complementary color
460 accent color 1
462 accent color 2

487

357

480

525

487 adjacent color
357 complementary color
480 accent color 1
525 accent color 2

582

463

567

572

582 adjacent color
463 complementary color
567 accent color 1
572 accent color 2

542

633

672

394

542 adjacent color
633 complementary color
672 accent color 1
394 accent color 2

542

618

662

639

542 adjacent color
618 complementary color
662 accent color 1
639 accent color 2

crowne hill yellow

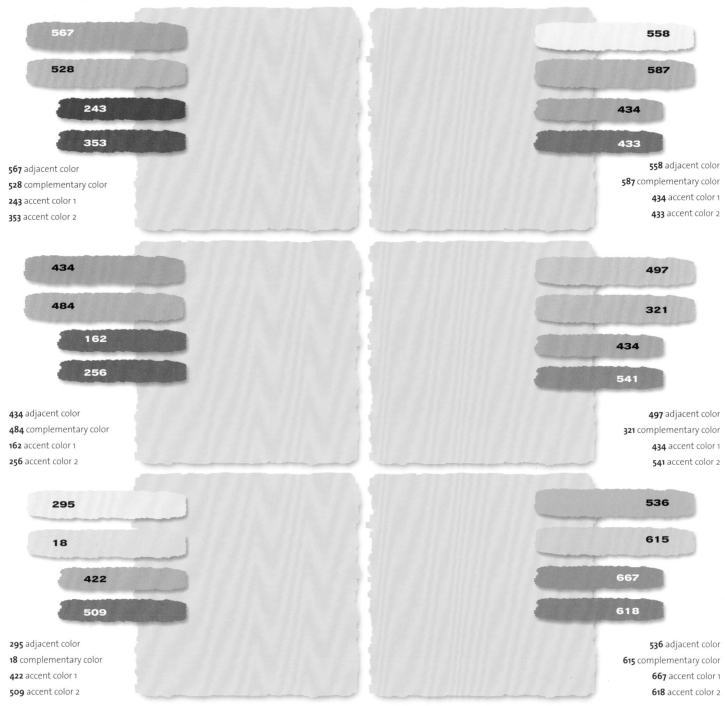

567
528
243
353

567 adjacent color
528 complementary color
243 accent color 1
353 accent color 2

558
587
434
433

558 adjacent color
587 complementary color
434 accent color 1
433 accent color 2

434
484
162
256

434 adjacent color
484 complementary color
162 accent color 1
256 accent color 2

497
321
434
541

497 adjacent color
321 complementary color
434 accent color 1
541 accent color 2

295
18
422
509

295 adjacent color
18 complementary color
422 accent color 1
509 accent color 2

536
615
667
618

536 adjacent color
615 complementary color
667 accent color 1
618 accent color 2

crowne hill yellow

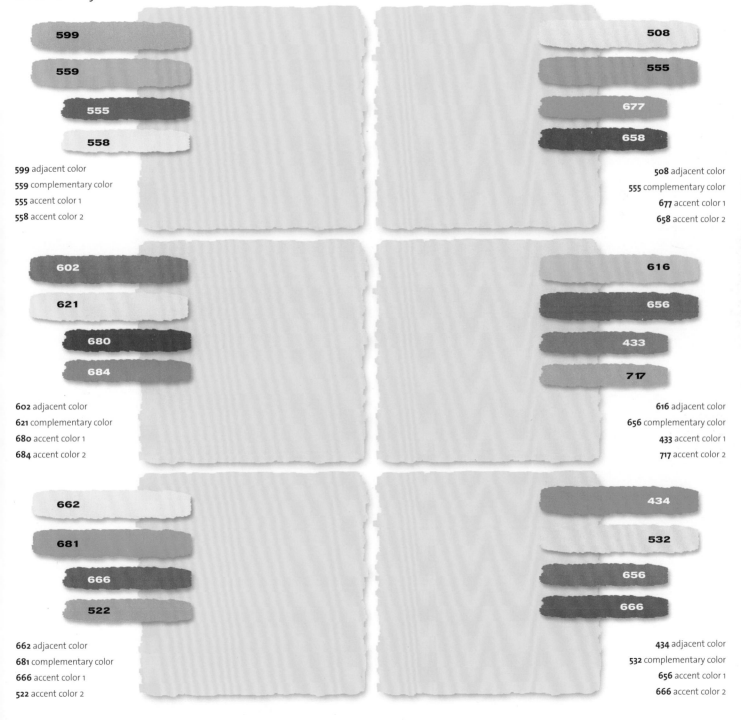

599
559
555
558

508
555
677
658

599 adjacent color
559 complementary color
555 accent color 1
558 accent color 2

508 adjacent color
555 complementary color
677 accent color 1
658 accent color 2

602
621
680
684

616
656
433
717

602 adjacent color
621 complementary color
680 accent color 1
684 accent color 2

616 adjacent color
656 complementary color
433 accent color 1
717 accent color 2

662
681
666
522

434
532
656
666

662 adjacent color
681 complementary color
666 accent color 1
522 accent color 2

434 adjacent color
532 complementary color
656 accent color 1
666 accent color 2

crowne hill yellow

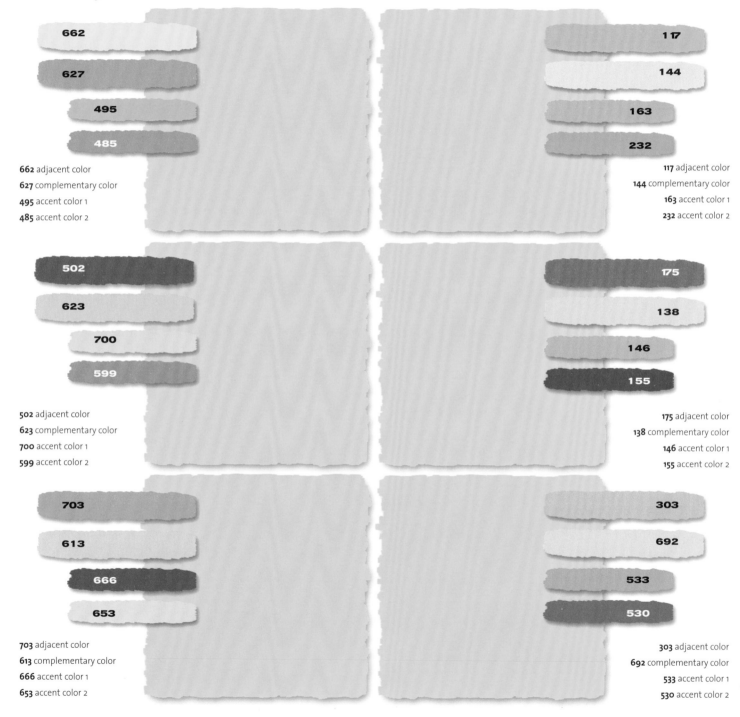

662
627
495
485

1 17
144
163
232

662 adjacent color
627 complementary color
495 accent color 1
485 accent color 2

117 adjacent color
144 complementary color
163 accent color 1
232 accent color 2

502
623
700
599

175
138
146
155

502 adjacent color
623 complementary color
700 accent color 1
599 accent color 2

175 adjacent color
138 complementary color
146 accent color 1
155 accent color 2

703
613
666
653

303
692
533
530

703 adjacent color
613 complementary color
666 accent color 1
653 accent color 2

303 adjacent color
692 complementary color
533 accent color 1
530 accent color 2

crowne hill yellow

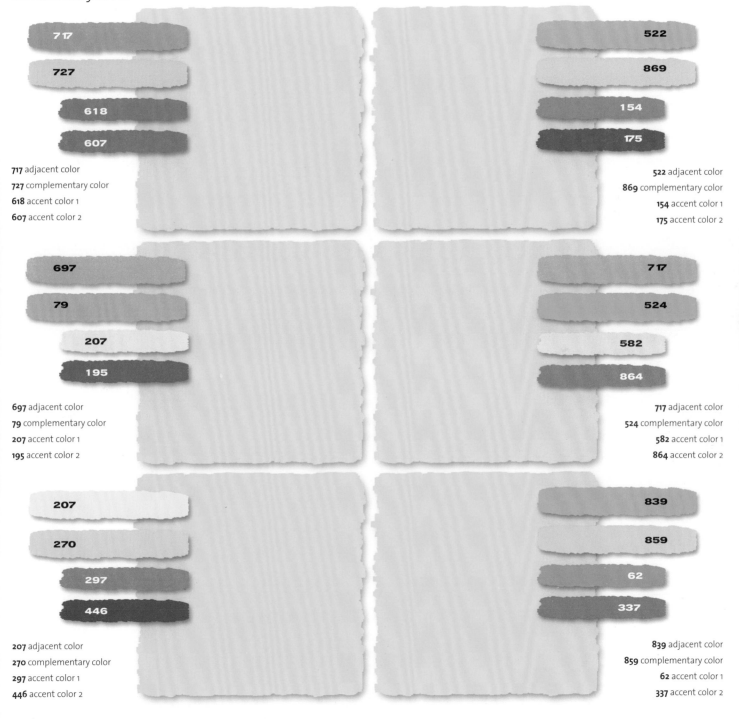

717
727
618
607

717 adjacent color
727 complementary color
618 accent color 1
607 accent color 2

522
869
154
175

522 adjacent color
869 complementary color
154 accent color 1
175 accent color 2

697
79
207
195

697 adjacent color
79 complementary color
207 accent color 1
195 accent color 2

717
524
582
864

717 adjacent color
524 complementary color
582 accent color 1
864 accent color 2

207
270
297
446

207 adjacent color
270 complementary color
297 accent color 1
446 accent color 2

839
859
62
337

839 adjacent color
859 complementary color
62 accent color 1
337 accent color 2

coral glow

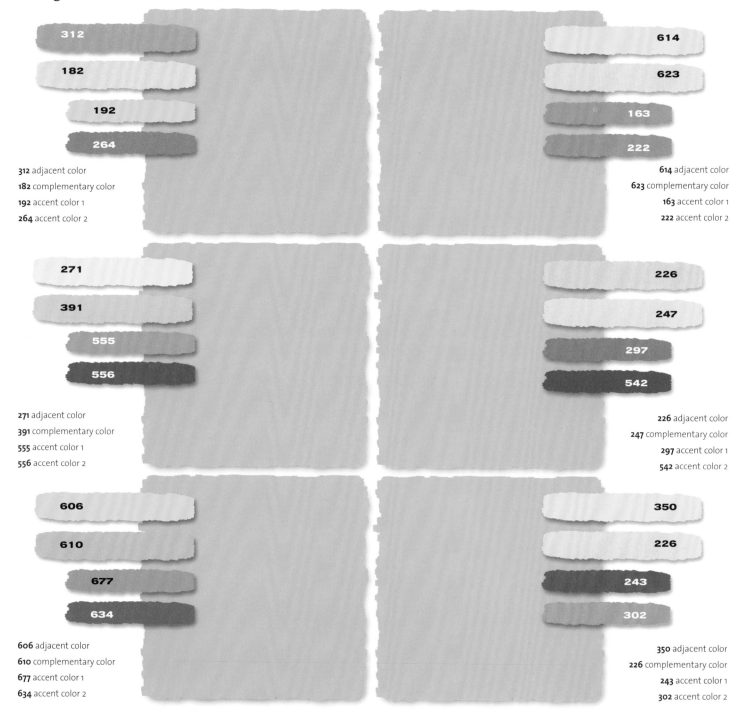

312

182

192

264

312 adjacent color
182 complementary color
192 accent color 1
264 accent color 2

614

623

163

222

614 adjacent color
623 complementary color
163 accent color 1
222 accent color 2

271

391

555

556

271 adjacent color
391 complementary color
555 accent color 1
556 accent color 2

226

247

297

542

226 adjacent color
247 complementary color
297 accent color 1
542 accent color 2

606

610

677

634

606 adjacent color
610 complementary color
677 accent color 1
634 accent color 2

350

226

243

302

350 adjacent color
226 complementary color
243 accent color 1
302 accent color 2

coral glow

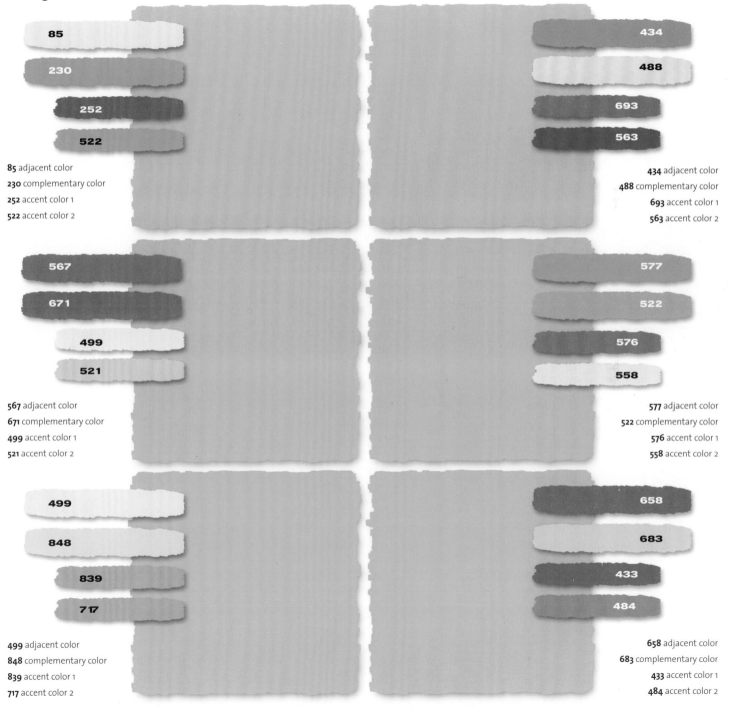

85 adjacent color
230 complementary color
252 accent color 1
522 accent color 2

434 adjacent color
488 complementary color
693 accent color 1
563 accent color 2

567 adjacent color
671 complementary color
499 accent color 1
521 accent color 2

577 adjacent color
522 complementary color
576 accent color 1
558 accent color 2

499 adjacent color
848 complementary color
839 accent color 1
717 accent color 2

658 adjacent color
683 complementary color
433 accent color 1
484 accent color 2

coral glow

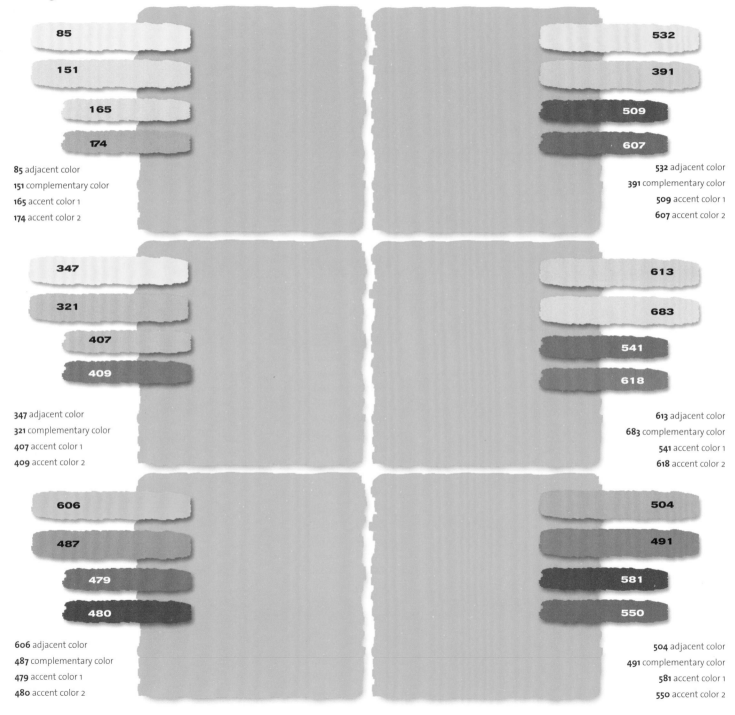

85

151

165

174

532

391

509

607

85 adjacent color
151 complementary color
165 accent color 1
174 accent color 2

532 adjacent color
391 complementary color
509 accent color 1
607 accent color 2

347

321

407

409

613

683

541

618

347 adjacent color
321 complementary color
407 accent color 1
409 accent color 2

613 adjacent color
683 complementary color
541 accent color 1
618 accent color 2

606

487

479

480

504

491

581

550

606 adjacent color
487 complementary color
479 accent color 1
480 accent color 2

504 adjacent color
491 complementary color
581 accent color 1
550 accent color 2

coral glow

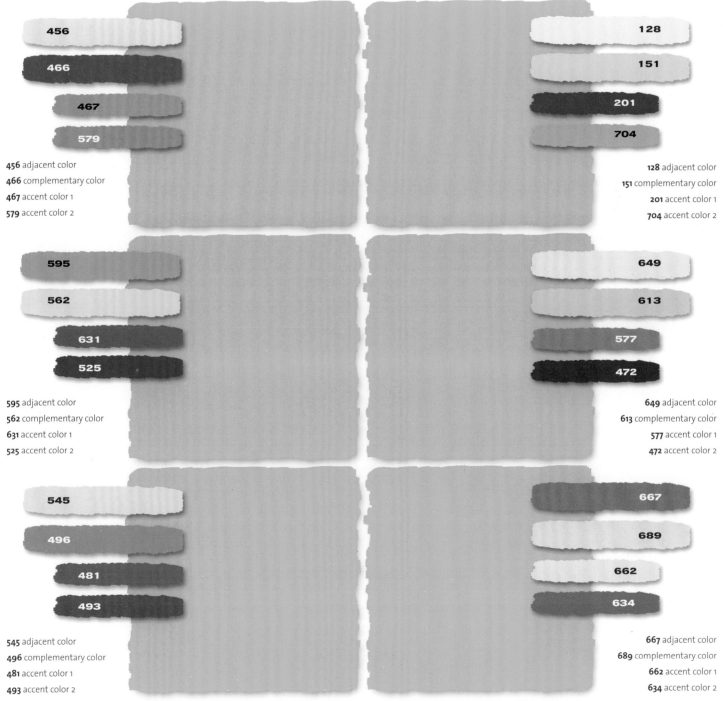

456

466

467

579

128

151

201

704

456 adjacent color
466 complementary color
467 accent color 1
579 accent color 2

128 adjacent color
151 complementary color
201 accent color 1
704 accent color 2

595

562

631

525

649

613

577

472

595 adjacent color
562 complementary color
631 accent color 1
525 accent color 2

649 adjacent color
613 complementary color
577 accent color 1
472 accent color 2

545

496

481

493

667

689

662

634

545 adjacent color
496 complementary color
481 accent color 1
493 accent color 2

667 adjacent color
689 complementary color
662 accent color 1
634 accent color 2

12	471
467	333

LEFT Gray is a much underrated color. It has so many subtle variations of hue and tone that it can be used in any and every situation. Here the warm gray is the perfect backdrop for the strong color in the art and the soft furnishings.

7	302
300	235

RIGHT Strong saturated colors, such as purple and orange, used in contrast, create a space that is physically sensual and welcoming, and in addition stimulates mental activity.

| 215 | 385 |
| 468 | 871 |

| 12 | 221 |
| 439 | 450 |

ABOVE The clean lines, neutral tones, and simple design of the bedside table and lamp sit in harmony with the neutral color scheme, providing a contemporary and sensual environment that will not dominate the room.

RIGHT The cool neutrals of the smooth walls and the reflections created in the polished floor help to create a beautiful contrast with the coarse-textured deep indigo material covering the bench, and the rich green raw silk drapes, that makes for a relaxing experience.

9	359	10	387
215	330	148	383

BELOW With its use of granite, stainless steel, and glass, set against the warm neutral color scheme, this kitchen provides the setting for a sensual cooking and eating experience.

RIGHT The somber tones of the sofa, cushions, and floor covering are brought to life by the contrast with the rich salmon pink walls, giving this room its welcoming appeal.

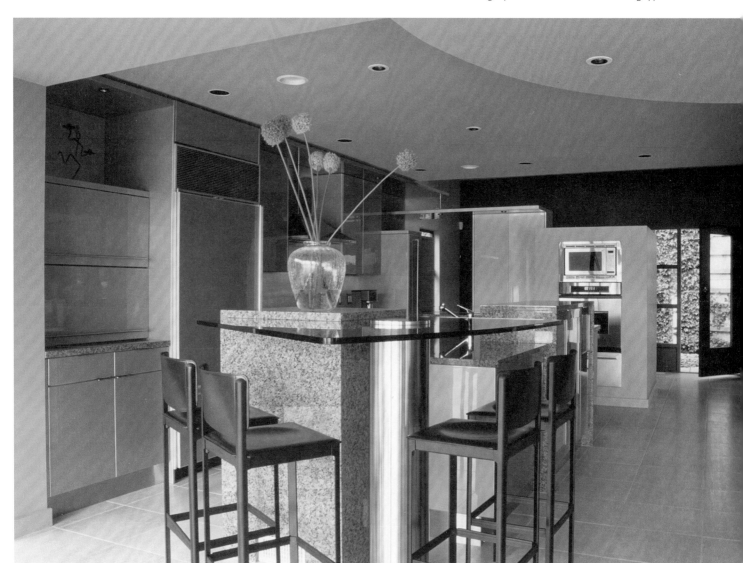

170	359
133	675

RIGHT The subtle combination of grays, fawns, browns, and black create a deeply sensual bedroom. The white bed linen is an essential addition in order to prevent the scheme becoming too overpowering.

203	195
215	382

RIGHT Using the colors from the garden to complement the rich yellow interior creates a sensual yet dynamic room that will be welcoming and also stimulating, making a perfect area for dining and entertaining.

8	333
337	128

LEFT Creating a sensual room can be achieved by simply adding accent colors with soft furnishings, such as cushions, drapes, and rugs. Thus allowing you to easily change your scheme should you wish to.

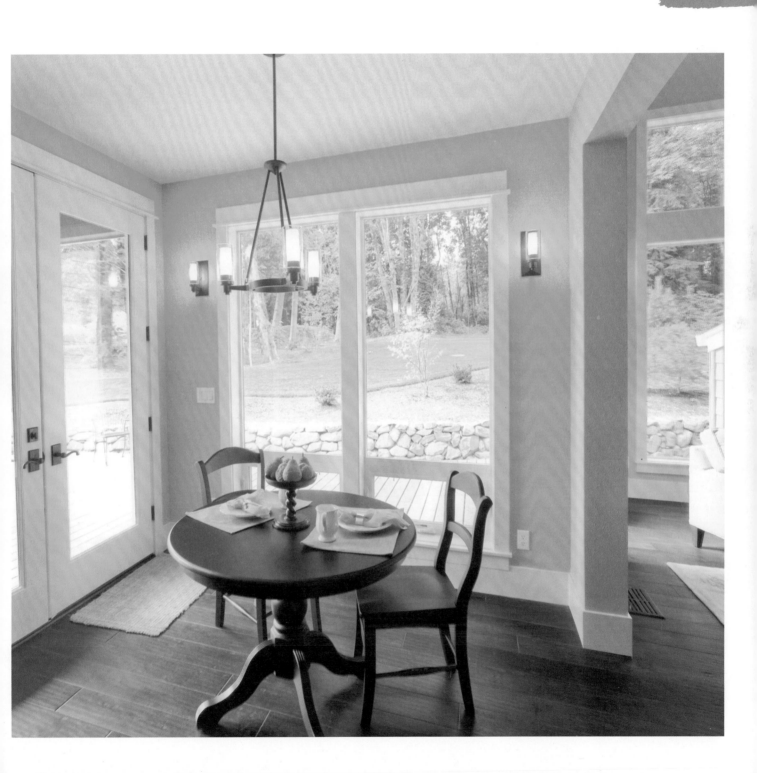

8	428
442	542

RIGHT Natural stone and the well-planted window boxes supply a beautiful complement to the rich terra-cotta of the door and window shutters

518	521
393	493

ABOVE Lavender can be used effectively when combined with neutral beiges and grays. The subtle combination of cushion colors used here makes for a calm, soothing living area.

95	68
642	376

RIGHT Selecting a scheme using adjacent colors on the color wheel, and balancing the strength of those colors creates a harmonious, soothing, and sensual room.

splendor

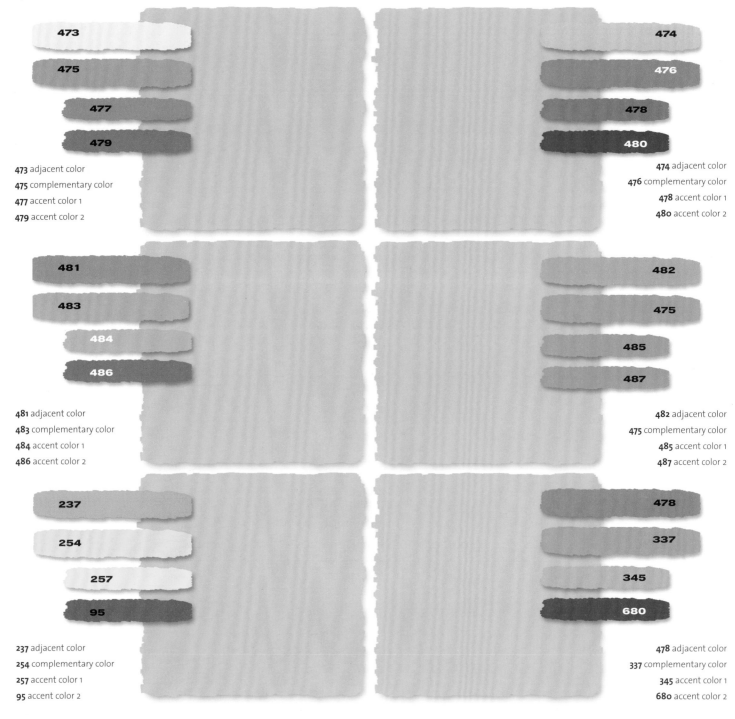

473
475
477
479

474
476
478
480

473 adjacent color
475 complementary color
477 accent color 1
479 accent color 2

474 adjacent color
476 complementary color
478 accent color 1
480 accent color 2

481
483
484
486

482
475
485
487

481 adjacent color
483 complementary color
484 accent color 1
486 accent color 2

482 adjacent color
475 complementary color
485 accent color 1
487 accent color 2

237
254
257
95

478
337
345
680

237 adjacent color
254 complementary color
257 accent color 1
95 accent color 2

478 adjacent color
337 complementary color
345 accent color 1
680 accent color 2

splendor

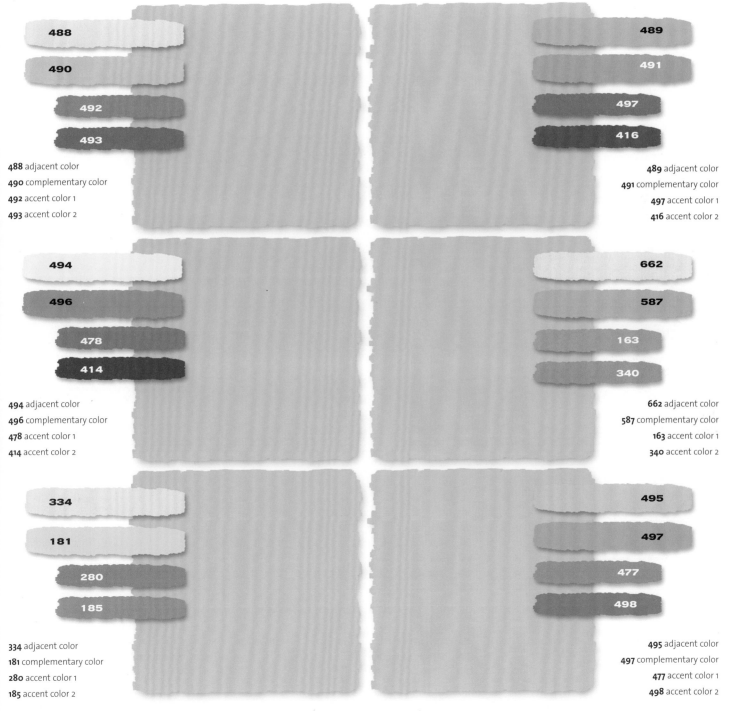

488
490
492
493

489
491
497
416

488 adjacent color
490 complementary color
492 accent color 1
493 accent color 2

489 adjacent color
491 complementary color
497 accent color 1
416 accent color 2

494
496
478
414

662
587
163
340

494 adjacent color
496 complementary color
478 accent color 1
414 accent color 2

662 adjacent color
587 complementary color
163 accent color 1
340 accent color 2

334
181
280
185

495
497
477
498

334 adjacent color
181 complementary color
280 accent color 1
185 accent color 2

495 adjacent color
497 complementary color
477 accent color 1
498 accent color 2

splendor

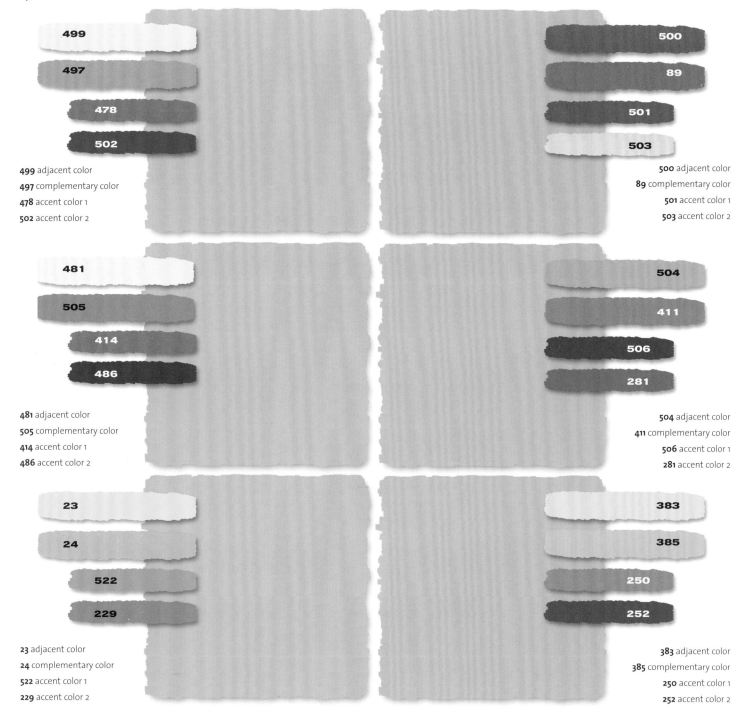

499
497
478
502

499 adjacent color
497 complementary color
478 accent color 1
502 accent color 2

500
89
501
503

500 adjacent color
89 complementary color
501 accent color 1
503 accent color 2

481
505
414
486

481 adjacent color
505 complementary color
414 accent color 1
486 accent color 2

504
411
506
281

504 adjacent color
411 complementary color
506 accent color 1
281 accent color 2

23
24
522
229

23 adjacent color
24 complementary color
522 accent color 1
229 accent color 2

383
385
250
252

383 adjacent color
385 complementary color
250 accent color 1
252 accent color 2

splendor

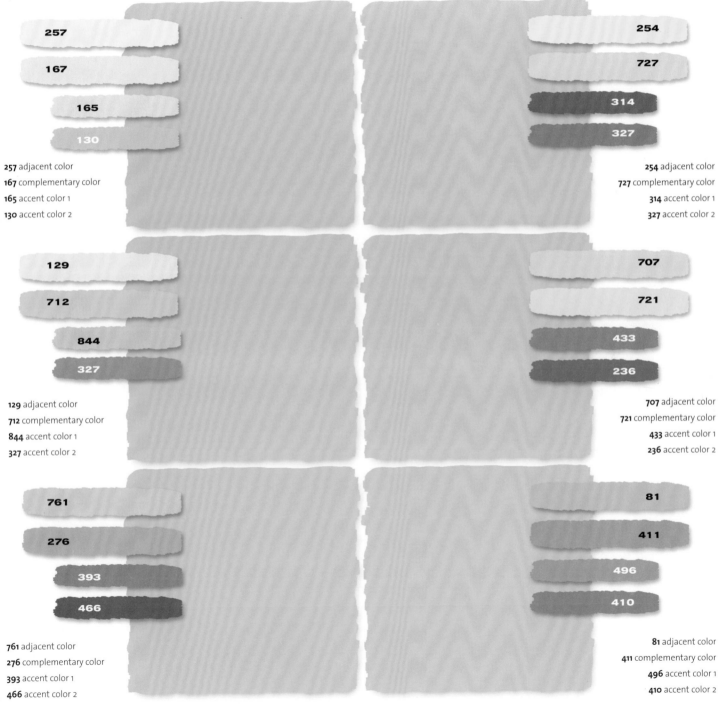

257

167

165

130

254

727

314

327

257 adjacent color
167 complementary color
165 accent color 1
130 accent color 2

254 adjacent color
727 complementary color
314 accent color 1
327 accent color 2

129

712

844

327

707

721

433

236

129 adjacent color
712 complementary color
844 accent color 1
327 accent color 2

707 adjacent color
721 complementary color
433 accent color 1
236 accent color 2

761

276

393

466

81

411

496

410

761 adjacent color
276 complementary color
393 accent color 1
466 accent color 2

81 adjacent color
411 complementary color
496 accent color 1
410 accent color 2

savannah clay

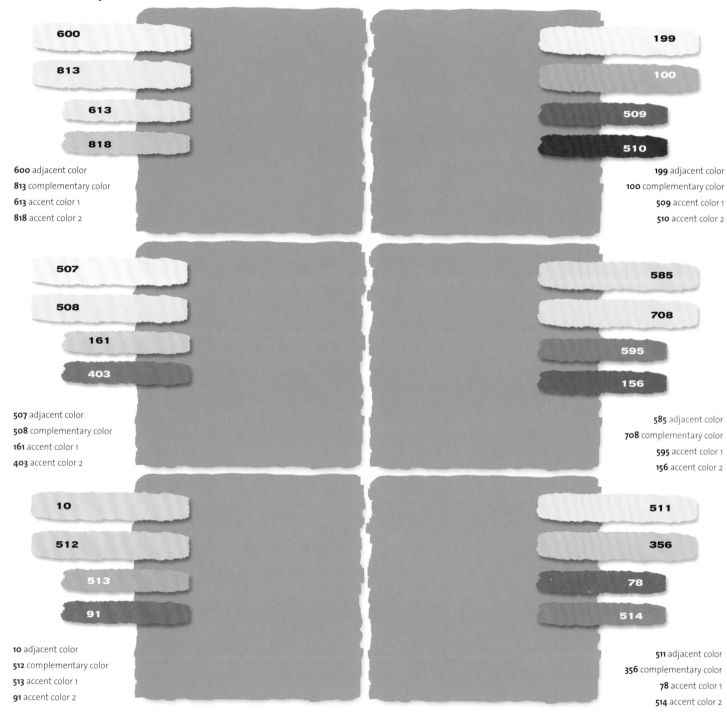

600

813

613

818

600 adjacent color
813 complementary color
613 accent color 1
818 accent color 2

199

100

509

510

199 adjacent color
100 complementary color
509 accent color 1
510 accent color 2

507

508

161

403

507 adjacent color
508 complementary color
161 accent color 1
403 accent color 2

585

708

595

156

585 adjacent color
708 complementary color
595 accent color 1
156 accent color 2

10

512

513

91

10 adjacent color
512 complementary color
513 accent color 1
91 accent color 2

511

356

78

514

511 adjacent color
356 complementary color
78 accent color 1
514 accent color 2

savannah clay

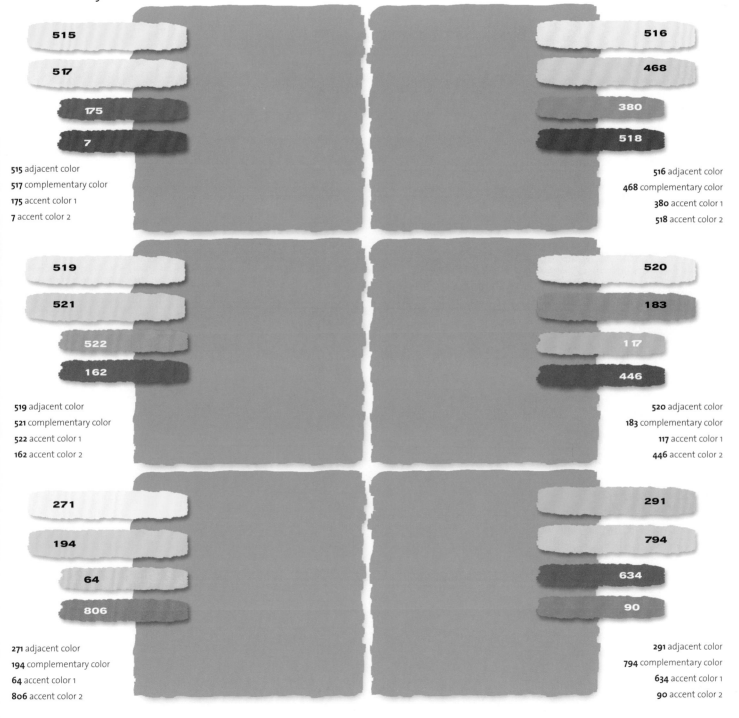

515 adjacent color
517 complementary color
175 accent color 1
7 accent color 2

516 adjacent color
468 complementary color
380 accent color 1
518 accent color 2

519 adjacent color
521 complementary color
522 accent color 1
162 accent color 2

520 adjacent color
183 complementary color
117 accent color 1
446 accent color 2

271 adjacent color
194 complementary color
64 accent color 1
806 accent color 2

291 adjacent color
794 complementary color
634 accent color 1
90 accent color 2

savannah clay

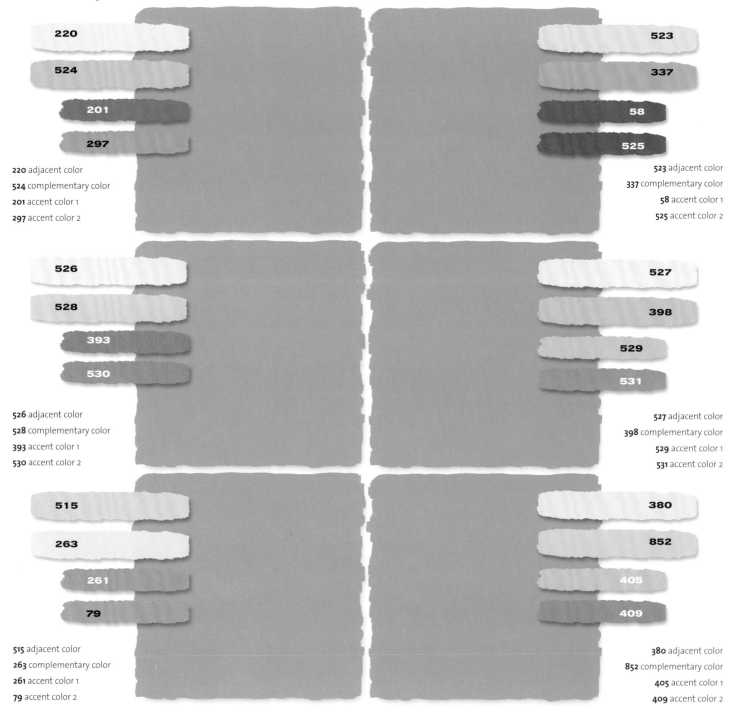

220
524
201
297

523
337
58
525

220 adjacent color
524 complementary color
201 accent color 1
297 accent color 2

523 adjacent color
337 complementary color
58 accent color 1
525 accent color 2

526
528
393
530

527
398
529
531

526 adjacent color
528 complementary color
393 accent color 1
530 accent color 2

527 adjacent color
398 complementary color
529 accent color 1
531 accent color 2

515
263
261
79

380
852
405
409

515 adjacent color
263 complementary color
261 accent color 1
79 accent color 2

380 adjacent color
852 complementary color
405 accent color 1
409 accent color 2

savannah clay

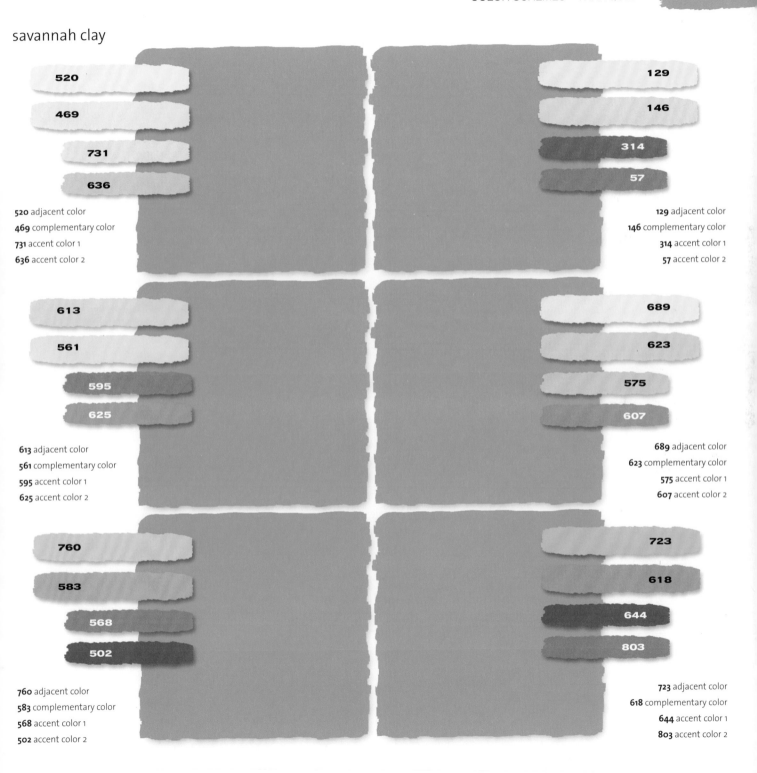

520 adjacent color
469 complementary color
731 accent color 1
636 accent color 2

129 adjacent color
146 complementary color
314 accent color 1
57 accent color 2

613 adjacent color
561 complementary color
595 accent color 1
625 accent color 2

689 adjacent color
623 complementary color
575 accent color 1
607 accent color 2

760 adjacent color
583 complementary color
568 accent color 1
502 accent color 2

723 adjacent color
618 complementary color
644 accent color 1
803 accent color 2

meadow pink

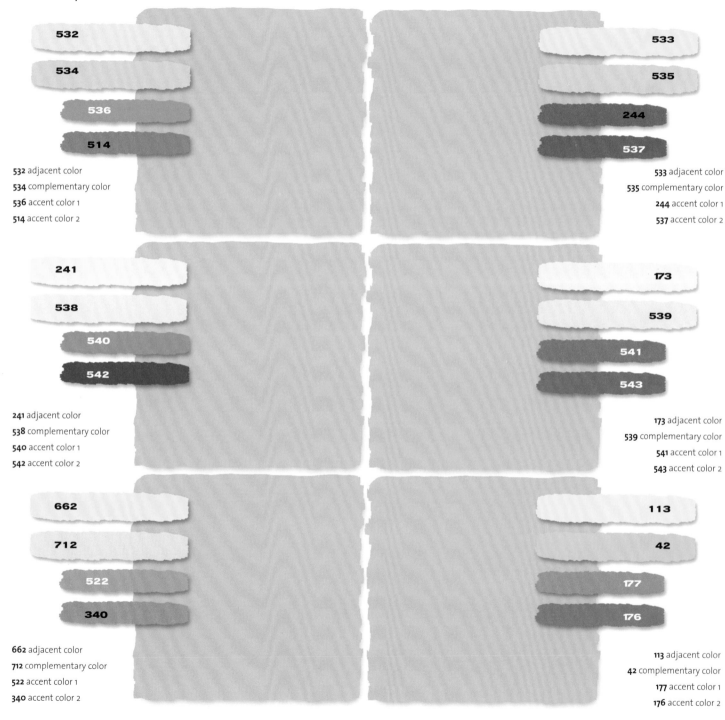

532
534
536
514

532 adjacent color
534 complementary color
536 accent color 1
514 accent color 2

533
535
244
537

533 adjacent color
535 complementary color
244 accent color 1
537 accent color 2

241
538
540
542

241 adjacent color
538 complementary color
540 accent color 1
542 accent color 2

173
539
541
543

173 adjacent color
539 complementary color
541 accent color 1
543 accent color 2

662
712
522
340

662 adjacent color
712 complementary color
522 accent color 1
340 accent color 2

113
42
177
176

113 adjacent color
42 complementary color
177 accent color 1
176 accent color 2

meadow pink

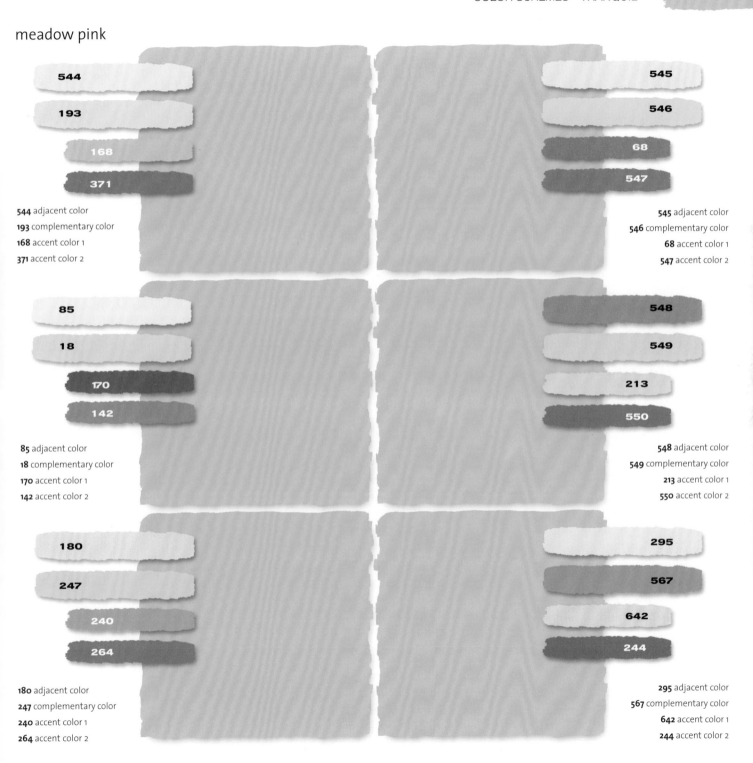

544

193

168

371

544 adjacent color
193 complementary color
168 accent color 1
371 accent color 2

545

546

68

547

545 adjacent color
546 complementary color
68 accent color 1
547 accent color 2

85

18

170

142

85 adjacent color
18 complementary color
170 accent color 1
142 accent color 2

548

549

213

550

548 adjacent color
549 complementary color
213 accent color 1
550 accent color 2

180

247

240

264

180 adjacent color
247 complementary color
240 accent color 1
264 accent color 2

295

567

642

244

295 adjacent color
567 complementary color
642 accent color 1
244 accent color 2

meadow pink

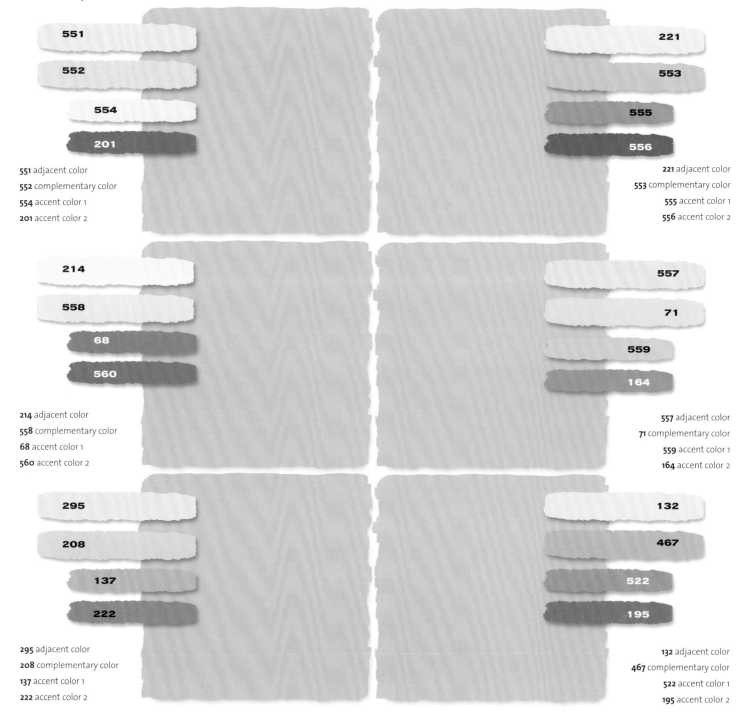

551

552

554

201

553 adjacent color

221

553

555

556

551 adjacent color
552 complementary color
554 accent color 1
201 accent color 2

221 adjacent color
553 complementary color
555 accent color 1
556 accent color 2

214

558

68

560

557

71

559

164

214 adjacent color
558 complementary color
68 accent color 1
560 accent color 2

557 adjacent color
71 complementary color
559 accent color 1
164 accent color 2

295

208

137

222

132

467

522

195

295 adjacent color
208 complementary color
137 accent color 1
222 accent color 2

132 adjacent color
467 complementary color
522 accent color 1
195 accent color 2

meadow pink

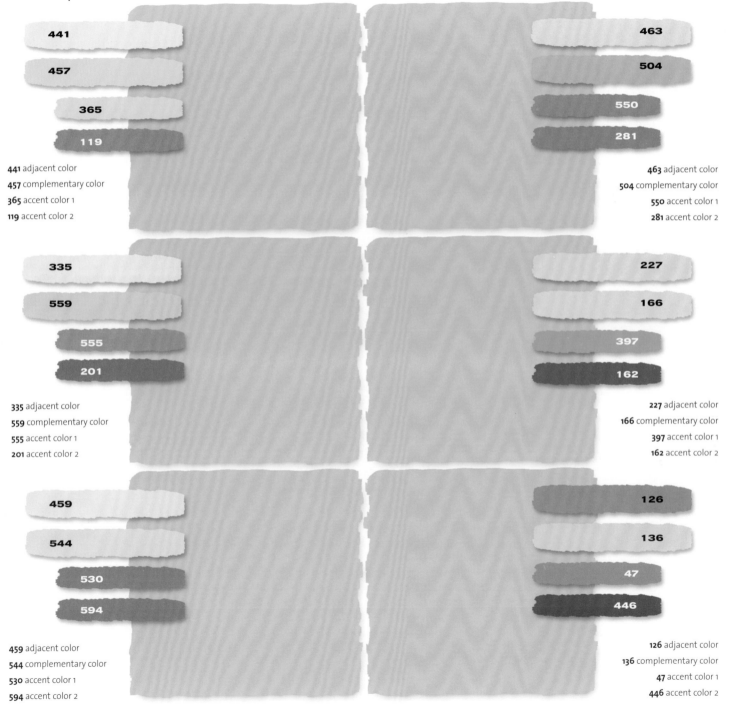

441
457
365
119

441 adjacent color
457 complementary color
365 accent color 1
119 accent color 2

463
504
550
281

463 adjacent color
504 complementary color
550 accent color 1
281 accent color 2

335
559
555
201

335 adjacent color
559 complementary color
555 accent color 1
201 accent color 2

227
166
397
162

227 adjacent color
166 complementary color
397 accent color 1
162 accent color 2

459
544
530
594

459 adjacent color
544 complementary color
530 accent color 1
594 accent color 2

126
136
47
446

126 adjacent color
136 complementary color
47 accent color 1
446 accent color 2

north cascades

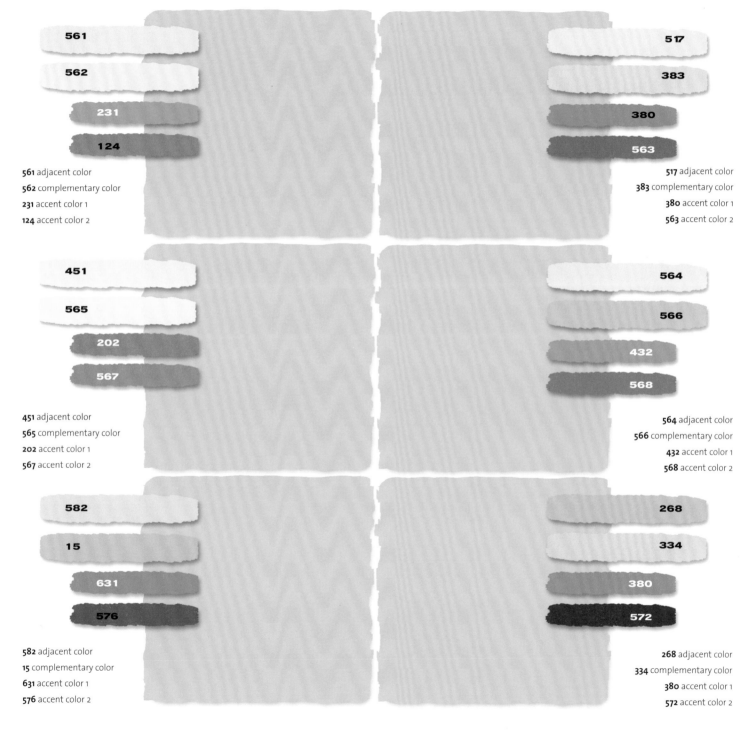

561

562

231

124

561 adjacent color
562 complementary color
231 accent color 1
124 accent color 2

517

383

380

563

517 adjacent color
383 complementary color
380 accent color 1
563 accent color 2

451

565

202

567

451 adjacent color
565 complementary color
202 accent color 1
567 accent color 2

564

566

432

568

564 adjacent color
566 complementary color
432 accent color 1
568 accent color 2

582

15

631

576

582 adjacent color
15 complementary color
631 accent color 1
576 accent color 2

268

334

380

572

268 adjacent color
334 complementary color
380 accent color 1
572 accent color 2

north cascades

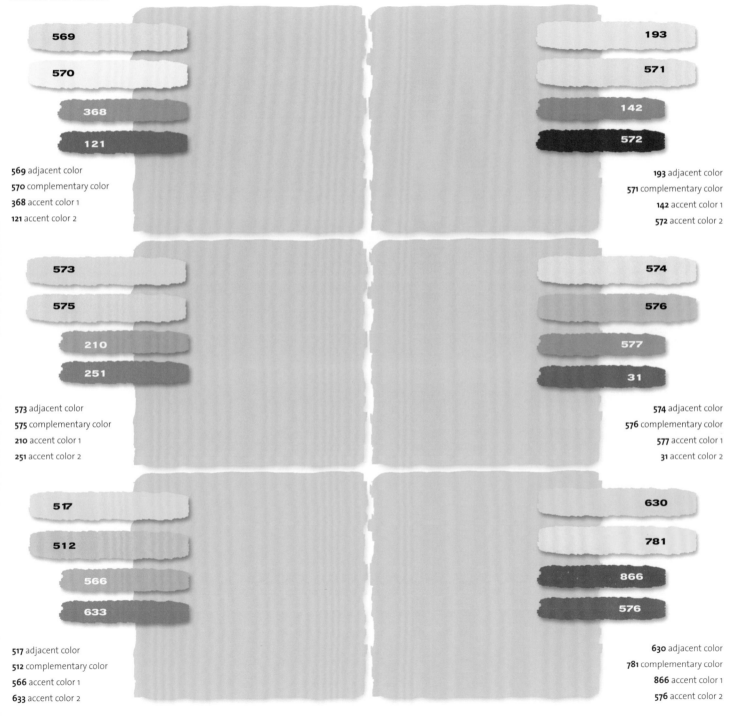

569 adjacent color
570 complementary color
368 accent color 1
121 accent color 2

193 adjacent color
571 complementary color
142 accent color 1
572 accent color 2

573 adjacent color
575 complementary color
210 accent color 1
251 accent color 2

574 adjacent color
576 complementary color
577 accent color 1
31 accent color 2

517 adjacent color
512 complementary color
566 accent color 1
633 accent color 2

630 adjacent color
781 complementary color
866 accent color 1
576 accent color 2

north cascades

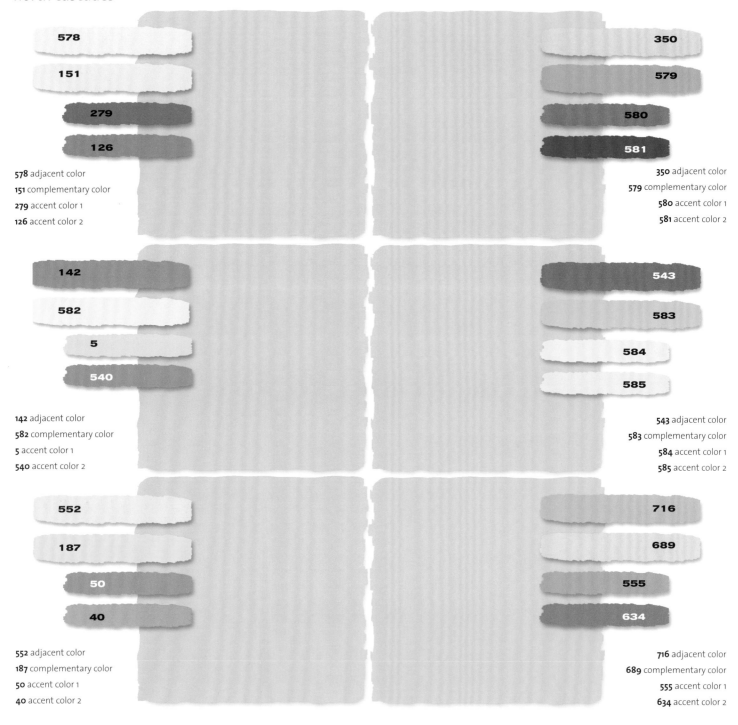

578

151

279

126

350

579

580

581

578 adjacent color
151 complementary color
279 accent color 1
126 accent color 2

350 adjacent color
579 complementary color
580 accent color 1
581 accent color 2

142

582

5

540

543

583

584

585

142 adjacent color
582 complementary color
5 accent color 1
540 accent color 2

543 adjacent color
583 complementary color
584 accent color 1
585 accent color 2

552

187

50

40

716

689

555

634

552 adjacent color
187 complementary color
50 accent color 1
40 accent color 2

716 adjacent color
689 complementary color
555 accent color 1
634 accent color 2

north cascades

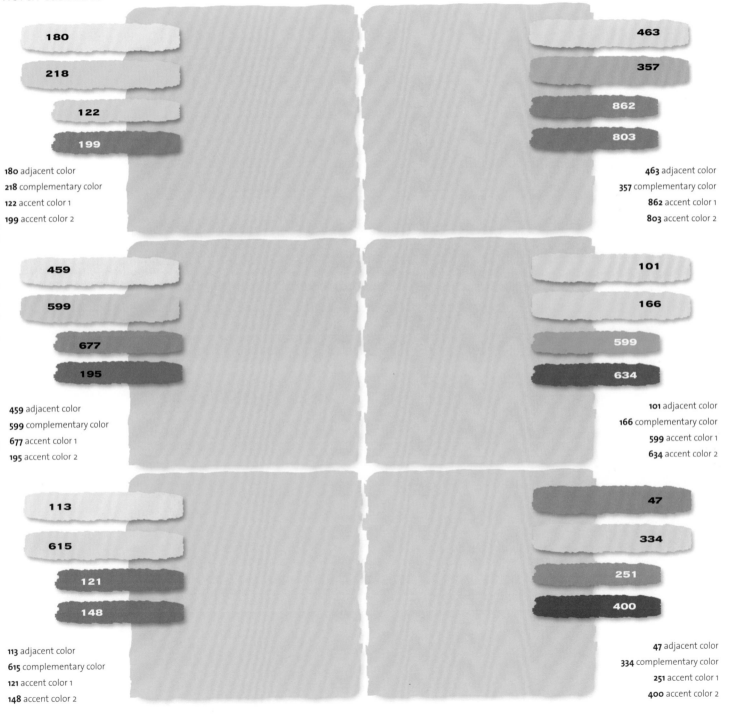

180
218
122
199

180 adjacent color
218 complementary color
122 accent color 1
199 accent color 2

463
357
862
803

463 adjacent color
357 complementary color
862 accent color 1
803 accent color 2

459
599
677
195

459 adjacent color
599 complementary color
677 accent color 1
195 accent color 2

101
166
599
634

101 adjacent color
166 complementary color
599 accent color 1
634 accent color 2

113
615
121
148

113 adjacent color
615 complementary color
121 accent color 1
148 accent color 2

47
334
251
400

47 adjacent color
334 complementary color
251 accent color 1
400 accent color 2

wispy green

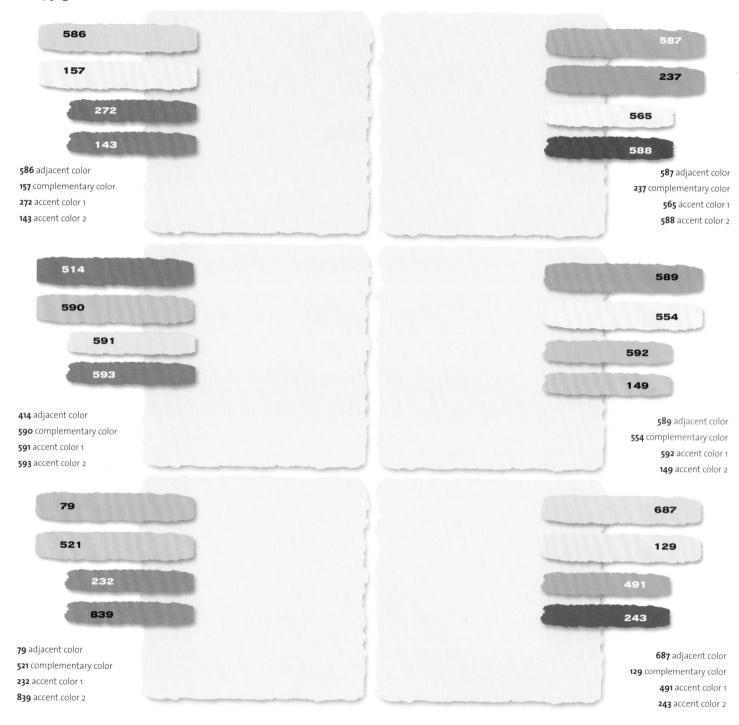

586

157

272

143

586 adjacent color
157 complementary color
272 accent color 1
143 accent color 2

587

237

565

588

587 adjacent color
237 complementary color
565 accent color 1
588 accent color 2

514

590

591

593

414 adjacent color
590 complementary color
591 accent color 1
593 accent color 2

589

554

592

149

589 adjacent color
554 complementary color
592 accent color 1
149 accent color 2

79

521

232

839

79 adjacent color
521 complementary color
232 accent color 1
839 accent color 2

687

129

491

243

687 adjacent color
129 complementary color
491 accent color 1
243 accent color 2

wispy green

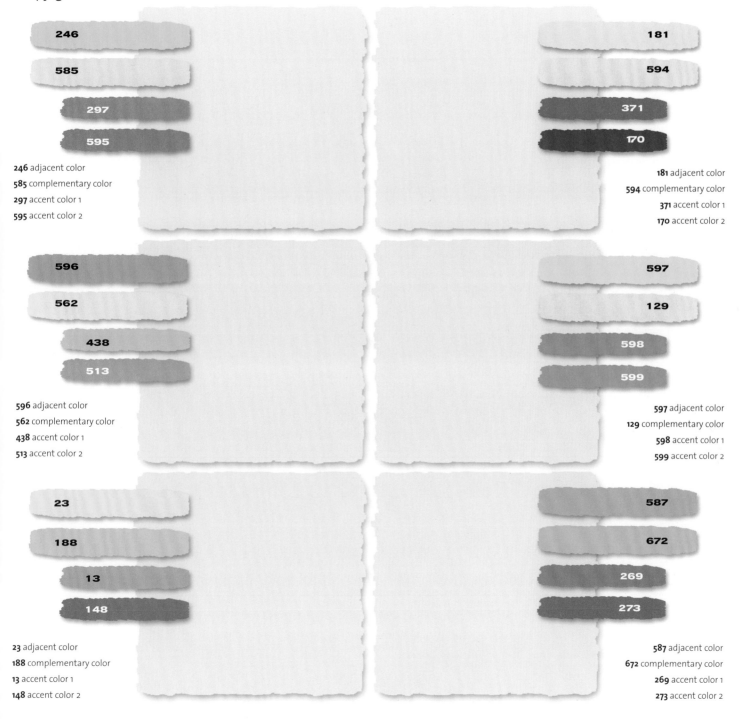

246 adjacent color
585 complementary color
297 accent color 1
595 accent color 2

181 adjacent color
594 complementary color
371 accent color 1
170 accent color 2

596 adjacent color
562 complementary color
438 accent color 1
513 accent color 2

597 adjacent color
129 complementary color
598 accent color 1
599 accent color 2

23 adjacent color
188 complementary color
13 accent color 1
148 accent color 2

587 adjacent color
672 complementary color
269 accent color 1
273 accent color 2

wispy green

247

9

601

602

462

600

135

161

247 adjacent color
9 complementary color
601 accent color 1
602 accent color 2

462 adjacent color
600 complementary color
135 accent color 1
161 accent color 2

603

144

605

606

604

207

52

607

603 adjacent color
144 complementary color
605 accent color 1
606 accent color 2

604 adjacent color
207 complementary color
52 accent color 1
607 accent color 2

138

223

572

400

524

746

804

568

138 adjacent color
223 complementary color
572 accent color 1
400 accent color 2

524 adjacent color
746 complementary color
804 accent color 1
568 accent color 2

wispy green

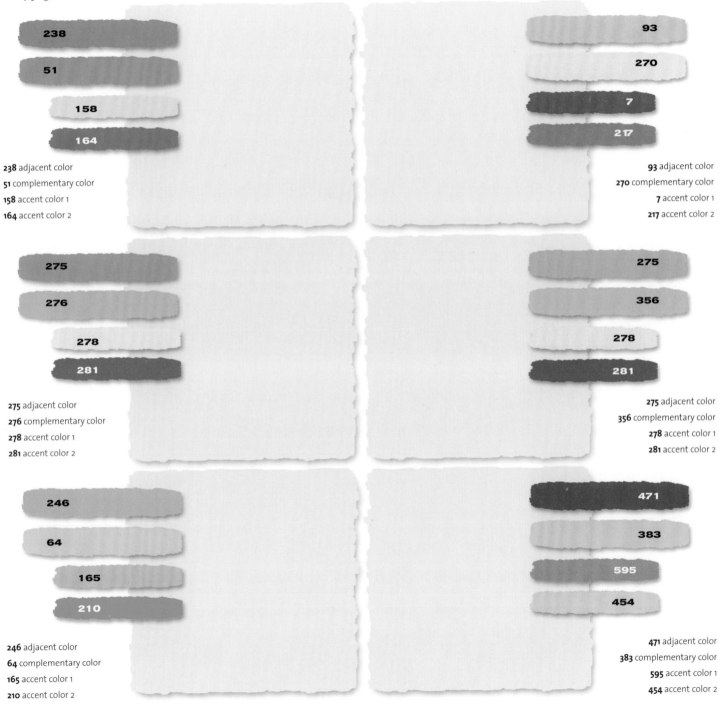

238
51
158
164

93
270
7
217

238 adjacent color
51 complementary color
158 accent color 1
164 accent color 2

93 adjacent color
270 complementary color
7 accent color 1
217 accent color 2

275
276
278
281

275
356
278
281

275 adjacent color
276 complementary color
278 accent color 1
281 accent color 2

275 adjacent color
356 complementary color
278 accent color 1
281 accent color 2

246
64
165
210

471
383
595
454

246 adjacent color
64 complementary color
165 accent color 1
210 accent color 2

471 adjacent color
383 complementary color
595 accent color 1
454 accent color 2

violet mist

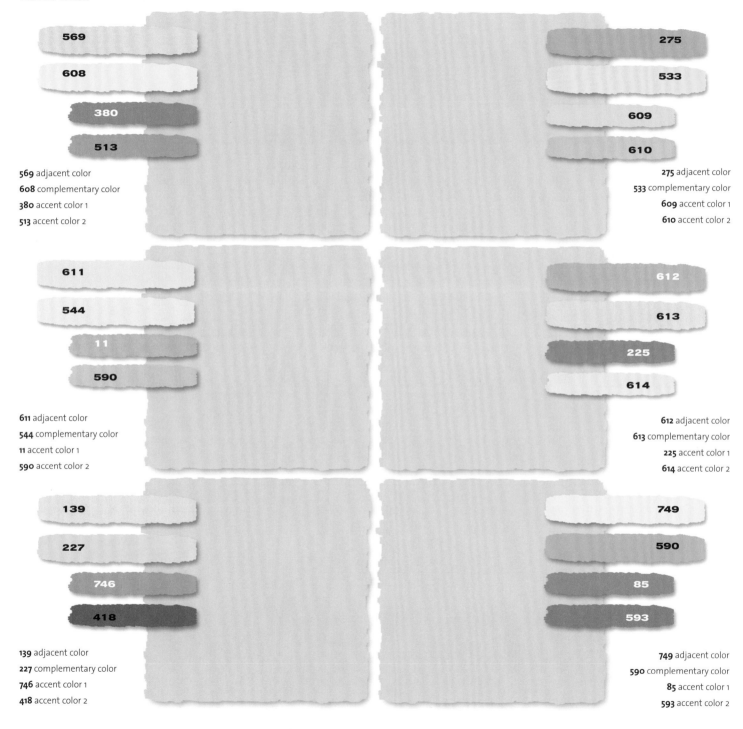

569

608

380

513

569 adjacent color
608 complementary color
380 accent color 1
513 accent color 2

275

533

609

610

275 adjacent color
533 complementary color
609 accent color 1
610 accent color 2

611

544

11

590

611 adjacent color
544 complementary color
11 accent color 1
590 accent color 2

612

613

225

614

612 adjacent color
613 complementary color
225 accent color 1
614 accent color 2

139

227

746

418

139 adjacent color
227 complementary color
746 accent color 1
418 accent color 2

749

590

85

593

749 adjacent color
590 complementary color
85 accent color 1
593 accent color 2

violet mist

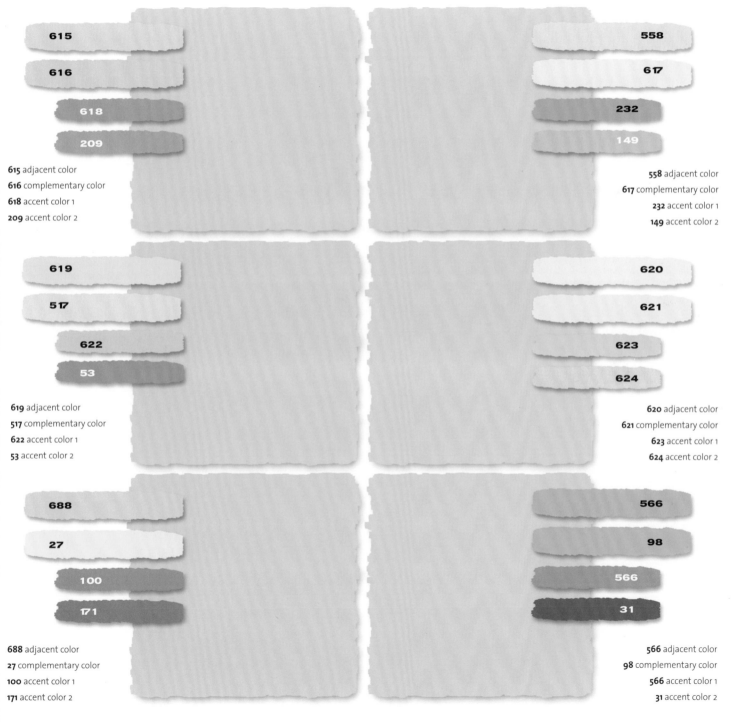

615
616
618
209

615 adjacent color
616 complementary color
618 accent color 1
209 accent color 2

558
617
232
149

558 adjacent color
617 complementary color
232 accent color 1
149 accent color 2

619
517
622
53

619 adjacent color
517 complementary color
622 accent color 1
53 accent color 2

620
621
623
624

620 adjacent color
621 complementary color
623 accent color 1
624 accent color 2

688
27
100
171

688 adjacent color
27 complementary color
100 accent color 1
171 accent color 2

566
98
566
31

566 adjacent color
98 complementary color
566 accent color 1
31 accent color 2

violet mist

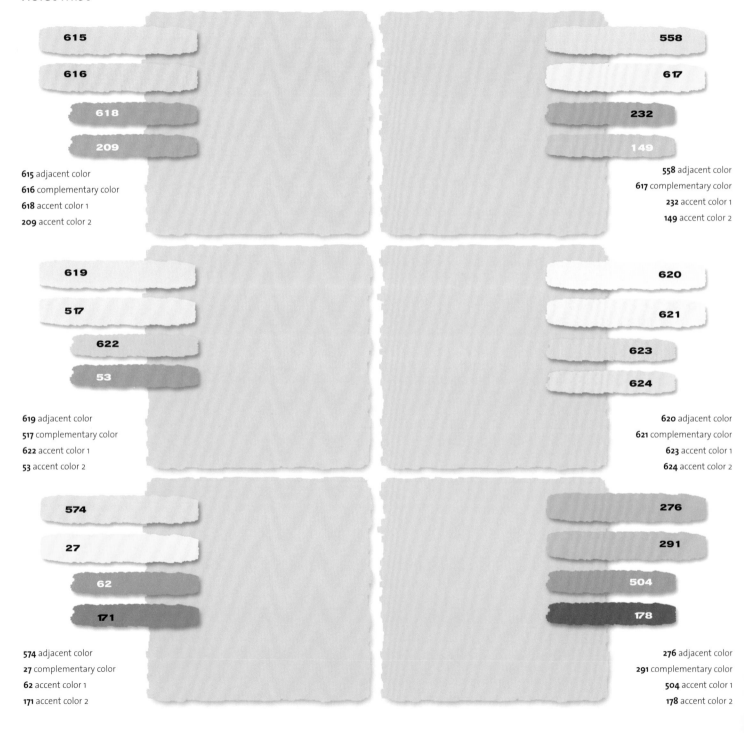

615

616

618

209

615 adjacent color
616 complementary color
618 accent color 1
209 accent color 2

558

617

232

149

558 adjacent color
617 complementary color
232 accent color 1
149 accent color 2

619

517

622

53

619 adjacent color
517 complementary color
622 accent color 1
53 accent color 2

620

621

623

624

620 adjacent color
621 complementary color
623 accent color 1
624 accent color 2

574

27

62

171

574 adjacent color
27 complementary color
62 accent color 1
171 accent color 2

276

291

504

178

276 adjacent color
291 complementary color
504 accent color 1
178 accent color 2

violet mist

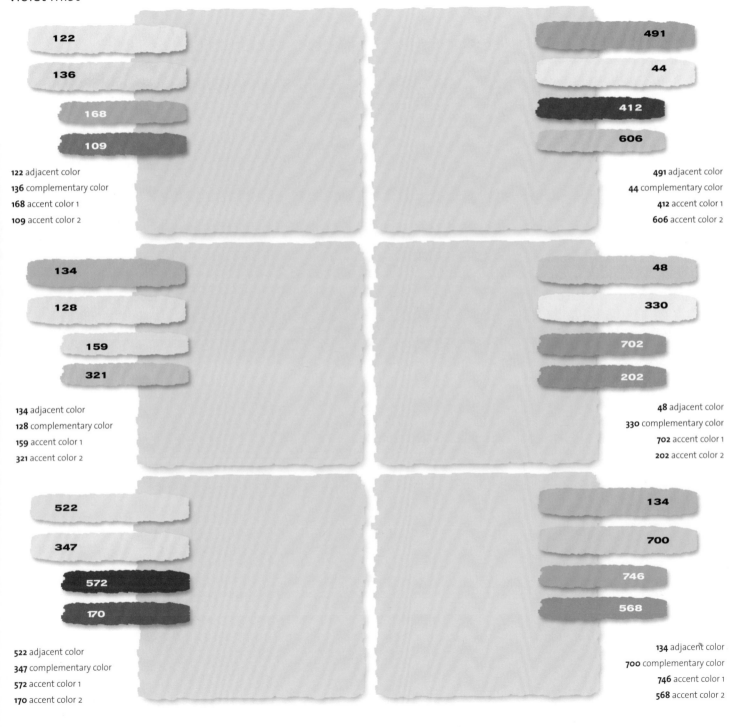

122
136
168
109

122 adjacent color
136 complementary color
168 accent color 1
109 accent color 2

491
44
412
606

491 adjacent color
44 complementary color
412 accent color 1
606 accent color 2

134
128
159
321

134 adjacent color
128 complementary color
159 accent color 1
321 accent color 2

48
330
702
202

48 adjacent color
330 complementary color
702 accent color 1
202 accent color 2

522
347
572
170

522 adjacent color
347 complementary color
572 accent color 1
170 accent color 2

134
700
746
568

134 adjacent color
700 complementary color
746 accent color 1
568 accent color 2

imperial gray

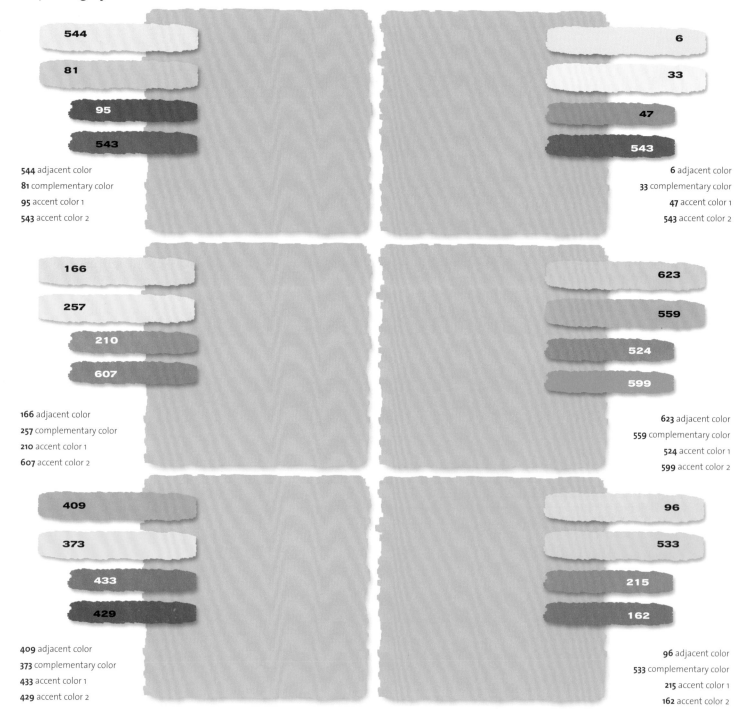

544

81

95

543

544 adjacent color
81 complementary color
95 accent color 1
543 accent color 2

6

33

47

543

6 adjacent color
33 complementary color
47 accent color 1
543 accent color 2

166

257

210

607

166 adjacent color
257 complementary color
210 accent color 1
607 accent color 2

623

559

524

599

623 adjacent color
559 complementary color
524 accent color 1
599 accent color 2

409

373

433

429

409 adjacent color
373 complementary color
433 accent color 1
429 accent color 2

96

533

215

162

96 adjacent color
533 complementary color
215 accent color 1
162 accent color 2

imperial gray

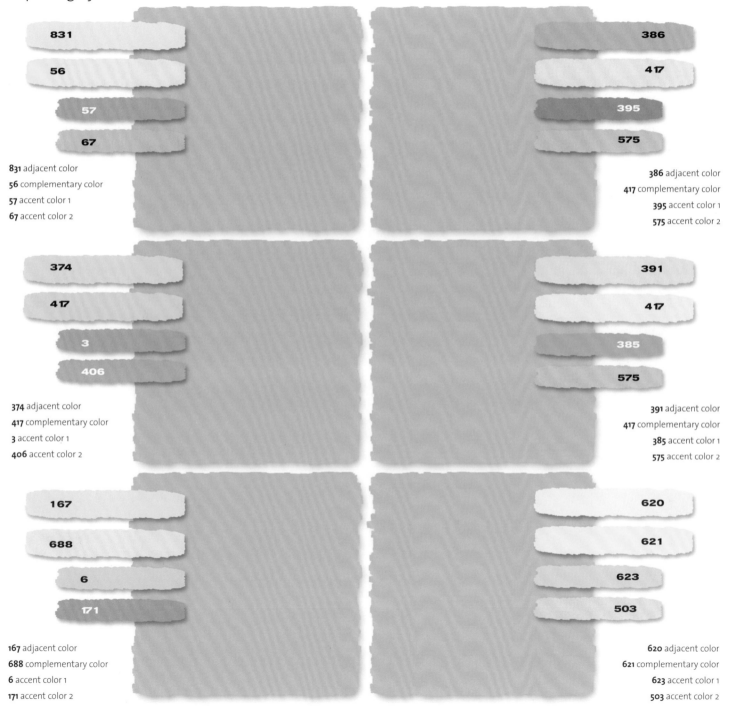

831

56

57

67

386

417

395

575

831 adjacent color
56 complementary color
57 accent color 1
67 accent color 2

386 adjacent color
417 complementary color
395 accent color 1
575 accent color 2

374

417

3

406

391

417

385

575

374 adjacent color
417 complementary color
3 accent color 1
406 accent color 2

391 adjacent color
417 complementary color
385 accent color 1
575 accent color 2

167

688

6

171

620

621

623

503

167 adjacent color
688 complementary color
6 accent color 1
171 accent color 2

620 adjacent color
621 complementary color
623 accent color 1
503 accent color 2

imperial gray

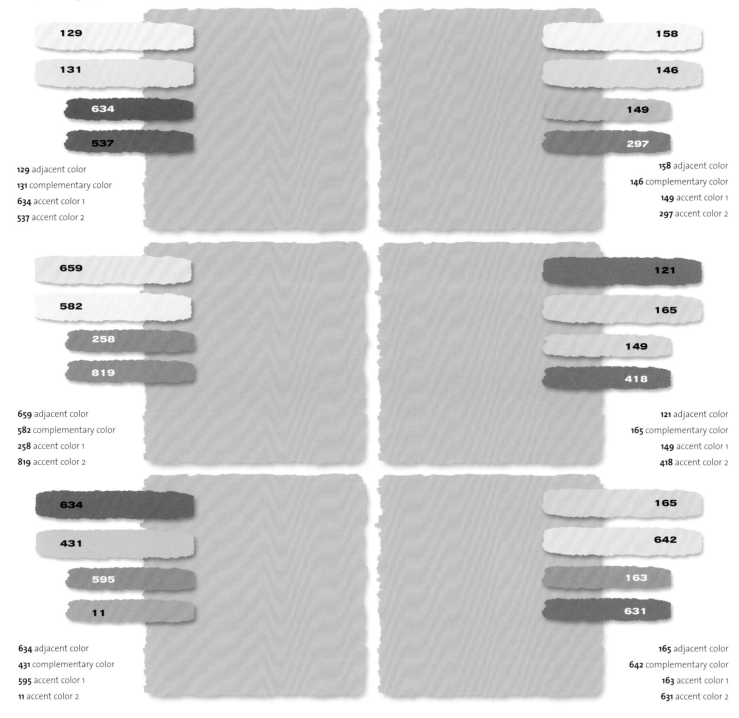

129 | 158

131 | 146

634 | 149

537 | 297

129 adjacent color
131 complementary color
634 accent color 1
537 accent color 2

158 adjacent color
146 complementary color
149 accent color 1
297 accent color 2

659 | 121

582 | 165

258 | 149

819 | 418

659 adjacent color
582 complementary color
258 accent color 1
819 accent color 2

121 adjacent color
165 complementary color
149 accent color 1
418 accent color 2

634 | 165

431 | 642

595 | 163

11 | 631

634 adjacent color
431 complementary color
595 accent color 1
11 accent color 2

165 adjacent color
642 complementary color
163 accent color 1
631 accent color 2

imperial gray

375

689

514

681

82

10

85

117

375 adjacent color
689 complementary color
514 accent color 1
681 accent color 2

82 adjacent color
10 complementary color
85 accent color 1
117 accent color 2

804

842

558

841

79

112

677

84

804 adjacent color
842 complementary color
558 accent color 1
841 accent color 2

79 adjacent color
112 complementary color
677 accent color 1
84 accent color 2

57

701

563

91

93

100

158

345

57 adjacent color
701 complementary color
563 accent color 1
91 accent color 2

93 adjacent color
100 complementary color
158 accent color 1
345 accent color 2

dreamcatcher

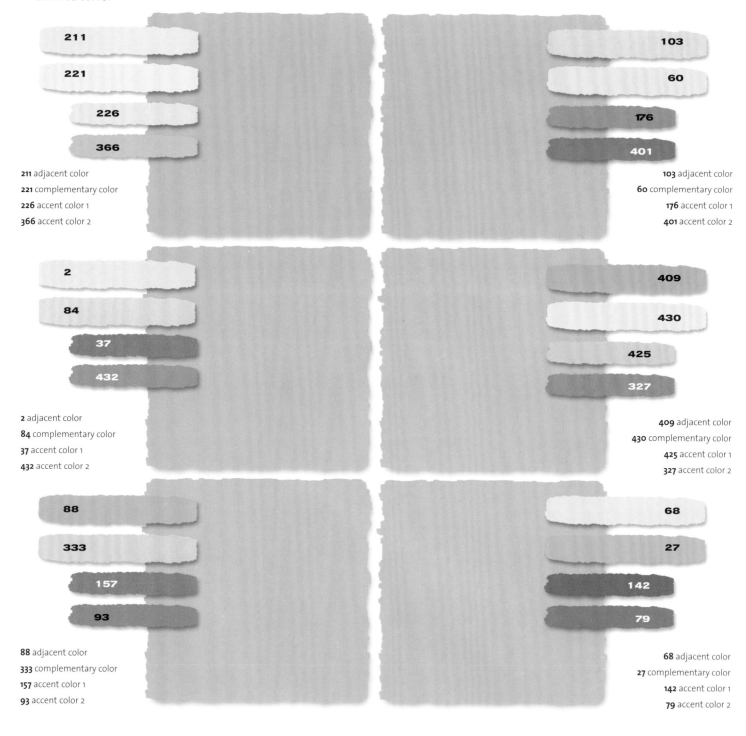

211

221

226

366

103

60

176

401

211 adjacent color
221 complementary color
226 accent color 1
366 accent color 2

103 adjacent color
60 complementary color
176 accent color 1
401 accent color 2

2

84

37

432

409

430

425

327

2 adjacent color
84 complementary color
37 accent color 1
432 accent color 2

409 adjacent color
430 complementary color
425 accent color 1
327 accent color 2

88

333

157

93

68

27

142

79

88 adjacent color
333 complementary color
157 accent color 1
93 accent color 2

68 adjacent color
27 complementary color
142 accent color 1
79 accent color 2

dreamcatcher

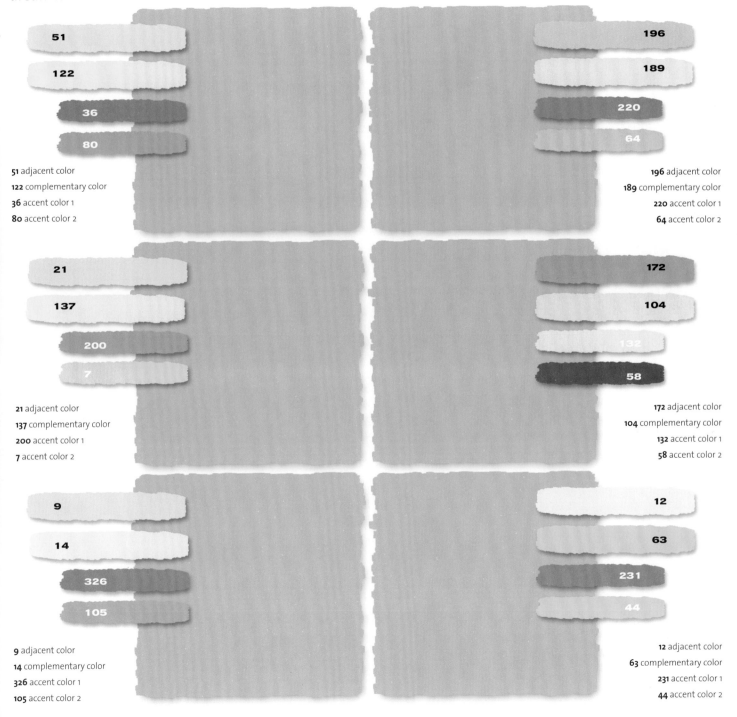

51

122

36

80

196

189

220

64

51 adjacent color
122 complementary color
36 accent color 1
80 accent color 2

196 adjacent color
189 complementary color
220 accent color 1
64 accent color 2

21

137

200

7

172

104

132

58

21 adjacent color
137 complementary color
200 accent color 1
7 accent color 2

172 adjacent color
104 complementary color
132 accent color 1
58 accent color 2

9

14

326

105

12

63

231

44

9 adjacent color
14 complementary color
326 accent color 1
105 accent color 2

12 adjacent color
63 complementary color
231 accent color 1
44 accent color 2

dreamcatcher

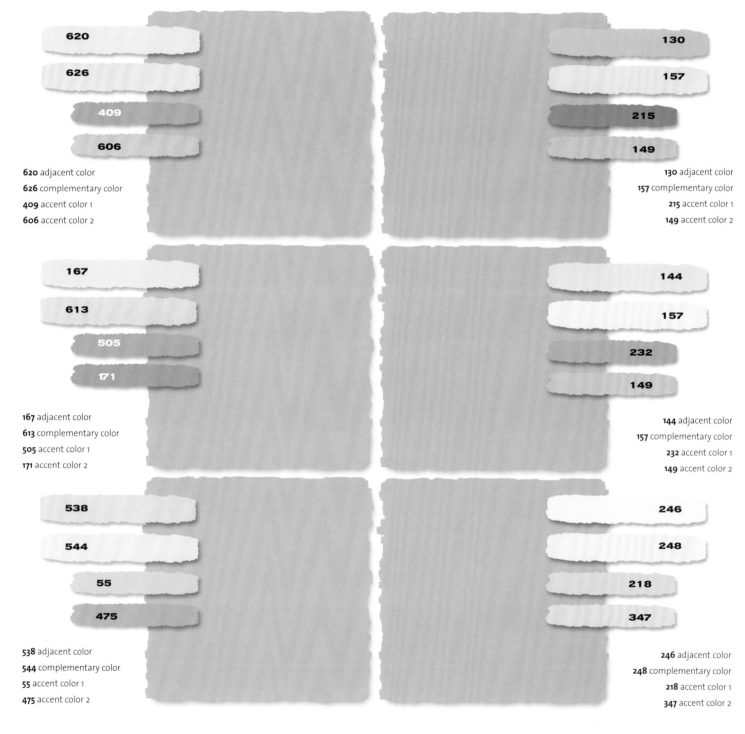

620

626

409

606

620 adjacent color
626 complementary color
409 accent color 1
606 accent color 2

130

157

215

149

130 adjacent color
157 complementary color
215 accent color 1
149 accent color 2

167

613

505

171

167 adjacent color
613 complementary color
505 accent color 1
171 accent color 2

144

157

232

149

144 adjacent color
157 complementary color
232 accent color 1
149 accent color 2

538

544

55

475

538 adjacent color
544 complementary color
55 accent color 1
475 accent color 2

246

248

218

347

246 adjacent color
248 complementary color
218 accent color 1
347 accent color 2

dreamcatcher

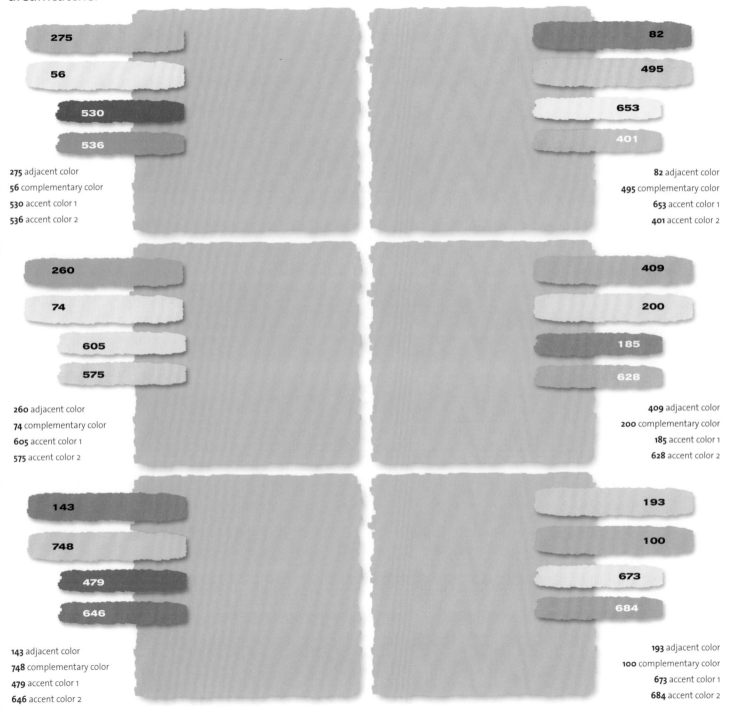

275 adjacent color
56 complementary color
530 accent color 1
536 accent color 2

82 adjacent color
495 complementary color
653 accent color 1
401 accent color 2

260 adjacent color
74 complementary color
605 accent color 1
575 accent color 2

409 adjacent color
200 complementary color
185 accent color 1
628 accent color 2

143 adjacent color
748 complementary color
479 accent color 1
646 accent color 2

193 adjacent color
100 complementary color
673 accent color 1
684 accent color 2

victoriana

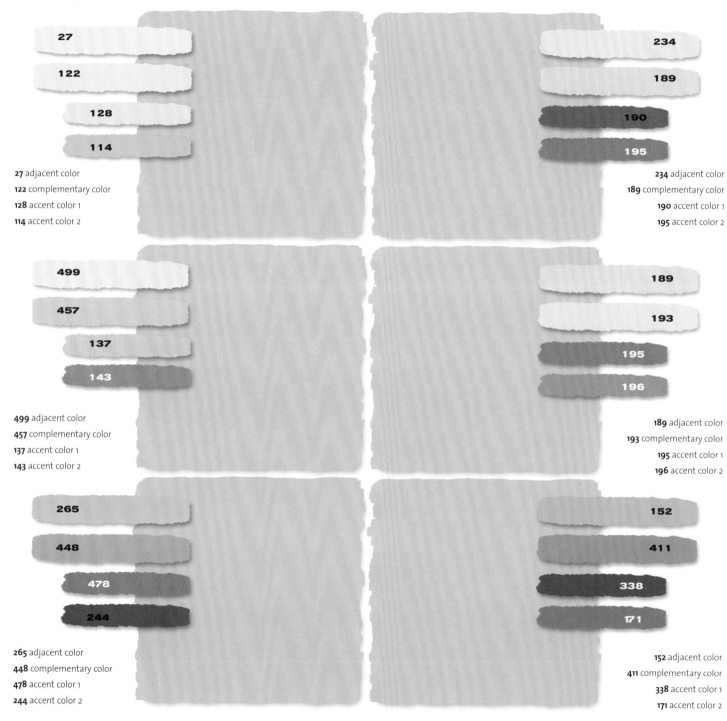

27

122

128

114

234

189

190

195

27 adjacent color
122 complementary color
128 accent color 1
114 accent color 2

234 adjacent color
189 complementary color
190 accent color 1
195 accent color 2

499

457

137

143

189

193

195

196

499 adjacent color
457 complementary color
137 accent color 1
143 accent color 2

189 adjacent color
193 complementary color
195 accent color 1
196 accent color 2

265

448

478

244

152

411

338

171

265 adjacent color
448 complementary color
478 accent color 1
244 accent color 2

152 adjacent color
411 complementary color
338 accent color 1
171 accent color 2

victoriana

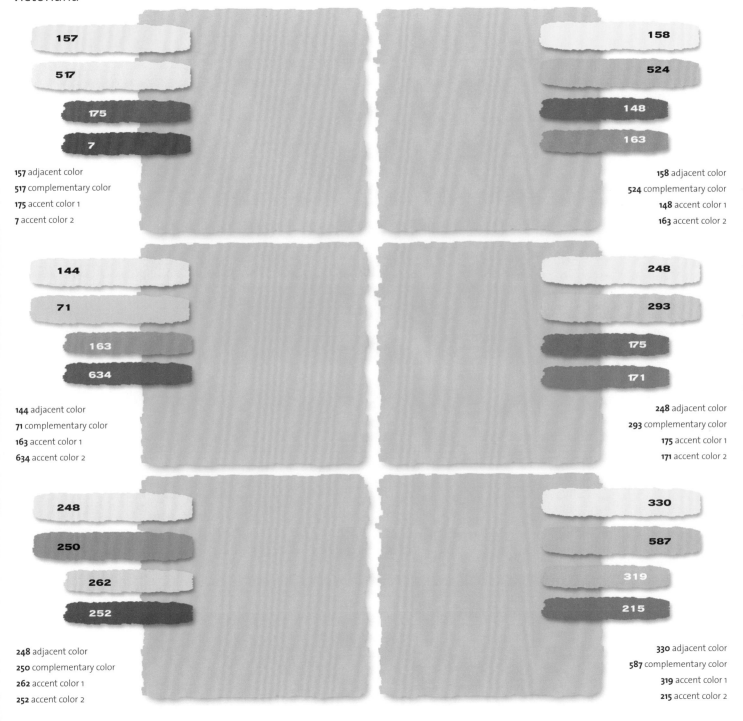

157

517

175

7

158

524

148

163

157 adjacent color
517 complementary color
175 accent color 1
7 accent color 2

158 adjacent color
524 complementary color
148 accent color 1
163 accent color 2

144

71

163

634

248

293

175

171

144 adjacent color
71 complementary color
163 accent color 1
634 accent color 2

248 adjacent color
293 complementary color
175 accent color 1
171 accent color 2

248

250

262

252

330

587

319

215

248 adjacent color
250 complementary color
262 accent color 1
252 accent color 2

330 adjacent color
587 complementary color
319 accent color 1
215 accent color 2

victoriana

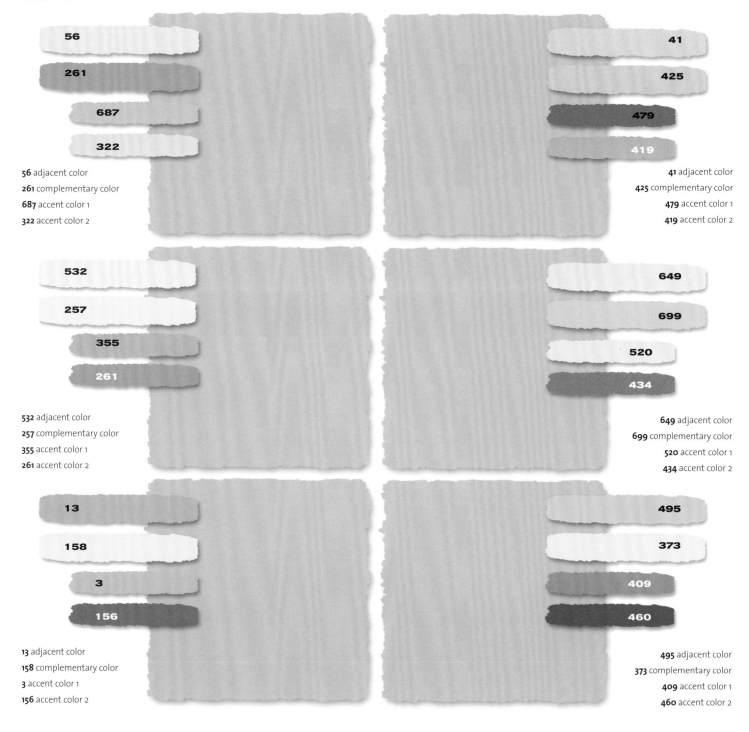

56 adjacent color
261 complementary color
687 accent color 1
322 accent color 2

41 adjacent color
425 complementary color
479 accent color 1
419 accent color 2

532 adjacent color
257 complementary color
355 accent color 1
261 accent color 2

649 adjacent color
699 complementary color
520 accent color 1
434 accent color 2

13 adjacent color
158 complementary color
3 accent color 1
156 accent color 2

495 adjacent color
373 complementary color
409 accent color 1
460 accent color 2

victoriana

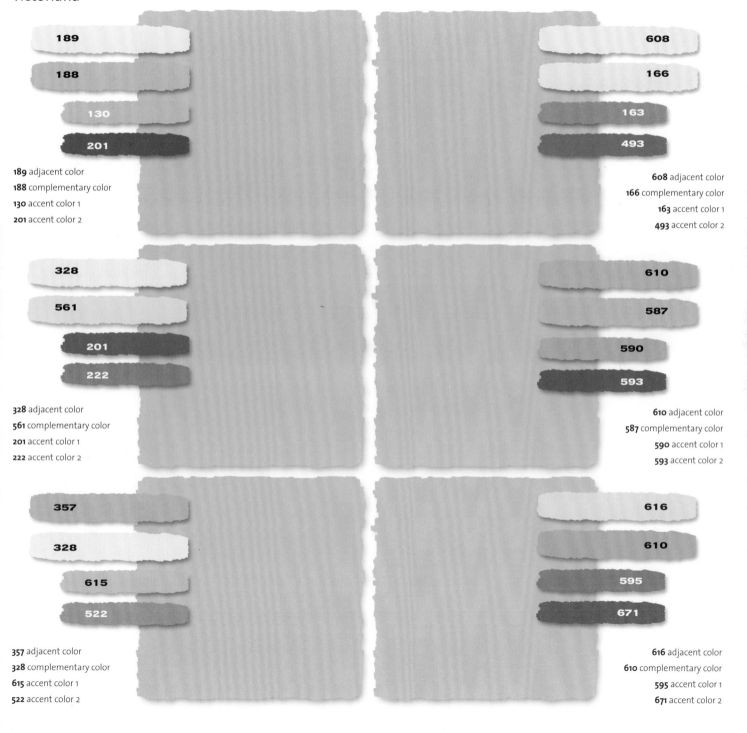

189
188
130
201

189 adjacent color
188 complementary color
130 accent color 1
201 accent color 2

608
166
163
493

608 adjacent color
166 complementary color
163 accent color 1
493 accent color 2

328
561
201
222

328 adjacent color
561 complementary color
201 accent color 1
222 accent color 2

610
587
590
593

610 adjacent color
587 complementary color
590 accent color 1
593 accent color 2

357
328
615
522

357 adjacent color
328 complementary color
615 accent color 1
522 accent color 2

616
610
595
671

616 adjacent color
610 complementary color
595 accent color 1
671 accent color 2

16	121	414	554
569	570	149	592

BELOW Using a cool neutral color in this kitchen helps to bring out the natural richness of the wooden cabinets and the stone worktops.

RIGHT A bright fresh bedroom using a cool green contrasted with the rich golden glow of the cushions prevent it from appearing too cold.

414	871
592	569

RIGHT Keeping the color scheme clean and simple makes for a space that is calm and peaceful, and that will benefit from small touches of accent color. Here the flowing lines of the vases soften the strong angular shapes of the television and shelving units.

18	149
121	570

LEFT Even small touches of accent color, such as these bright red, orange, and yellow lamp shades, have a dramatic effect on a room, here setting off the neutral walls and dark worktops.

15	16

RIGHT A color scheme that uses tones of the same hue is the ultimate in conveying tranquilty; everything works together to create a space that is gentle to the eye.

14	515
175	570

LEFT Using a variety of shades of adjacent colors, this scheme conveys a sense of warmth, naturally drawing the eye to the contrasting shower, emphasized by daylight flooding in through a glass wall.

16	570
175	2

RIGHT A rich purple can be softened by using broken paint effects and paler tones. Combine this with dark woods and touches of white to create a hint of the exotic.

| 739 | 666 |
| 806 | 813 |

RIGHT This traditional kitchen benefits from a simple color scheme. The soft color of the walls sets off the classic lines of the white units and island, while the warm tones of the floor, chairs, and dresser are brought alive by the bright green of the fruit and potted plants.

592	677		449	582
642	600		576	665

LEFT A picture of tranquility, the soft green walls of this bedroom are prevented from becoming cold and uninviting by using rich warm accent colors in the drapes and the bed linen. The hardness of the wooden floor is also contrasted by the use of a luxurious deep-pile rug.

ABOVE Cool green-yellow walls are a perfect partner to the rich wood of the dining furniture. Accent colors are abundant in the paintings on the wall and the soft furnishings. All this combines to achieve a tranquil space that invites conversation.

| 168 | 572 | 307 | 130 |
| 210 | 548 | 212 | 151 |

LEFT Warm, rich colors are used to contrast and enrich the otherwise cool, gray walls. The great advantage of creating a color scheme with accessories and soft furnishing is that you can alter the feel of a room as often as you wish.

ABOVE Decorating in colors that are reminiscent of water can really improve the way you use and enjoy your bathroom. They make it look fresh and clean. Aquamarine and dark blue, as used here, are partuicularly good at creating a tranquil space as they are reminders of revitalizing places by the sea.

moroccan spice

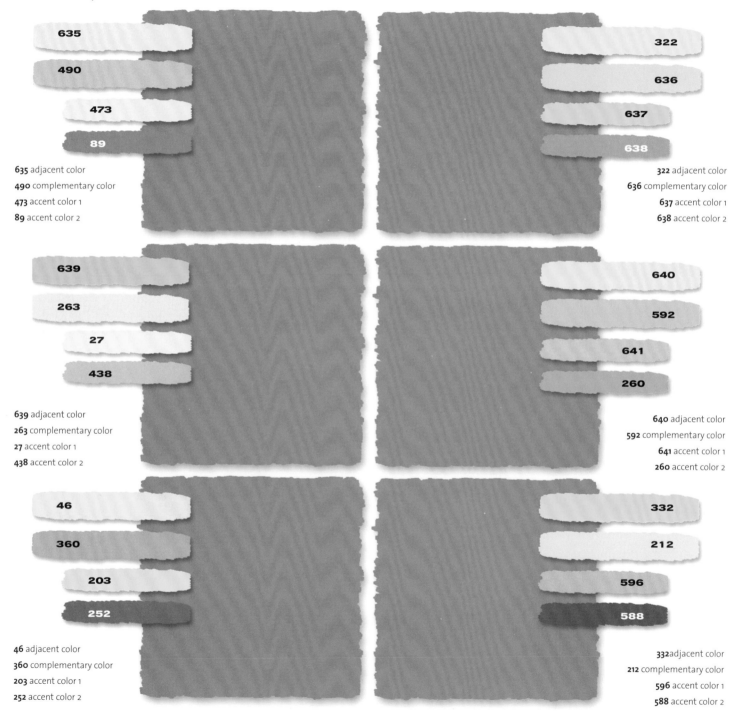

635
490
473
89

635 adjacent color
490 complementary color
473 accent color 1
89 accent color 2

322
636
637
638

322 adjacent color
636 complementary color
637 accent color 1
638 accent color 2

639
263
27
438

639 adjacent color
263 complementary color
27 accent color 1
438 accent color 2

640
592
641
260

640 adjacent color
592 complementary color
641 accent color 1
260 accent color 2

46
360
203
252

46 adjacent color
360 complementary color
203 accent color 1
252 accent color 2

332
212
596
588

332 adjacent color
212 complementary color
596 accent color 1
588 accent color 2

moroccan spice

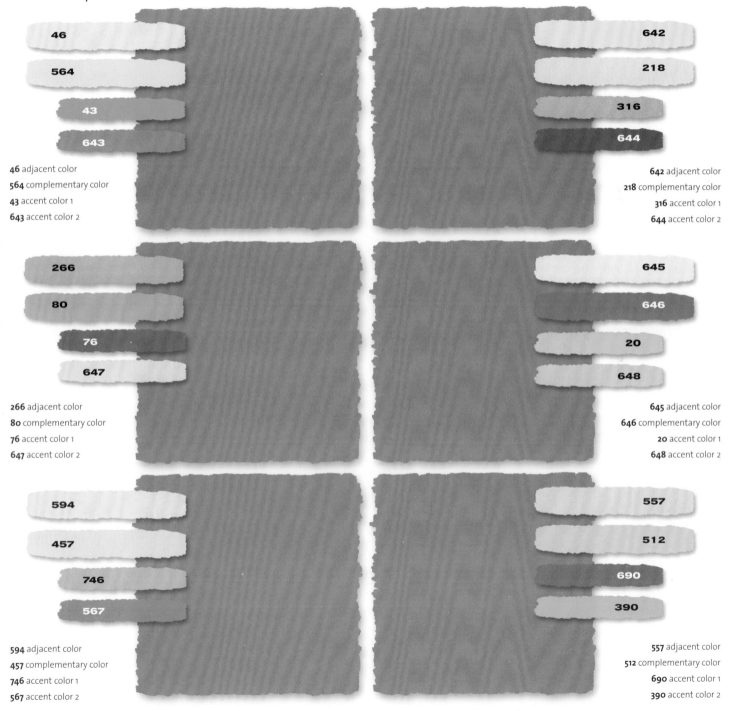

46

564

43

643

642

218

316

644

46 adjacent color
564 complementary color
43 accent color 1
643 accent color 2

642 adjacent color
218 complementary color
316 accent color 1
644 accent color 2

266

80

76

647

645

646

20

648

266 adjacent color
80 complementary color
76 accent color 1
647 accent color 2

645 adjacent color
646 complementary color
20 accent color 1
648 accent color 2

594

457

746

567

557

512

690

390

594 adjacent color
457 complementary color
746 accent color 1
567 accent color 2

557 adjacent color
512 complementary color
690 accent color 1
390 accent color 2

moroccan spice

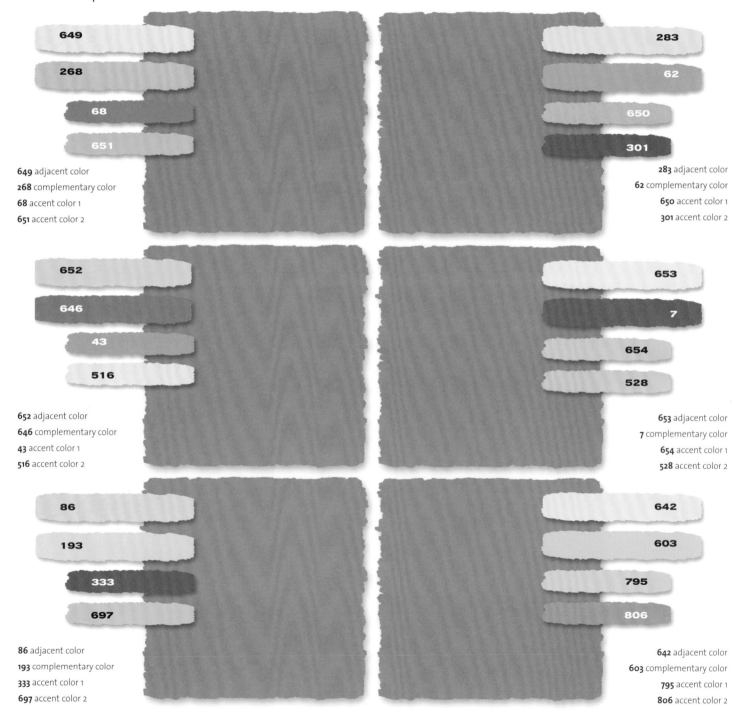

649 adjacent color
268 complementary color
68 accent color 1
651 accent color 2

283 adjacent color
62 complementary color
650 accent color 1
301 accent color 2

652 adjacent color
646 complementary color
43 accent color 1
516 accent color 2

653 adjacent color
7 complementary color
654 accent color 1
528 accent color 2

86 adjacent color
193 complementary color
333 accent color 1
697 accent color 2

642 adjacent color
603 complementary color
795 accent color 1
806 accent color 2

moroccan spice

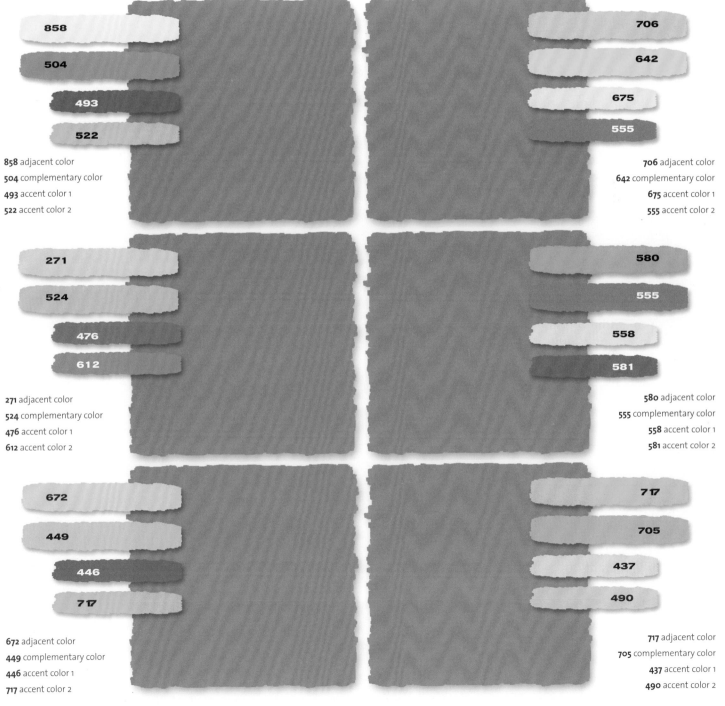

858 adjacent color
504 complementary color
493 accent color 1
522 accent color 2

706 adjacent color
642 complementary color
675 accent color 1
555 accent color 2

271 adjacent color
524 complementary color
476 accent color 1
612 accent color 2

580 adjacent color
555 complementary color
558 accent color 1
581 accent color 2

672 adjacent color
449 complementary color
446 accent color 1
717 accent color 2

717 adjacent color
705 complementary color
437 accent color 1
490 accent color 2

sunrays

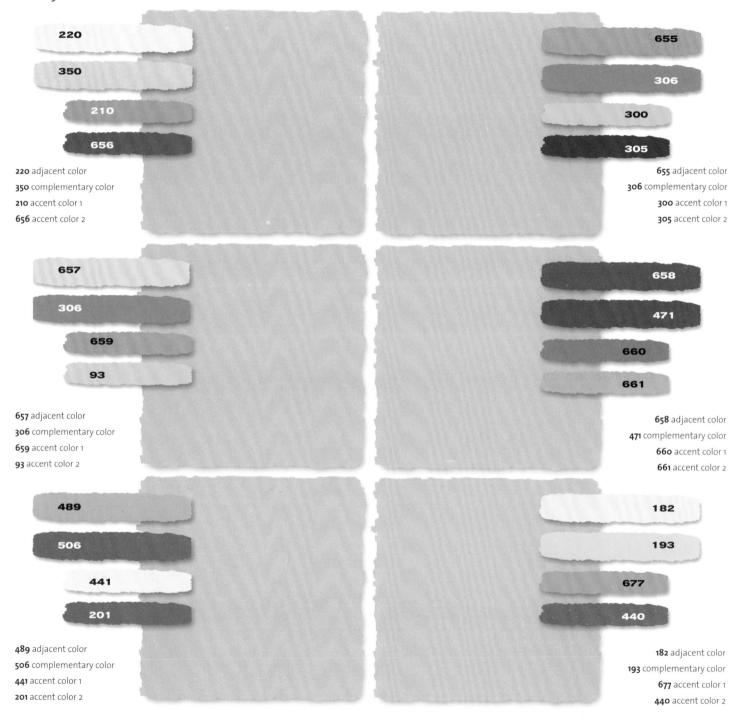

220
350
210
656

220 adjacent color
350 complementary color
210 accent color 1
656 accent color 2

655
306
300
305

655 adjacent color
306 complementary color
300 accent color 1
305 accent color 2

657
306
659
93

657 adjacent color
306 complementary color
659 accent color 1
93 accent color 2

658
471
660
661

658 adjacent color
471 complementary color
660 accent color 1
661 accent color 2

489
506
441
201

489 adjacent color
506 complementary color
441 accent color 1
201 accent color 2

182
193
677
440

182 adjacent color
193 complementary color
677 accent color 1
440 accent color 2

sunrays

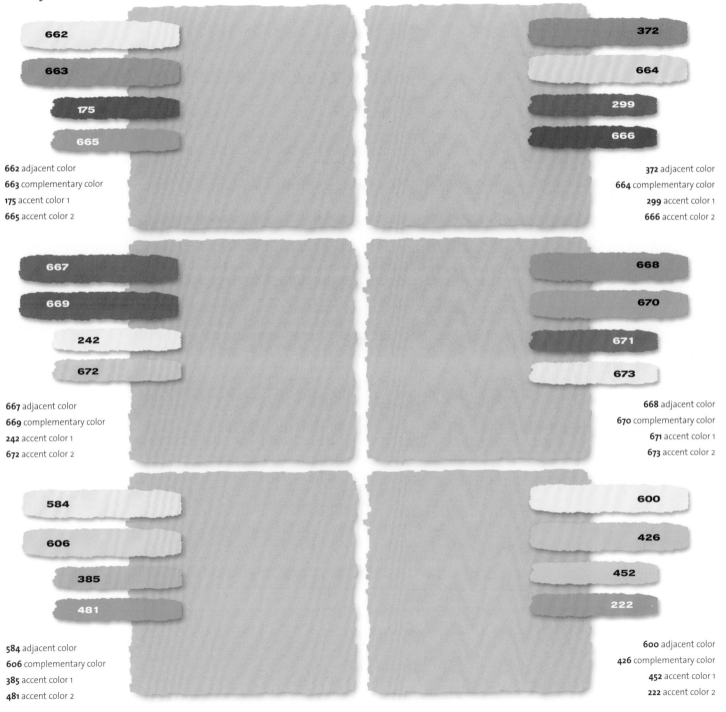

662
663
175
665

662 adjacent color
663 complementary color
175 accent color 1
665 accent color 2

372
664
299
666

372 adjacent color
664 complementary color
299 accent color 1
666 accent color 2

667
669
242
672

667 adjacent color
669 complementary color
242 accent color 1
672 accent color 2

668
670
671
673

668 adjacent color
670 complementary color
671 accent color 1
673 accent color 2

584
606
385
481

584 adjacent color
606 complementary color
385 accent color 1
481 accent color 2

600
426
452
222

600 adjacent color
426 complementary color
452 accent color 1
222 accent color 2

sunrays

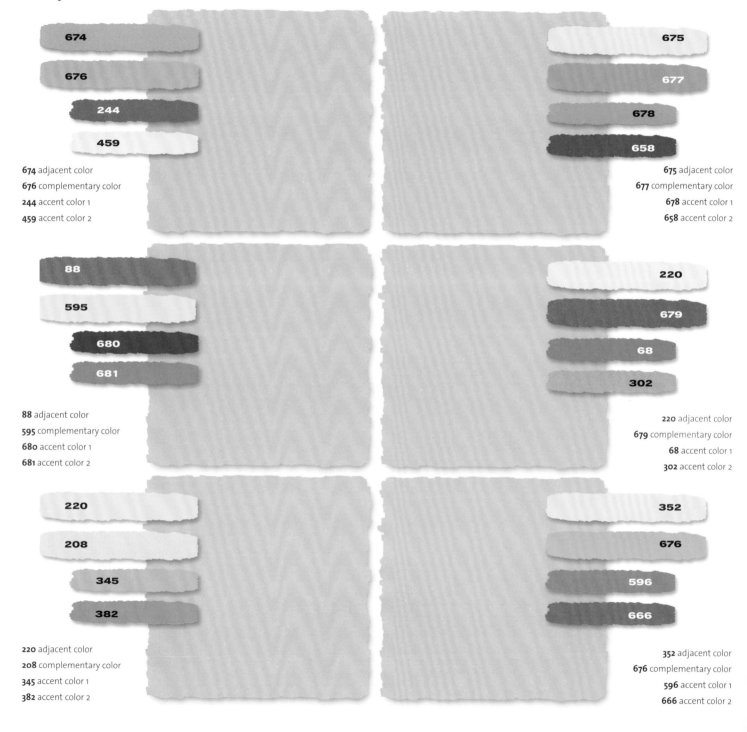

674

676

244

459

675

677

678

658

674 adjacent color
676 complementary color
244 accent color 1
459 accent color 2

675 adjacent color
677 complementary color
678 accent color 1
658 accent color 2

88

595

680

681

220

679

68

302

88 adjacent color
595 complementary color
680 accent color 1
681 accent color 2

220 adjacent color
679 complementary color
68 accent color 1
302 accent color 2

220

208

345

382

352

676

596

666

220 adjacent color
208 complementary color
345 accent color 1
382 accent color 2

352 adjacent color
676 complementary color
596 accent color 1
666 accent color 2

sunrays

634
699
826
52

158
534
650
525

634 adjacent color
699 complementary color
826 accent color 1
52 accent color 2

158 adjacent color
534 complementary color
650 accent color 1
525 accent color 2

98
194
202
195

492
450
399
509

98 adjacent color
194 complementary color
202 accent color 1
195 accent color 2

492 adjacent color
450 complementary color
399 accent color 1
509 accent color 2

1
80
85
142

295
386
631
367

1 adjacent color
80 complementary color
85 accent color 1
142 accent color 2

295 adjacent color
386 complementary color
631 accent color 1
367 accent color 2

nova scotia blue

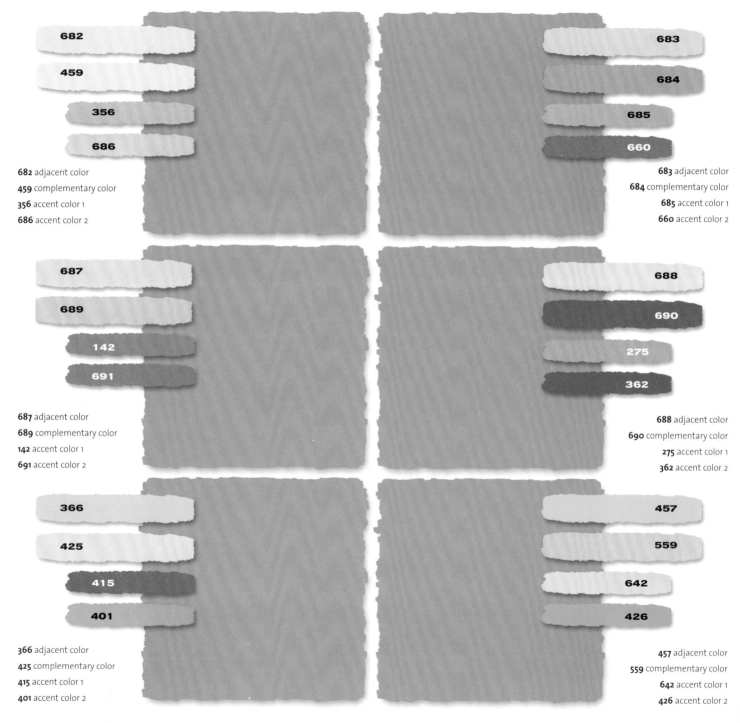

682 | **683**
459 | **684**
356 | **685**
686 | **660**

682 adjacent color
459 complementary color
356 accent color 1
686 accent color 2

683 adjacent color
684 complementary color
685 accent color 1
660 accent color 2

687 | **688**
689 | **690**
142 | **275**
691 | **362**

687 adjacent color
689 complementary color
142 accent color 1
691 accent color 2

688 adjacent color
690 complementary color
275 accent color 1
362 accent color 2

366 | **457**
425 | **559**
415 | **642**
401 | **426**

366 adjacent color
425 complementary color
415 accent color 1
401 accent color 2

457 adjacent color
559 complementary color
642 accent color 1
426 accent color 2

nova scotia blue

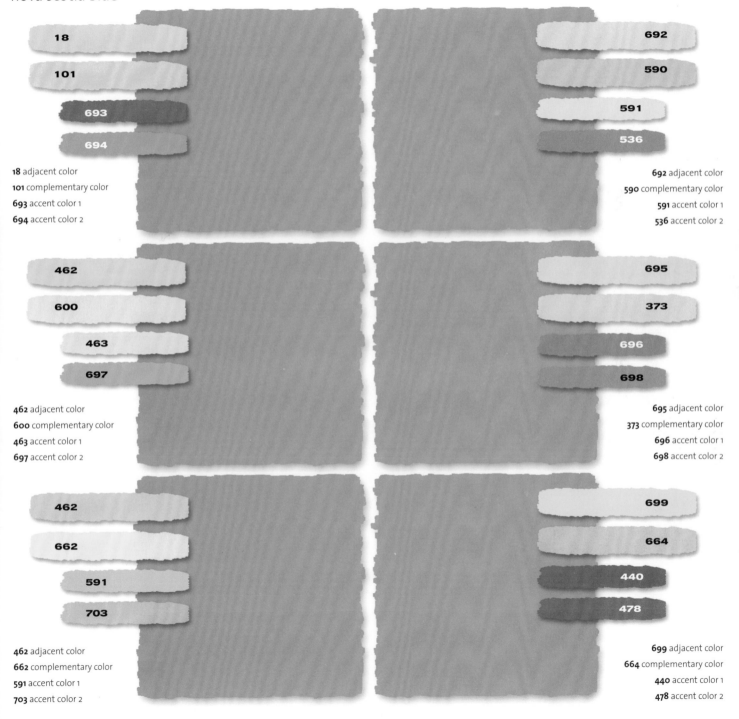

18 | **692**
101 | **590**
693 | **591**
694 | **536**

18 adjacent color
101 complementary color
693 accent color 1
694 accent color 2

692 adjacent color
590 complementary color
591 accent color 1
536 accent color 2

462 | **695**
600 | **373**
463 | **696**
697 | **698**

462 adjacent color
600 complementary color
463 accent color 1
697 accent color 2

695 adjacent color
373 complementary color
696 accent color 1
698 accent color 2

462 | **699**
662 | **664**
591 | **440**
703 | **478**

462 adjacent color
662 complementary color
591 accent color 1
703 accent color 2

699 adjacent color
664 complementary color
440 accent color 1
478 accent color 2

nova scotia blue

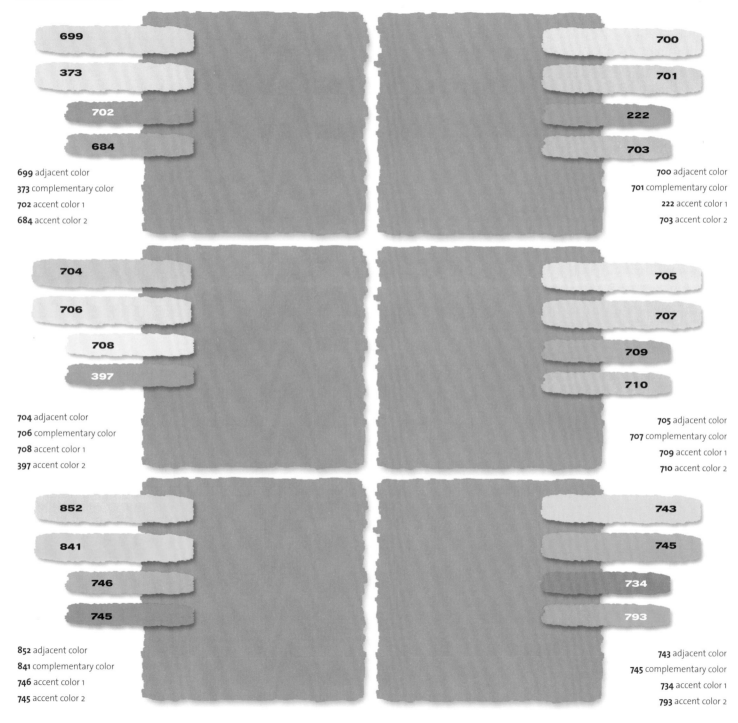

699
373
702
684

700
701
222
703

699 adjacent color
373 complementary color
702 accent color 1
684 accent color 2

700 adjacent color
701 complementary color
222 accent color 1
703 accent color 2

704
706
708
397

705
707
709
710

704 adjacent color
706 complementary color
708 accent color 1
397 accent color 2

705 adjacent color
707 complementary color
709 accent color 1
710 accent color 2

852
841
746
745

743
745
734
793

852 adjacent color
841 complementary color
746 accent color 1
745 accent color 2

743 adjacent color
745 complementary color
734 accent color 1
793 accent color 2

nova scotia blue

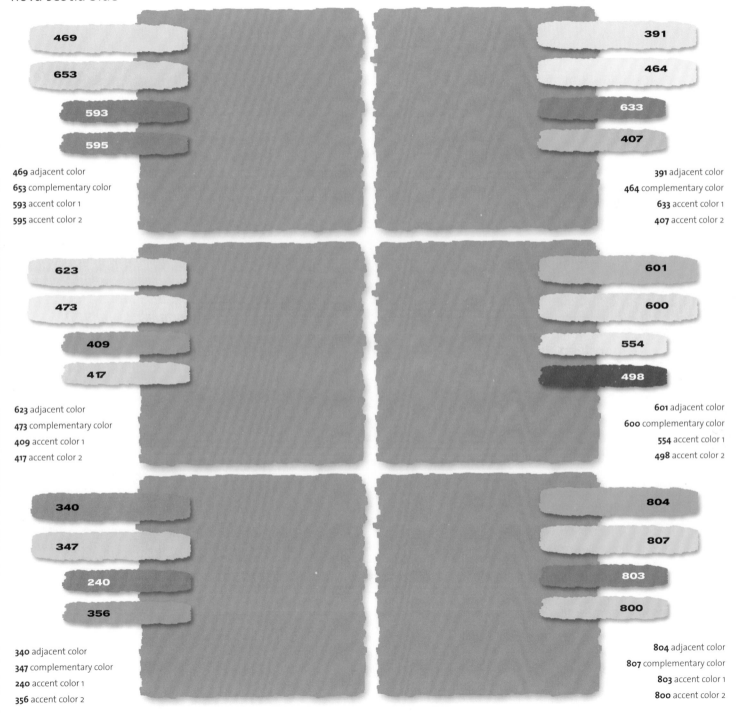

469

653

593

595

469 adjacent color
653 complementary color
593 accent color 1
595 accent color 2

391

464

633

407

391 adjacent color
464 complementary color
633 accent color 1
407 accent color 2

623

473

409

417

623 adjacent color
473 complementary color
409 accent color 1
417 accent color 2

601

600

554

498

601 adjacent color
600 complementary color
554 accent color 1
498 accent color 2

340

347

240

356

340 adjacent color
347 complementary color
240 accent color 1
356 accent color 2

804

807

803

800

804 adjacent color
807 complementary color
803 accent color 1
800 accent color 2

warm apple crisp

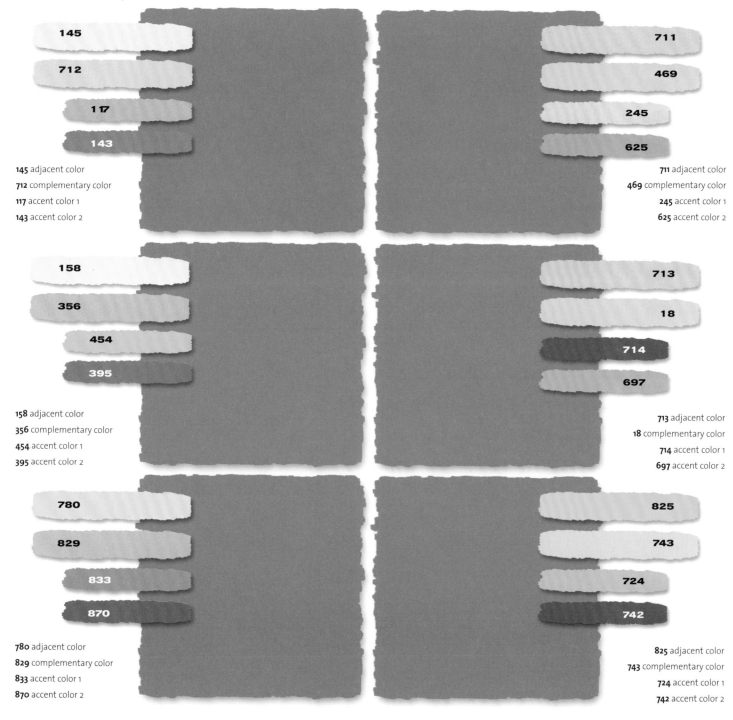

145

712

1 17

143

145 adjacent color
712 complementary color
117 accent color 1
143 accent color 2

711

469

245

625

711 adjacent color
469 complementary color
245 accent color 1
625 accent color 2

158

356

454

395

158 adjacent color
356 complementary color
454 accent color 1
395 accent color 2

713

18

714

697

713 adjacent color
18 complementary color
714 accent color 1
697 accent color 2

780

829

833

870

780 adjacent color
829 complementary color
833 accent color 1
870 accent color 2

825

743

724

742

825 adjacent color
743 complementary color
724 accent color 1
742 accent color 2

warm apple crisp

600
716
717
718

715
369
162
377

600 adjacent color
716 complementary color
717 accent color 1
718 accent color 2

715 adjacent color
369 complementary color
162 accent color 1
377 accent color 2

544
18
121
11

9
596
719
395

544 adjacent color
18 complementary color
121 accent color 1
11 accent color 2

9 adjacent color
596 complementary color
719 accent color 1
395 accent color 2

456
623
606
426

473
534
541
684

456 adjacent color
623 complementary color
606 accent color 1
426 accent color 2

473 adjacent color
534 complementary color
541 accent color 1
684 accent color 2

warm apple crisp

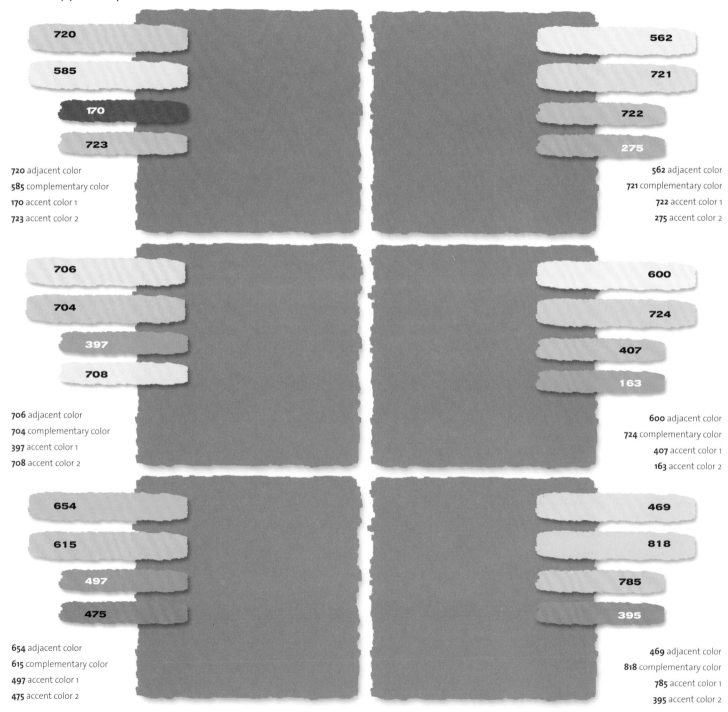

720
585
170
723

720 adjacent color
585 complementary color
170 accent color 1
723 accent color 2

562
721
722
275

562 adjacent color
721 complementary color
722 accent color 1
275 accent color 2

706
704
397
708

706 adjacent color
704 complementary color
397 accent color 1
708 accent color 2

600
724
407
163

600 adjacent color
724 complementary color
407 accent color 1
163 accent color 2

654
615
497
475

654 adjacent color
615 complementary color
497 accent color 1
475 accent color 2

469
818
785
395

469 adjacent color
818 complementary color
785 accent color 1
395 accent color 2

warm apple crisp

454

571

581

565

454 adjacent color
571 complementary color
581 accent color 1
565 accent color 2

783

451

194

208

783 adjacent color
451 complementary color
194 accent color 1
208 accent color 2

576

623

700

691

576 adjacent color
623 complementary color
700 accent color 1
691 accent color 2

13

683

687

281

13 adjacent color
683 complementary color
687 accent color 1
281 accent color 2

600

553

710

599

600 adjacent color
553 complementary color
710 accent color 1
599 accent color 2

363

508

695

320

363 adjacent color
508 complementary color
695 accent color 1
320 accent color 2

lemon grass

737

539

79

135

737 adjacent color
539 complementary color
79 accent color 1
135 accent color 2

645

443

738

222

645 adjacent color
443 complementary color
738 accent color 1
222 accent color 2

102

449

740

340

102 adjacent color
449 complementary color
740 accent color 1
340 accent color 2

675

739

741

742

675 adjacent color
739 complementary color
741 accent color 1
742 accent color 2

271

604

639

632

271 adjacent color
604 complementary color
639 accent color 1
632 accent color 2

309

603

659

690

309 adjacent color
603 complementary color
659 accent color 1
690 accent color 2

lemon grass

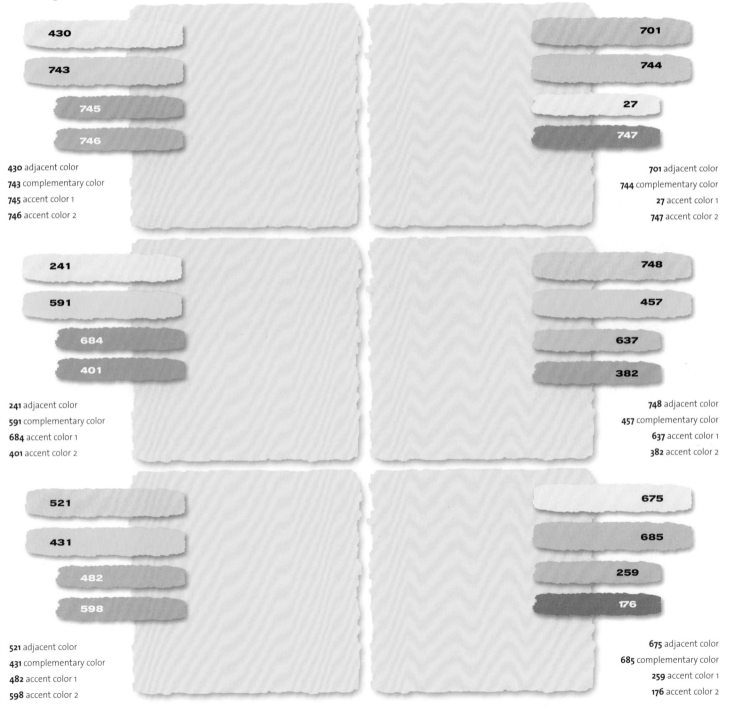

430

743

745

746

701

744

27

747

430 adjacent color
743 complementary color
745 accent color 1
746 accent color 2

701 adjacent color
744 complementary color
27 accent color 1
747 accent color 2

241

591

684

401

748

457

637

382

241 adjacent color
591 complementary color
684 accent color 1
401 accent color 2

748 adjacent color
457 complementary color
637 accent color 1
382 accent color 2

521

431

482

598

675

685

259

176

521 adjacent color
431 complementary color
482 accent color 1
598 accent color 2

675 adjacent color
685 complementary color
259 accent color 1
176 accent color 2

lemon grass

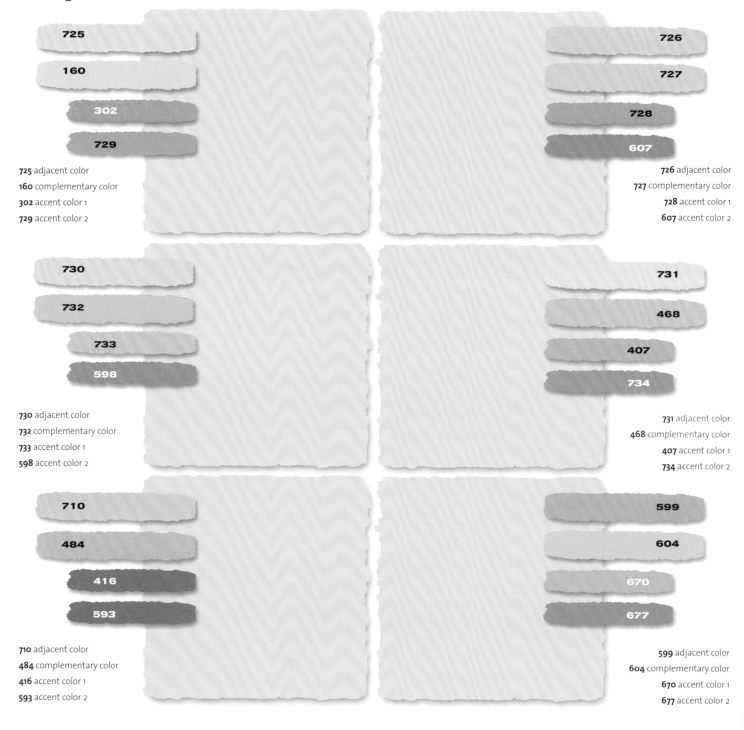

725

160

302

729

726

727

728

607

725 adjacent color
160 complementary color
302 accent color 1
729 accent color 2

726 adjacent color
727 complementary color
728 accent color 1
607 accent color 2

730

732

733

598

731

468

407

734

730 adjacent color
732 complementary color
733 accent color 1
598 accent color 2

731 adjacent color
468 complementary color
407 accent color 1
734 accent color 2

710

484

416

593

599

604

670

677

710 adjacent color
484 complementary color
416 accent color 1
593 accent color 2

599 adjacent color
604 complementary color
670 accent color 1
677 accent color 2

lemon grass

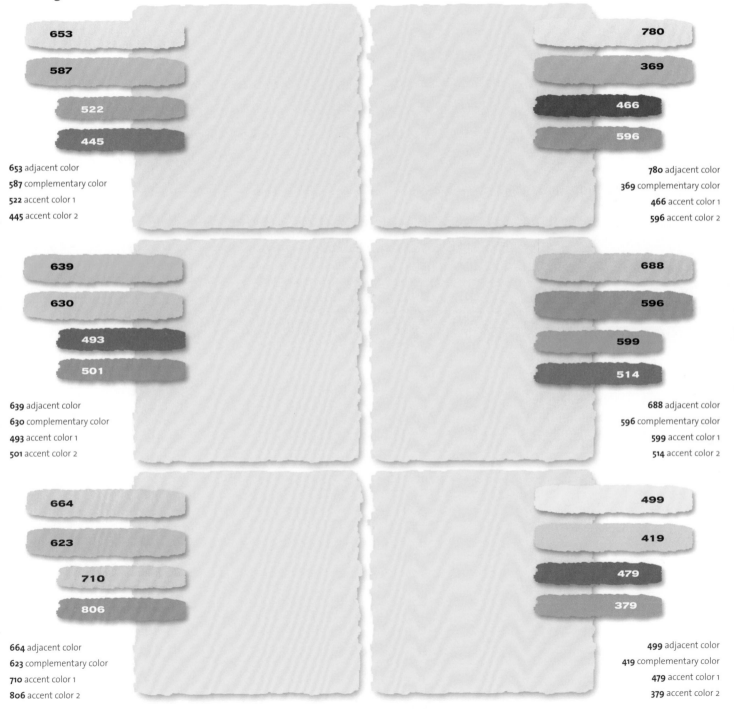

653

587

522

445

653 adjacent color
587 complementary color
522 accent color 1
445 accent color 2

780

369

466

596

780 adjacent color
369 complementary color
466 accent color 1
596 accent color 2

639

630

493

501

639 adjacent color
630 complementary color
493 accent color 1
501 accent color 2

688

596

599

514

688 adjacent color
596 complementary color
599 accent color 1
514 accent color 2

664

623

710

806

664 adjacent color
623 complementary color
710 accent color 1
806 accent color 2

499

419

479

379

499 adjacent color
419 complementary color
479 accent color 1
379 accent color 2

chic lime

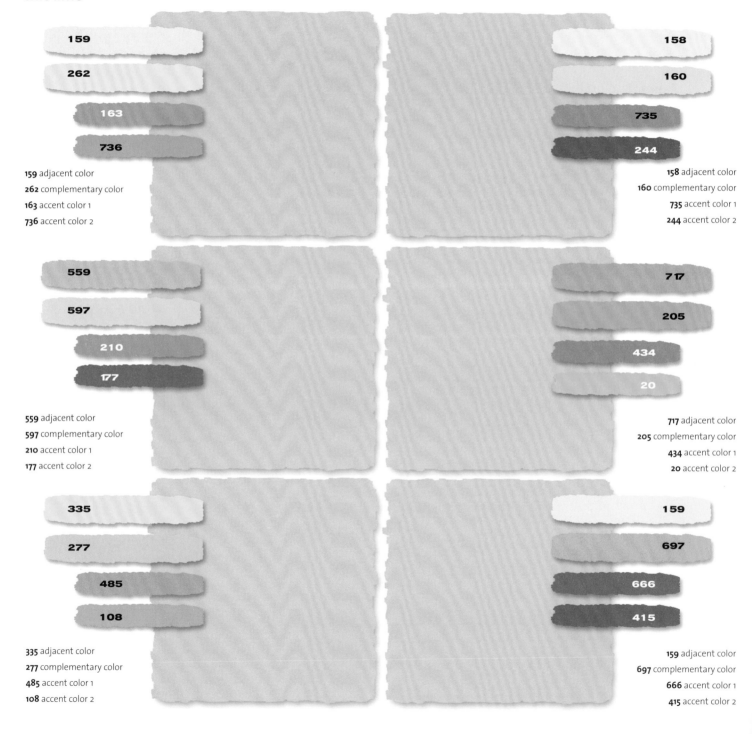

159

262

163

736

159 adjacent color
262 complementary color
163 accent color 1
736 accent color 2

158

160

735

244

158 adjacent color
160 complementary color
735 accent color 1
244 accent color 2

559

597

210

177

559 adjacent color
597 complementary color
210 accent color 1
177 accent color 2

717

205

434

20

717 adjacent color
205 complementary color
434 accent color 1
20 accent color 2

335

277

485

108

335 adjacent color
277 complementary color
485 accent color 1
108 accent color 2

159

697

666

415

159 adjacent color
697 complementary color
666 accent color 1
415 accent color 2

chic lime

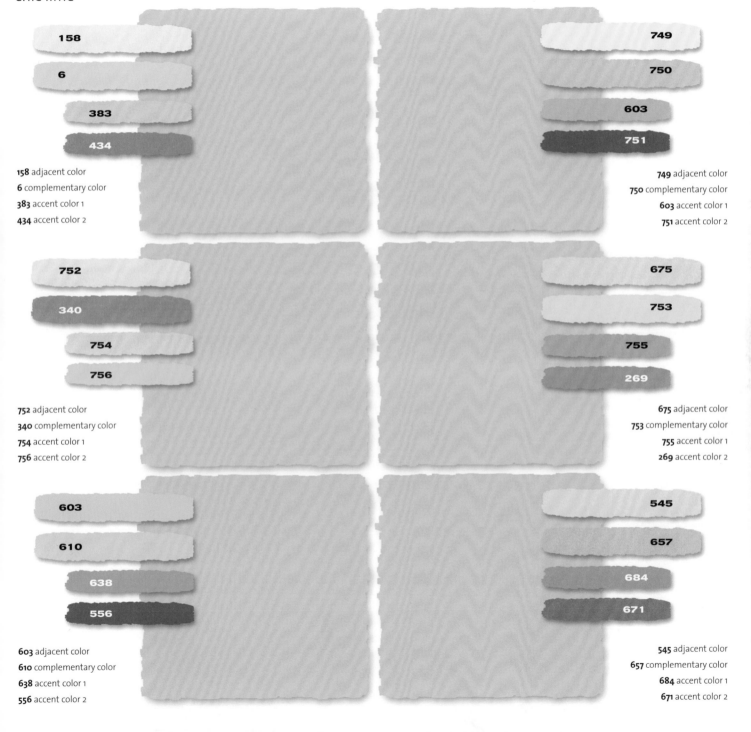

158

6

383

434

158 adjacent color
6 complementary color
383 accent color 1
434 accent color 2

749

750

603

751

749 adjacent color
750 complementary color
603 accent color 1
751 accent color 2

752

340

754

756

752 adjacent color
340 complementary color
754 accent color 1
756 accent color 2

675

753

755

269

675 adjacent color
753 complementary color
755 accent color 1
269 accent color 2

603

610

638

556

603 adjacent color
610 complementary color
638 accent color 1
556 accent color 2

545

657

684

671

545 adjacent color
657 complementary color
684 accent color 1
671 accent color 2

chic lime

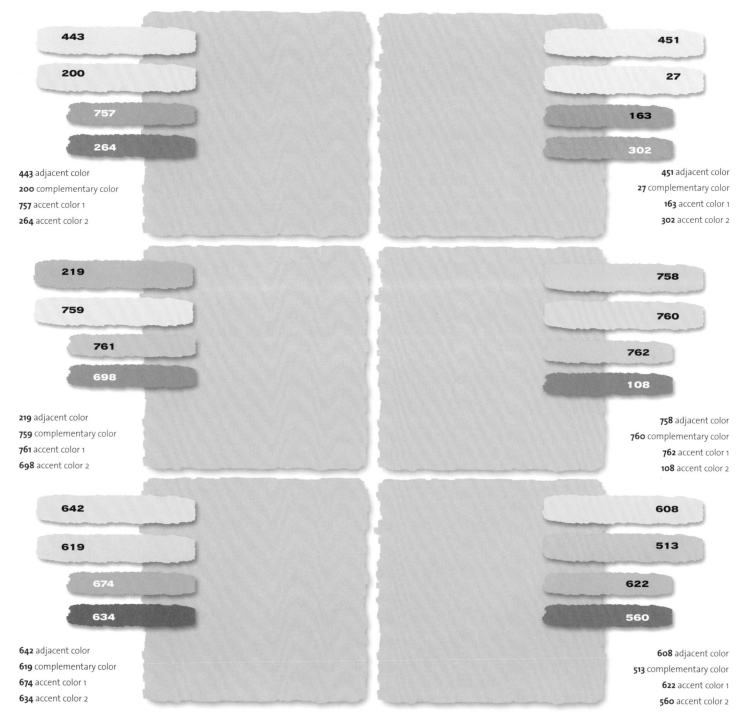

443

200

757

264

451

27

163

302

443 adjacent color
200 complementary color
757 accent color 1
264 accent color 2

451 adjacent color
27 complementary color
163 accent color 1
302 accent color 2

219

759

761

698

758

760

762

108

219 adjacent color
759 complementary color
761 accent color 1
698 accent color 2

758 adjacent color
760 complementary color
762 accent color 1
108 accent color 2

642

619

674

634

608

513

622

560

642 adjacent color
619 complementary color
674 accent color 1
634 accent color 2

608 adjacent color
513 complementary color
622 accent color 1
560 accent color 2

chic lime

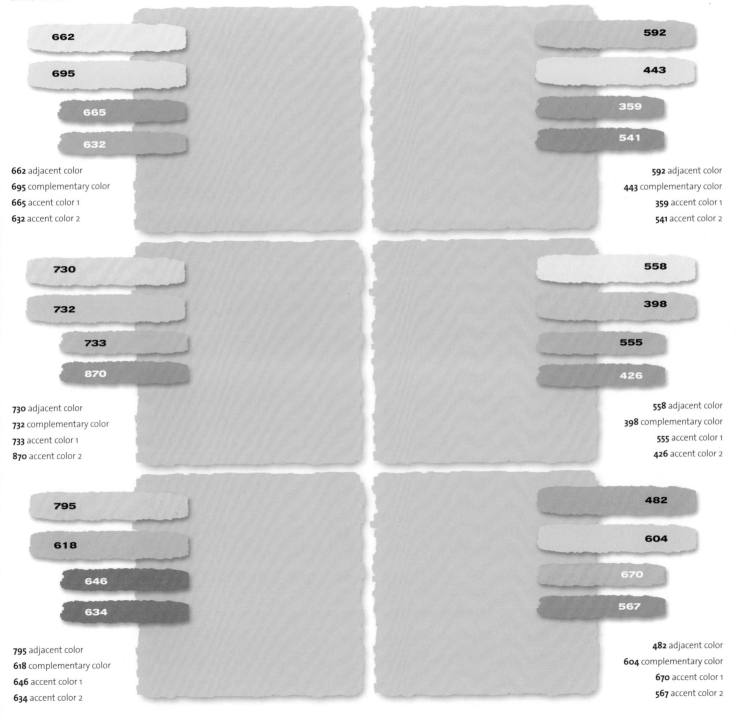

662

695

665

632

662 adjacent color
695 complementary color
665 accent color 1
632 accent color 2

592

443

359

541

592 adjacent color
443 complementary color
359 accent color 1
541 accent color 2

730

732

733

870

730 adjacent color
732 complementary color
733 accent color 1
870 accent color 2

558

398

555

426

558 adjacent color
398 complementary color
555 accent color 1
426 accent color 2

795

618

646

634

795 adjacent color
618 complementary color
646 accent color 1
634 accent color 2

482

604

670

567

482 adjacent color
604 complementary color
670 accent color 1
567 accent color 2

sounds of nature

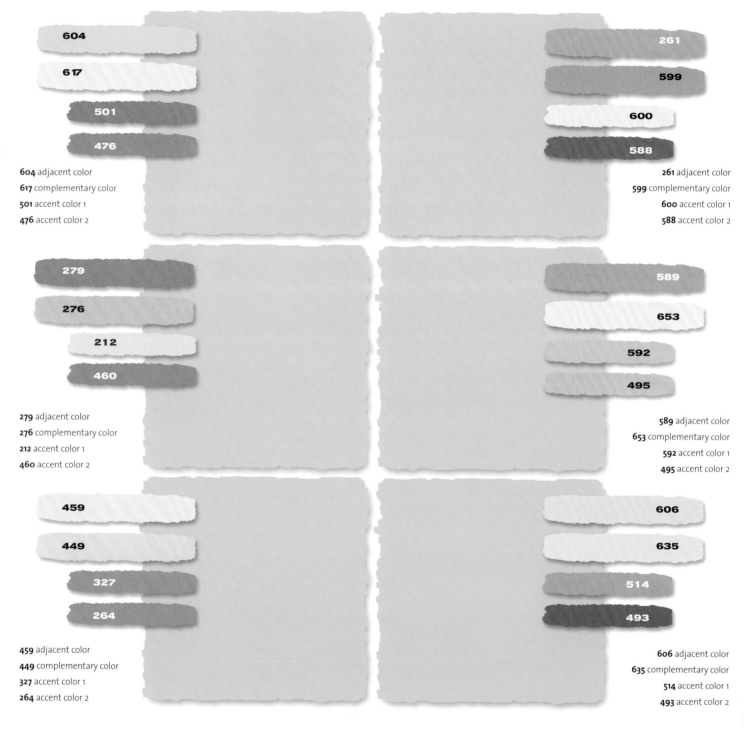

604

617

501

476

261

599

600

588

604 adjacent color
617 complementary color
501 accent color 1
476 accent color 2

261 adjacent color
599 complementary color
600 accent color 1
588 accent color 2

279

276

212

460

589

653

592

495

279 adjacent color
276 complementary color
212 accent color 1
460 accent color 2

589 adjacent color
653 complementary color
592 accent color 1
495 accent color 2

459

449

327

264

606

635

514

493

459 adjacent color
449 complementary color
327 accent color 1
264 accent color 2

606 adjacent color
635 complementary color
514 accent color 1
493 accent color 2

sounds of nature

662

391

521

369

662 adjacent color
391 complementary color
521 accent color 1
369 accent color 2

590

649

656

634

590 adjacent color
649 complementary color
656 accent color 1
634 accent color 2

383

521

593

598

383 adjacent color
521 complementary color
593 accent color 1
598 accent color 2

514

720

711

696

514 adjacent color
720 complementary color
711 accent color 1
696 accent color 2

84

595

478

502

84 adjacent color
595 complementary color
478 accent color 1
502 accent color 2

449

504

566

486

449 adjacent color
504 complementary color
566 accent color 1
486 accent color 2

sounds of nature

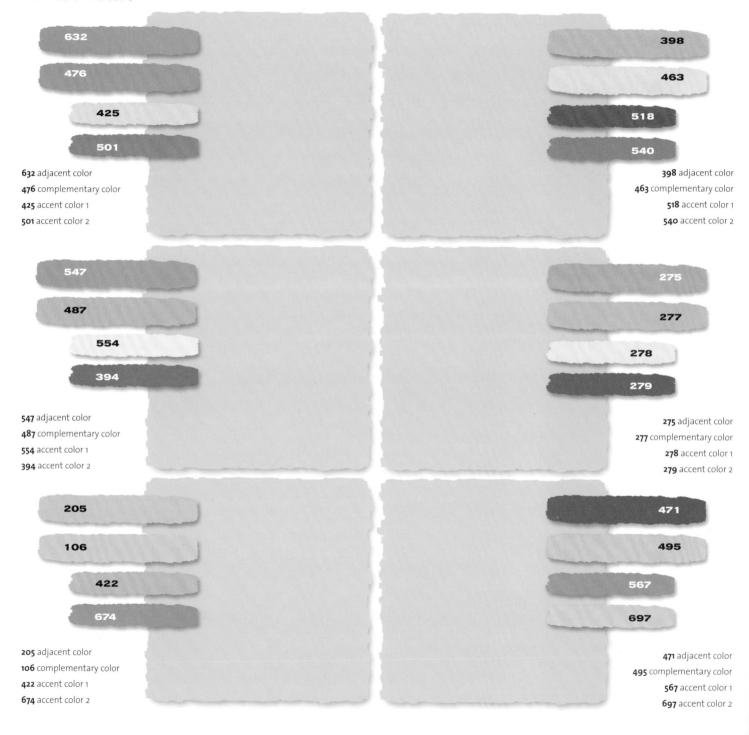

632
476
425
501

632 adjacent color
476 complementary color
425 accent color 1
501 accent color 2

398
463
518
540

398 adjacent color
463 complementary color
518 accent color 1
540 accent color 2

547
487
554
394

547 adjacent color
487 complementary color
554 accent color 1
394 accent color 2

275
277
278
279

275 adjacent color
277 complementary color
278 accent color 1
279 accent color 2

205
106
422
674

205 adjacent color
106 complementary color
422 accent color 1
674 accent color 2

471
495
567
697

471 adjacent color
495 complementary color
567 accent color 1
697 accent color 2

sounds of nature

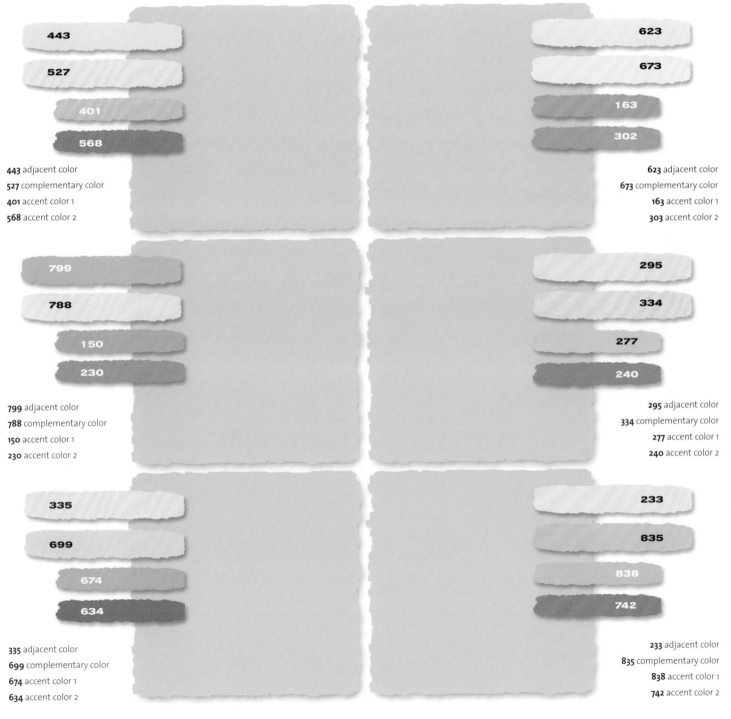

443
527
401
568

443 adjacent color
527 complementary color
401 accent color 1
568 accent color 2

623
673
163
302

623 adjacent color
673 complementary color
163 accent color 1
303 accent color 2

799
788
150
230

799 adjacent color
788 complementary color
150 accent color 1
230 accent color 2

295
334
277
240

295 adjacent color
334 complementary color
277 accent color 1
240 accent color 2

335
699
674
634

335 adjacent color
699 complementary color
674 accent color 1
634 accent color 2

233
835
838
742

233 adjacent color
835 complementary color
838 accent color 1
742 accent color 2

tooty fruity

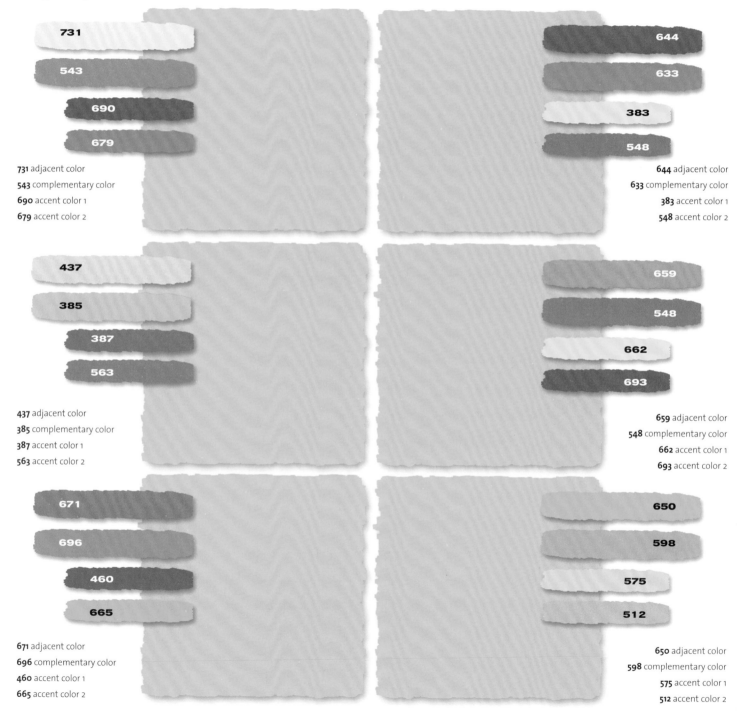

731

543

690

679

731 adjacent color
543 complementary color
690 accent color 1
679 accent color 2

644

633

383

548

644 adjacent color
633 complementary color
383 accent color 1
548 accent color 2

437

385

387

563

437 adjacent color
385 complementary color
387 accent color 1
563 accent color 2

659

548

662

693

659 adjacent color
548 complementary color
662 accent color 1
693 accent color 2

671

696

460

665

671 adjacent color
696 complementary color
460 accent color 1
665 accent color 2

650

598

575

512

650 adjacent color
598 complementary color
575 accent color 1
512 accent color 2

tooty fruity

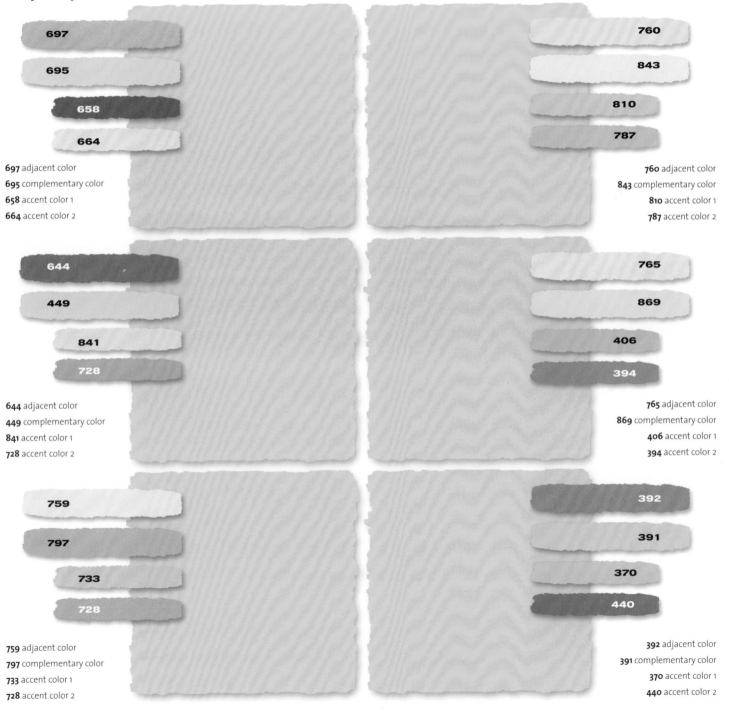

697

695

658

664

760

843

810

787

697 adjacent color
695 complementary color
658 accent color 1
664 accent color 2

760 adjacent color
843 complementary color
810 accent color 1
787 accent color 2

644

449

841

728

765

869

406

394

644 adjacent color
449 complementary color
841 accent color 1
728 accent color 2

765 adjacent color
869 complementary color
406 accent color 1
394 accent color 2

759

797

733

728

392

391

370

440

759 adjacent color
797 complementary color
733 accent color 1
728 accent color 2

392 adjacent color
391 complementary color
370 accent color 1
440 accent color 2

tooty fruity

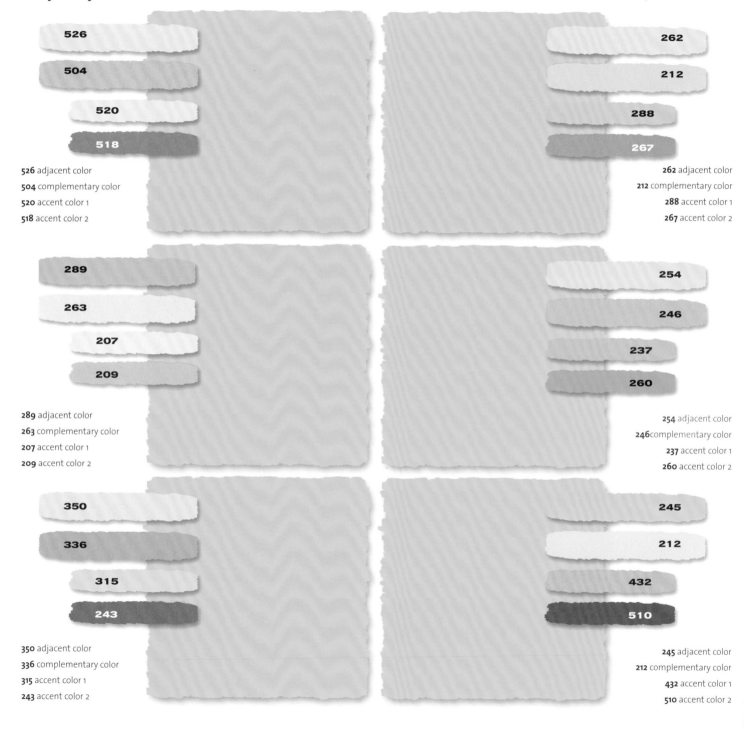

526

504

520

518

262

212

288

267

289

263

207

209

254

246

237

260

350

336

315

243

245

212

432

510

526 adjacent color
504 complementary color
520 accent color 1
518 accent color 2

262 adjacent color
212 complementary color
288 accent color 1
267 accent color 2

289 adjacent color
263 complementary color
207 accent color 1
209 accent color 2

254 adjacent color
246 complementary color
237 accent color 1
260 accent color 2

350 adjacent color
336 complementary color
315 accent color 1
243 accent color 2

245 adjacent color
212 complementary color
432 accent color 1
510 accent color 2

tooty fruity

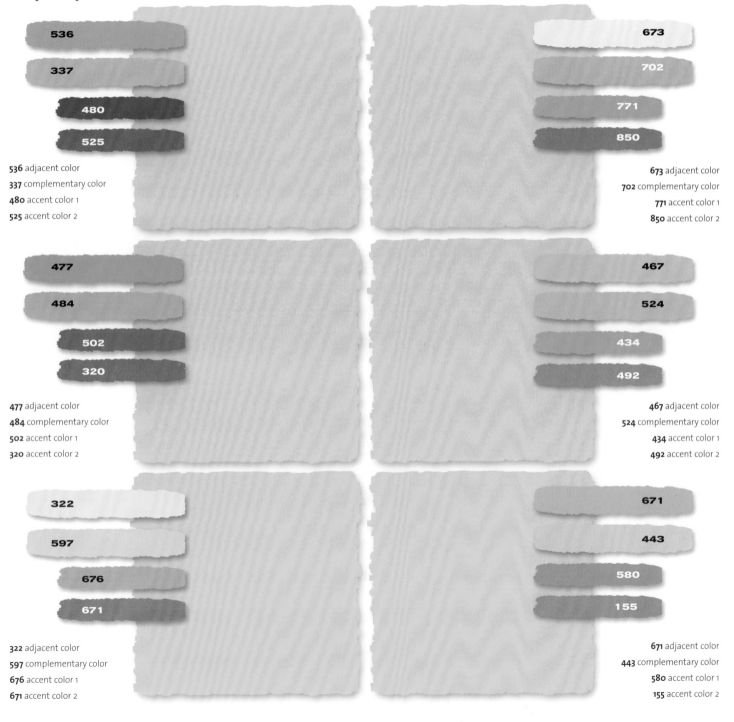

536

337

480

525

536 adjacent color
337 complementary color
480 accent color 1
525 accent color 2

673

702

771

850

673 adjacent color
702 complementary color
771 accent color 1
850 accent color 2

477

484

502

320

477 adjacent color
484 complementary color
502 accent color 1
320 accent color 2

467

524

434

492

467 adjacent color
524 complementary color
434 accent color 1
492 accent color 2

322

597

676

671

322 adjacent color
597 complementary color
676 accent color 1
671 accent color 2

671

443

580

155

671 adjacent color
443 complementary color
580 accent color 1
155 accent color 2

rose garden

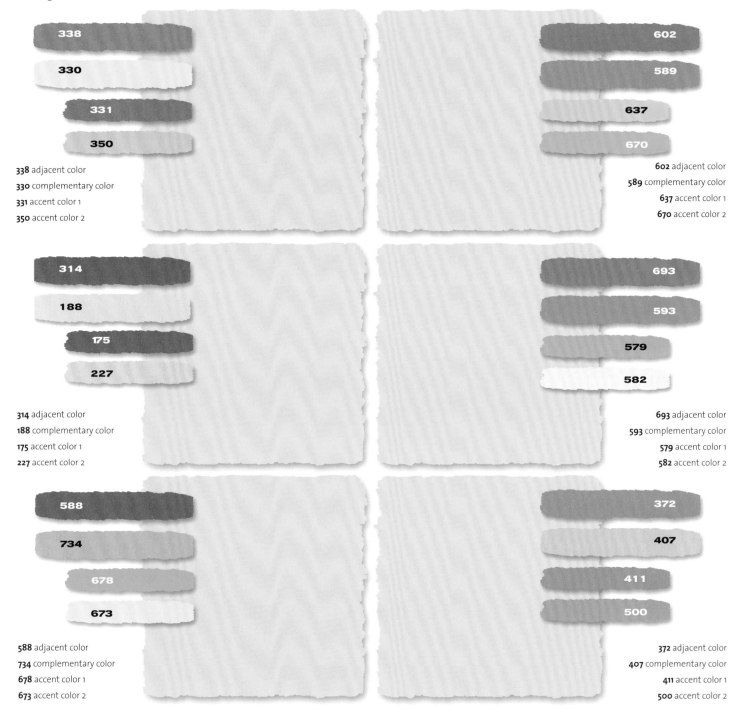

338

330

331

350

602

589

637

670

338 adjacent color
330 complementary color
331 accent color 1
350 accent color 2

602 adjacent color
589 complementary color
637 accent color 1
670 accent color 2

314

188

175

227

693

593

579

582

314 adjacent color
188 complementary color
175 accent color 1
227 accent color 2

693 adjacent color
593 complementary color
579 accent color 1
582 accent color 2

588

734

678

673

372

407

411

500

588 adjacent color
734 complementary color
678 accent color 1
673 accent color 2

372 adjacent color
407 complementary color
411 accent color 1
500 accent color 2

rose garden

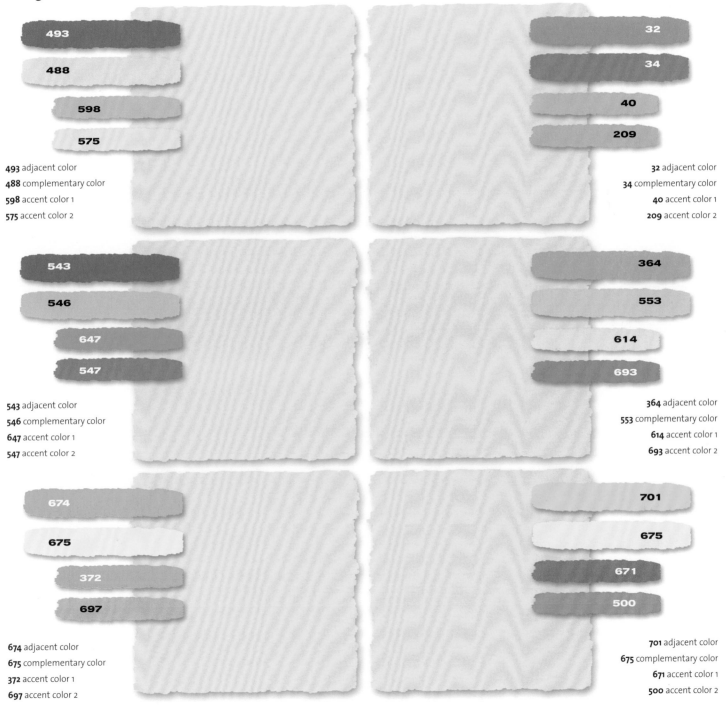

493 adjacent color
488 complementary color
598 accent color 1
575 accent color 2

32 adjacent color
34 complementary color
40 accent color 1
209 accent color 2

543 adjacent color
546 complementary color
647 accent color 1
547 accent color 2

364 adjacent color
553 complementary color
614 accent color 1
693 accent color 2

674 adjacent color
675 complementary color
372 accent color 1
697 accent color 2

701 adjacent color
675 complementary color
671 accent color 1
500 accent color 2

rose garden

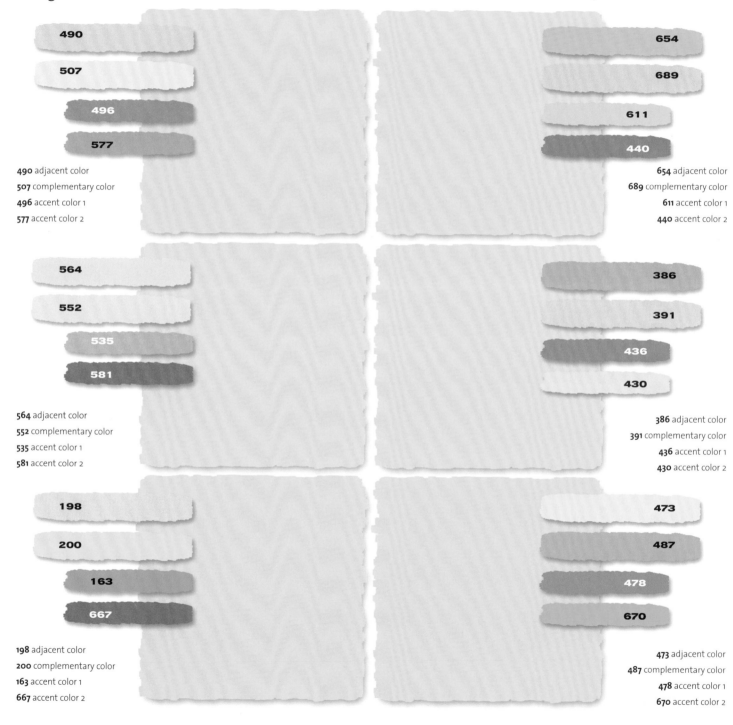

490
507
496
577

654
689
611
440

490 adjacent color
507 complementary color
496 accent color 1
577 accent color 2

654 adjacent color
689 complementary color
611 accent color 1
440 accent color 2

564
552
535
581

386
391
436
430

564 adjacent color
552 complementary color
535 accent color 1
581 accent color 2

386 adjacent color
391 complementary color
436 accent color 1
430 accent color 2

198
200
163
667

473
487
478
670

198 adjacent color
200 complementary color
163 accent color 1
667 accent color 2

473 adjacent color
487 complementary color
478 accent color 1
670 accent color 2

rose garden

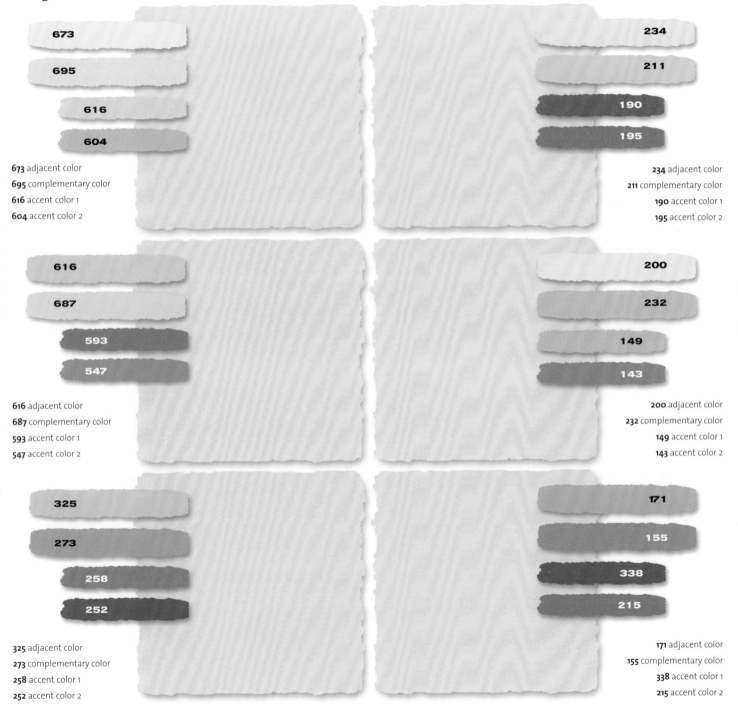

673

695

616

604

234

211

190

195

673 adjacent color
695 complementary color
616 accent color 1
604 accent color 2

234 adjacent color
211 complementary color
190 accent color 1
195 accent color 2

616

687

593

547

200

232

149

143

616 adjacent color
687 complementary color
593 accent color 1
547 accent color 2

200 adjacent color
232 complementary color
149 accent color 1
143 accent color 2

325

273

258

252

171

155

338

215

325 adjacent color
273 complementary color
258 accent color 1
252 accent color 2

171 adjacent color
155 complementary color
338 accent color 1
215 accent color 2

24	302
163	27

20	175
663	665

ABOVE The tones of the colors used here work perfectly together in creating a bathing space that is peaceful, but that will help you to feel refreshed and ready for the day ahead.

RIGHT Here the strong sand-colored walls and contrasting white provide balance so that the large patterned sofa does not overpower the room.

20	339
175	21

RIGHT Strong contrasts such as blue and yellow work well, particularly if one is used for accents such as pillows. This scheme is kept from being overpowering by the soft warm wall, which breaks up the intensity of the stronger contrasting tones.

20	662
443	871

LEFT The combination of cream, white, and yellow offset the black work surface and give this room a fresh quality and a golden glow making it a pleasant space to spend time.

21	471
368	175

RIGHT By varying the tones of blue from light to dark and by adding touches of contrast, as in the full bowl of fruit, this cool kitchen is brought to life.

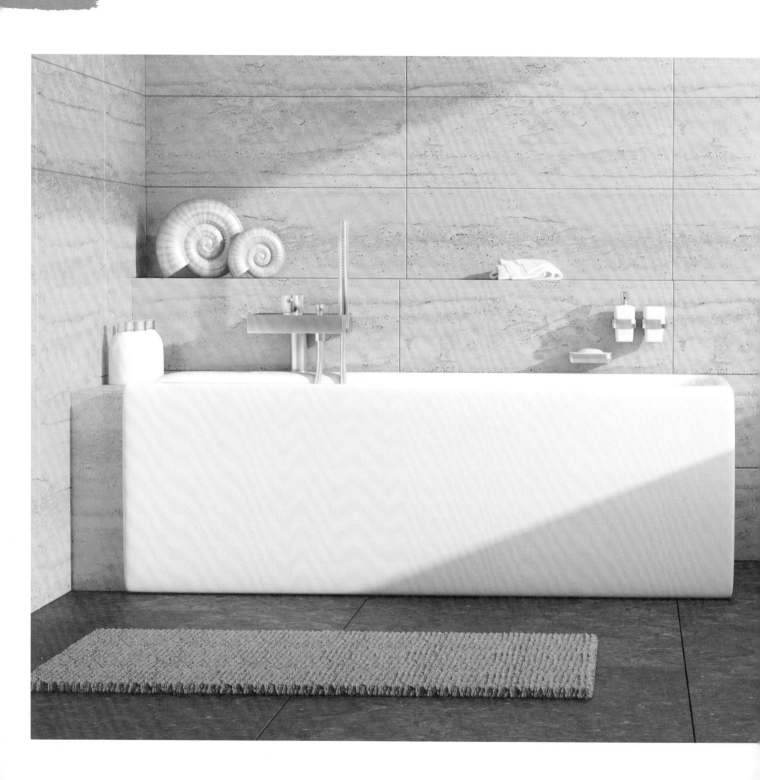

348	270	603	82
279	522	616	235

LEFT Bathrooms can benefit from simple color schemes, here the white bath and chrome faucet are enlivened with a striking contrast of rich yellow wall tiles and a dark blue-gray floor tiles. The bath mat and accessories bring the whole scheme together.

ABOVE Using colors inspired by nature always works well. The bright green used here lends an energetic feel, making this kitchen a stimulating place for cooking, socializing and entertaining.

135	776
133	841

RIGHT With its array of shiny and mat surfaces, and the use of complementary colors, this bathroom will energise and refresh. The strong patterns used throughout create a stimulating environment.

382	471
400	375

LEFT The combination of two colors that sit along side each other on the color wheel, in this case blue and green, produces a harmonious scheme. The brighter the tone of the colors used the more invigorating the space will become.

656	630
614	682

LEFT The strong red accent color used on the feature wall define the "work area" of this kitchen, echoing the red with the stools and glassware, unites the whole scheme.

384	476
461	383

RIGHT A monochrome scheme combining various shades of brown is given a vitality by the intensity of the greens supplied by the couch, chair and plant. All these natural tones ensure that this color scheme looks harmonious and balanced.

389	392	462	440
495	463	461	454

LEFT A very cool contemporary space featuring a patterned gray wall covering, and a white and chrome couch. The solid wooden floor begins to add warmth to the room, but the whole concept is energized by the rich red of the roses placed in a clear vase to allow as much color to contrast the neutral walls.

RIGHT A child's room is a space that requires an energy to promote creativity. The bright colors complementing each other make for a clean, fresh, and stimulating room that can be both calming and invigorating.

buttered yam

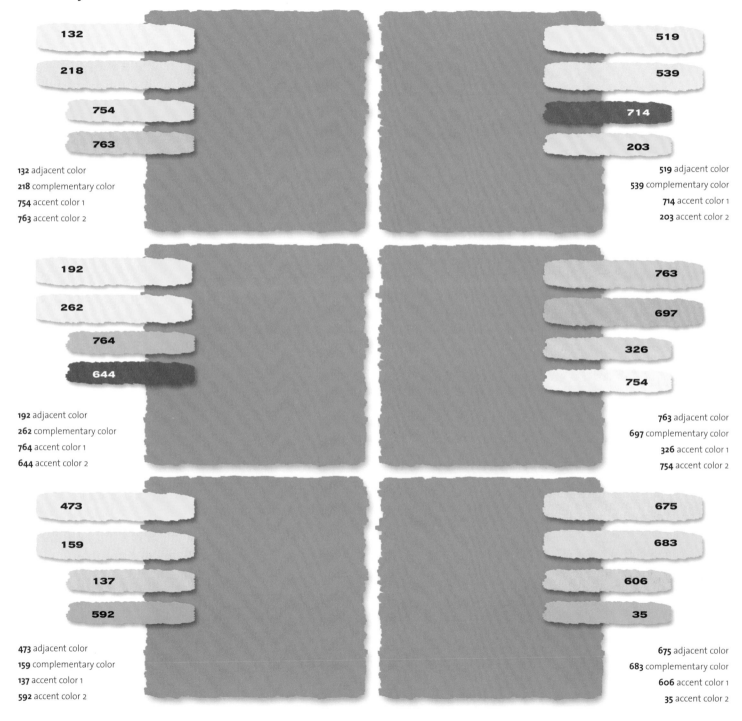

132 adjacent color
218 complementary color
754 accent color 1
763 accent color 2

519 adjacent color
539 complementary color
714 accent color 1
203 accent color 2

192 adjacent color
262 complementary color
764 accent color 1
644 accent color 2

763 adjacent color
697 complementary color
326 accent color 1
754 accent color 2

473 adjacent color
159 complementary color
137 accent color 1
592 accent color 2

675 adjacent color
683 complementary color
606 accent color 1
35 accent color 2

buttered yam

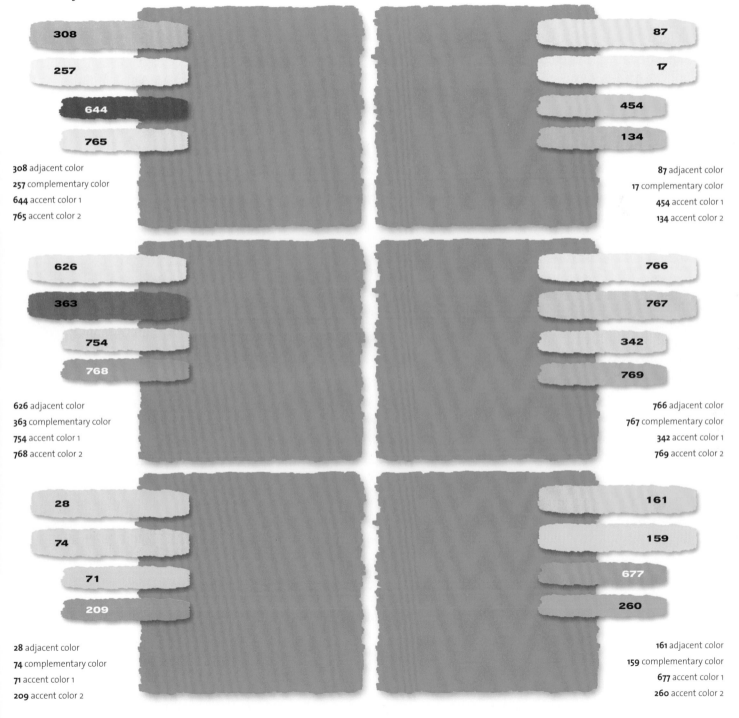

308 | **87**
257 | **17**
644 | **454**
765 | **134**

308 adjacent color
257 complementary color
644 accent color 1
765 accent color 2

87 adjacent color
17 complementary color
454 accent color 1
134 accent color 2

626 | **766**
363 | **767**
754 | **342**
768 | **769**

626 adjacent color
363 complementary color
754 accent color 1
768 accent color 2

766 adjacent color
767 complementary color
342 accent color 1
769 accent color 2

28 | **161**
74 | **159**
71 | **677**
209 | **260**

28 adjacent color
74 complementary color
71 accent color 1
209 accent color 2

161 adjacent color
159 complementary color
677 accent color 1
260 accent color 2

buttered yam

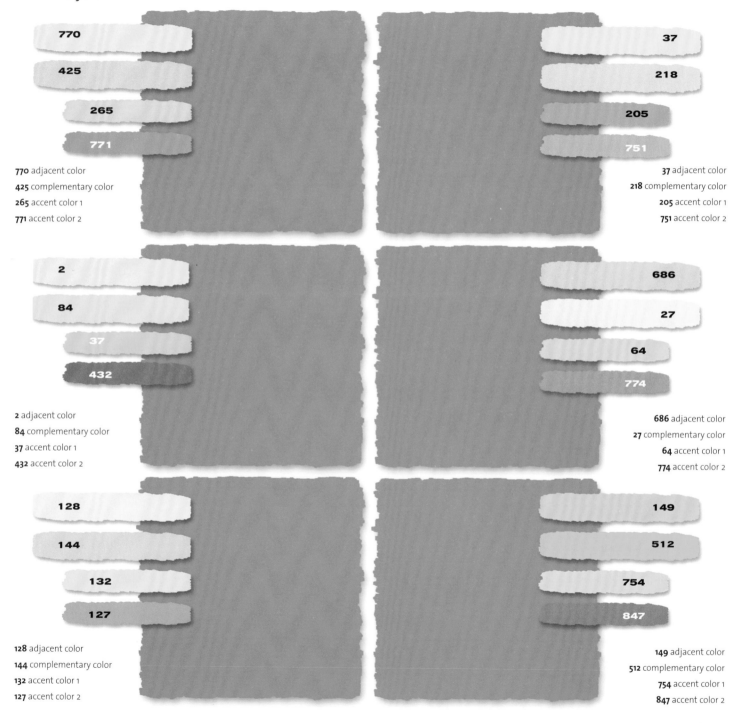

770 adjacent color
425 complementary color
265 accent color 1
771 accent color 2

37 adjacent color
218 complementary color
205 accent color 1
751 accent color 2

2 adjacent color
84 complementary color
37 accent color 1
432 accent color 2

686 adjacent color
27 complementary color
64 accent color 1
774 accent color 2

128 adjacent color
144 complementary color
132 accent color 1
127 accent color 2

149 adjacent color
512 complementary color
754 accent color 1
847 accent color 2

buttered yam

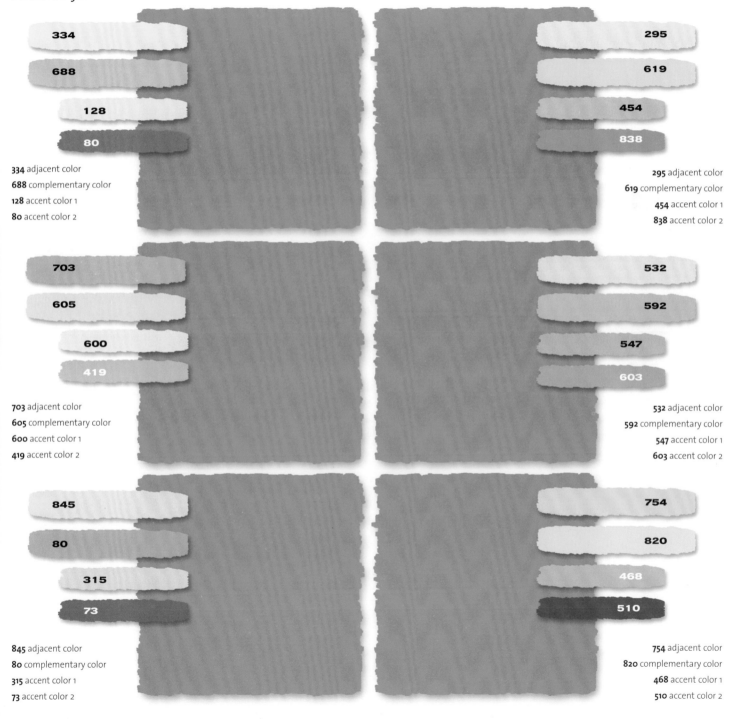

334
688
128
80

334 adjacent color
688 complementary color
128 accent color 1
80 accent color 2

295
619
454
838

295 adjacent color
619 complementary color
454 accent color 1
838 accent color 2

703
605
600
419

703 adjacent color
605 complementary color
600 accent color 1
419 accent color 2

532
592
547
603

532 adjacent color
592 complementary color
547 accent color 1
603 accent color 2

845
80
315
73

845 adjacent color
80 complementary color
315 accent color 1
73 accent color 2

754
820
468
510

754 adjacent color
820 complementary color
468 accent color 1
510 accent color 2

sailor's delight

324

27

775

1 17

245

554

776

777

653

77

14

780

778

651

137

781

36

592

656

746

112

131

32

154

324 adjacent color
27 complementary color
775 accent color 1
117 accent color 2

245 adjacent color
554 complementary color
776 accent color 1
777 accent color 2

653 adjacent color
77 complementary color
14 accent color 1
780 accent color 2

778 adjacent color
651 complementary color
137 accent color 1
781 accent color 2

36 adjacent color
592 complementary color
656 accent color 1
746 accent color 2

112 adjacent color
131 complementary color
32 accent color 1
154 accent color 2

sailor's delight

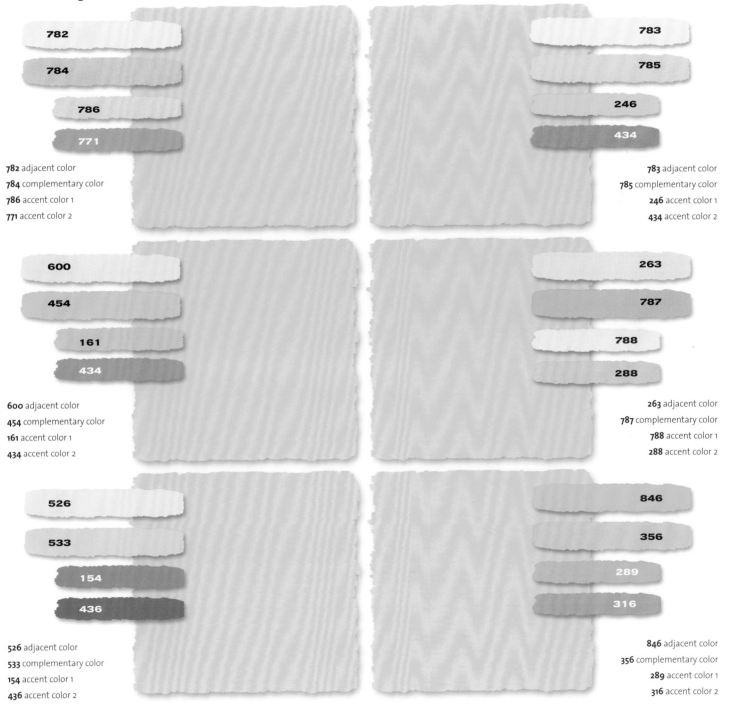

782
784
786
771

782 adjacent color
784 complementary color
786 accent color 1
771 accent color 2

783
785
246
434

783 adjacent color
785 complementary color
246 accent color 1
434 accent color 2

600
454
161
434

600 adjacent color
454 complementary color
161 accent color 1
434 accent color 2

263
787
788
288

263 adjacent color
787 complementary color
788 accent color 1
288 accent color 2

526
533
154
436

526 adjacent color
533 complementary color
154 accent color 1
436 accent color 2

846
356
289
316

846 adjacent color
356 complementary color
289 accent color 1
316 accent color 2

sailor's delight

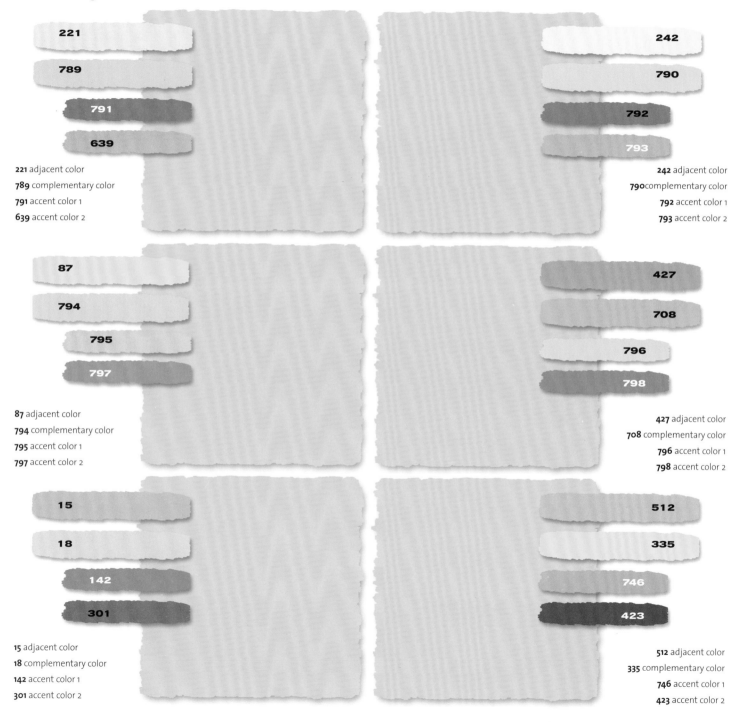

221

789

791

639

221 adjacent color
789 complementary color
791 accent color 1
639 accent color 2

242

790

792

793

242 adjacent color
790 complementary color
792 accent color 1
793 accent color 2

87

794

795

797

87 adjacent color
794 complementary color
795 accent color 1
797 accent color 2

427

708

796

798

427 adjacent color
708 complementary color
796 accent color 1
798 accent color 2

15

18

142

301

15 adjacent color
18 complementary color
142 accent color 1
301 accent color 2

512

335

746

423

512 adjacent color
335 complementary color
746 accent color 1
423 accent color 2

sailor's delight

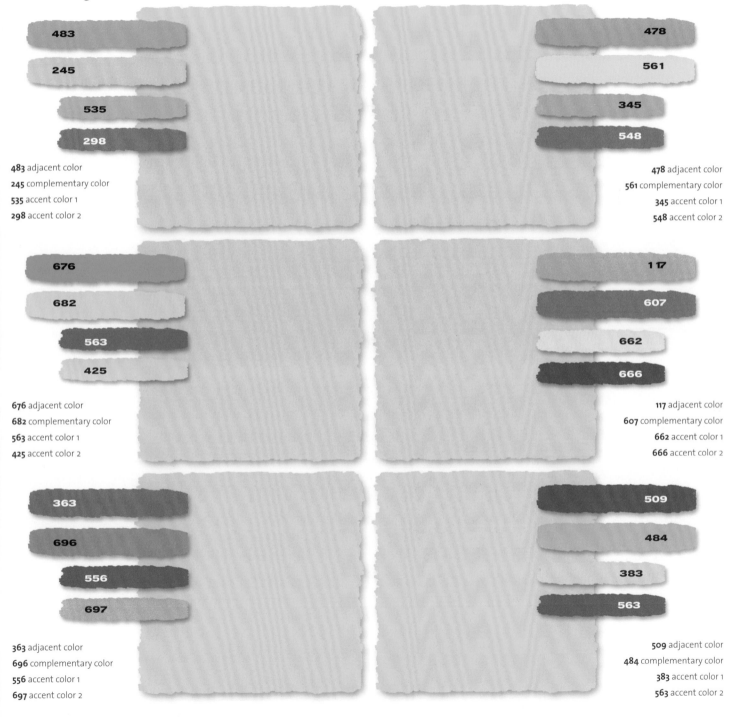

483
245
535
298

483 adjacent color
245 complementary color
535 accent color 1
298 accent color 2

478
561
345
548

478 adjacent color
561 complementary color
345 accent color 1
548 accent color 2

676
682
563
425

676 adjacent color
682 complementary color
563 accent color 1
425 accent color 2

1 17
607
662
666

117 adjacent color
607 complementary color
662 accent color 1
666 accent color 2

363
696
556
697

363 adjacent color
696 complementary color
556 accent color 1
697 accent color 2

509
484
383
563

509 adjacent color
484 complementary color
383 accent color 1
563 accent color 2

old straw hat

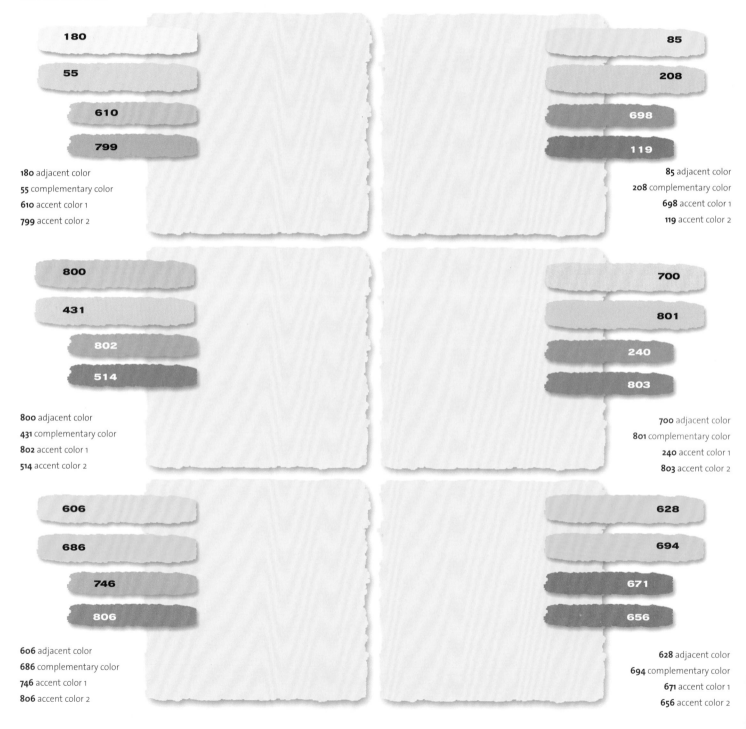

180

55

610

799

85

208

698

119

180 adjacent color
55 complementary color
610 accent color 1
799 accent color 2

85 adjacent color
208 complementary color
698 accent color 1
119 accent color 2

800

431

802

514

700

801

240

803

800 adjacent color
431 complementary color
802 accent color 1
514 accent color 2

700 adjacent color
801 complementary color
240 accent color 1
803 accent color 2

606

686

746

806

628

694

671

656

606 adjacent color
686 complementary color
746 accent color 1
806 accent color 2

628 adjacent color
694 complementary color
671 accent color 1
656 accent color 2

old straw hat

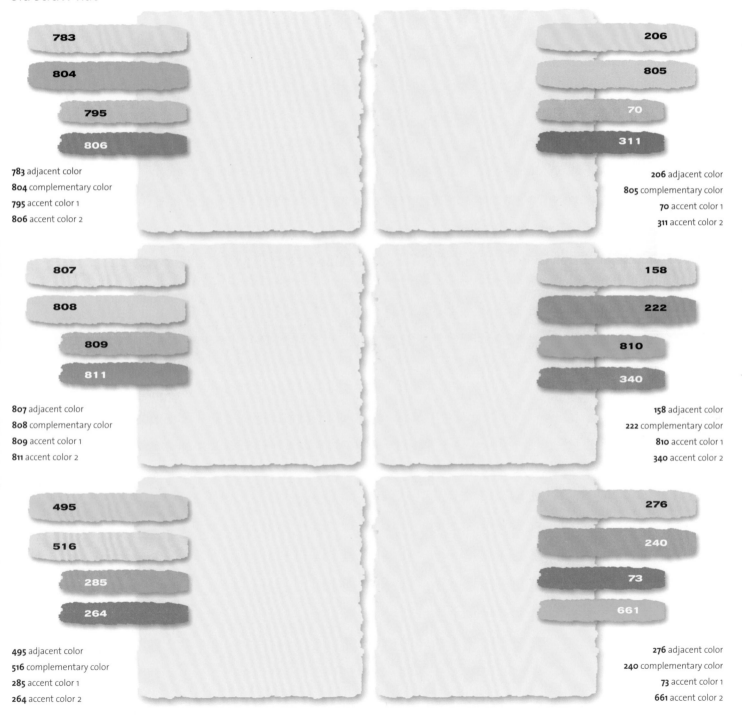

783

804

795

806

206

805

70

311

783 adjacent color
804 complementary color
795 accent color 1
806 accent color 2

206 adjacent color
805 complementary color
70 accent color 1
311 accent color 2

807

808

809

811

158

222

810

340

807 adjacent color
808 complementary color
809 accent color 1
811 accent color 2

158 adjacent color
222 complementary color
810 accent color 1
340 accent color 2

495

516

285

264

276

240

73

661

495 adjacent color
516 complementary color
285 accent color 1
264 accent color 2

276 adjacent color
240 complementary color
73 accent color 1
661 accent color 2

old straw hat

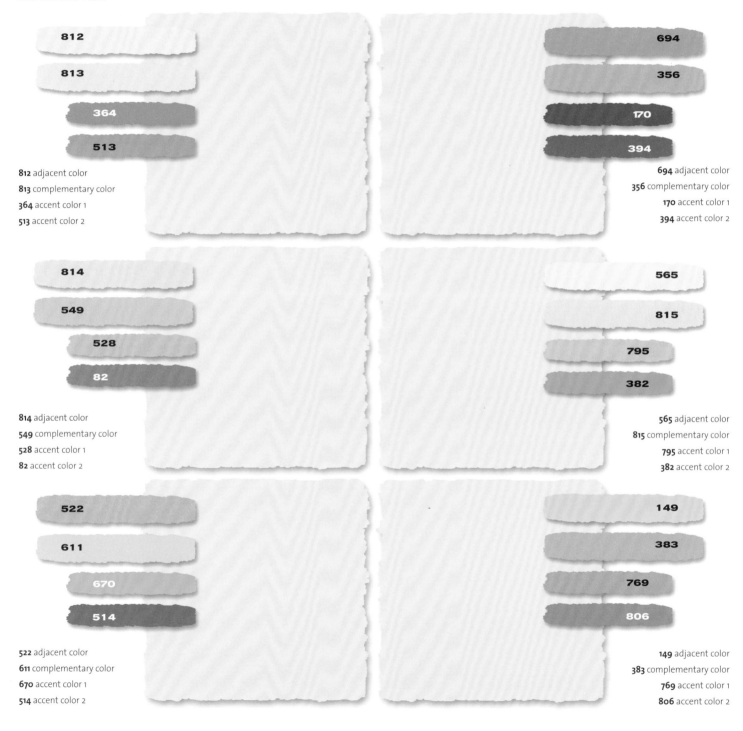

812

813

364

513

694

356

170

394

812 adjacent color
813 complementary color
364 accent color 1
513 accent color 2

694 adjacent color
356 complementary color
170 accent color 1
394 accent color 2

814

549

528

82

565

815

795

382

814 adjacent color
549 complementary color
528 accent color 1
82 accent color 2

565 adjacent color
815 complementary color
795 accent color 1
382 accent color 2

522

611

670

514

149

383

769

806

522 adjacent color
611 complementary color
670 accent color 1
514 accent color 2

149 adjacent color
383 complementary color
769 accent color 1
806 accent color 2

old straw hat

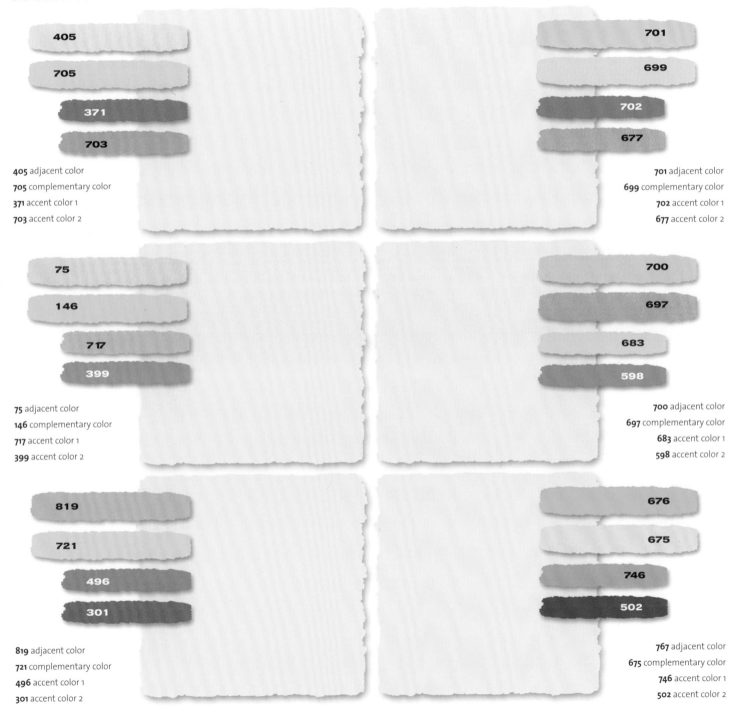

405
705
371
703

405 adjacent color
705 complementary color
371 accent color 1
703 accent color 2

701
699
702
677

701 adjacent color
699 complementary color
702 accent color 1
677 accent color 2

75
146
717
399

75 adjacent color
146 complementary color
717 accent color 1
399 accent color 2

700
697
683
598

700 adjacent color
697 complementary color
683 accent color 1
598 accent color 2

819
721
496
301

819 adjacent color
721 complementary color
496 accent color 1
301 accent color 2

676
675
746
502

767 adjacent color
675 complementary color
746 accent color 1
502 accent color 2

hushed hue

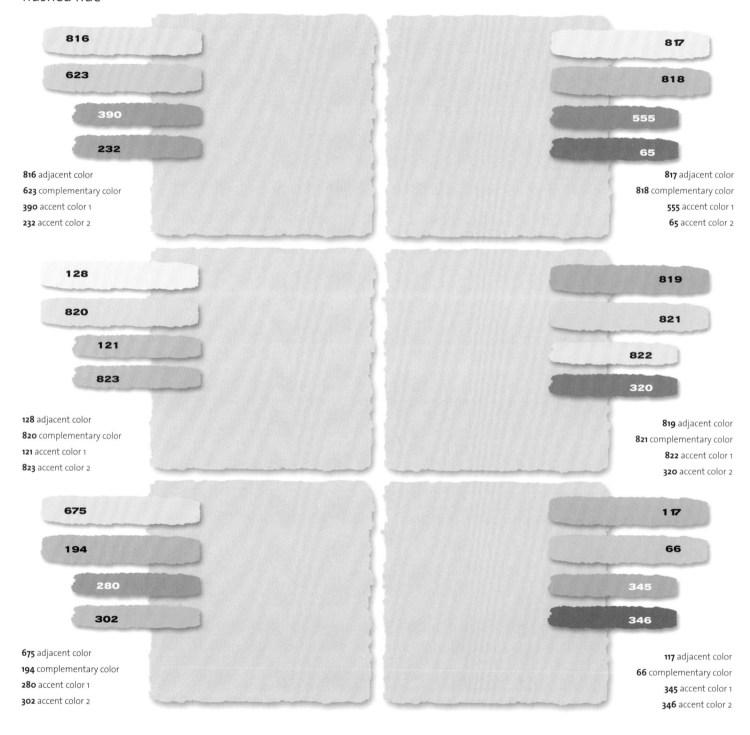

816
623
390
232

817
818
555
65

816 adjacent color
623 complementary color
390 accent color 1
232 accent color 2

817 adjacent color
818 complementary color
555 accent color 1
65 accent color 2

128
820
121
823

819
821
822
320

128 adjacent color
820 complementary color
121 accent color 1
823 accent color 2

819 adjacent color
821 complementary color
822 accent color 1
320 accent color 2

675
194
280
302

117
66
345
346

675 adjacent color
194 complementary color
280 accent color 1
302 accent color 2

117 adjacent color
66 complementary color
345 accent color 1
346 accent color 2

hushed hue

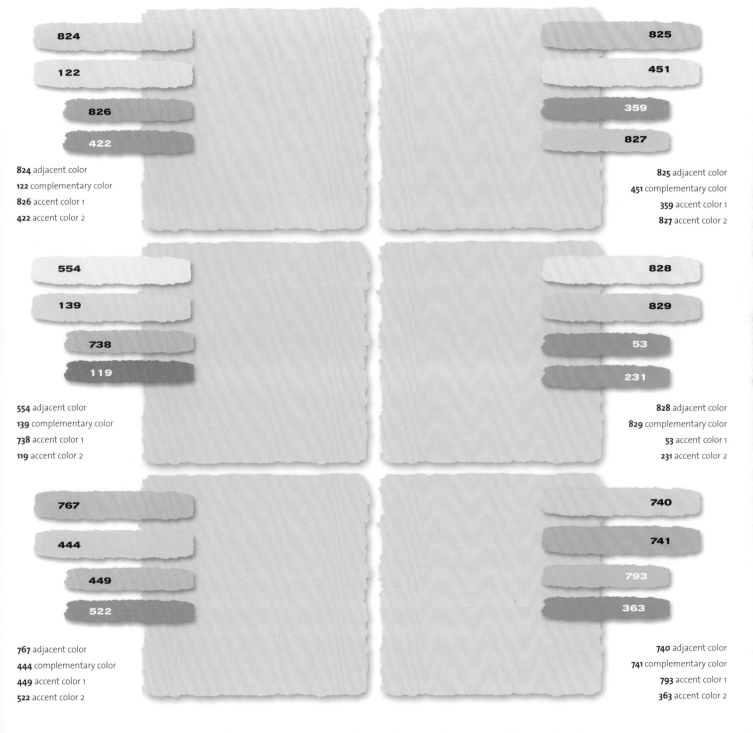

824 adjacent color
122 complementary color
826 accent color 1
422 accent color 2

825 adjacent color
451 complementary color
359 accent color 1
827 accent color 2

554 adjacent color
139 complementary color
738 accent color 1
119 accent color 2

828 adjacent color
829 complementary color
53 accent color 1
231 accent color 2

767 adjacent color
444 complementary color
449 accent color 1
522 accent color 2

740 adjacent color
741 complementary color
793 accent color 1
363 accent color 2

hushed hue

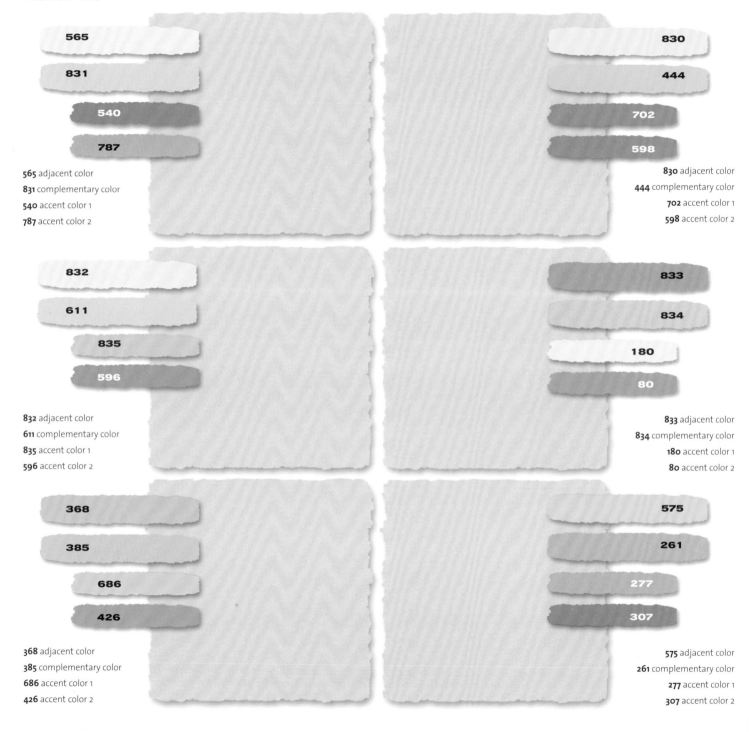

565

831

540

787

830

444

702

598

565 adjacent color
831 complementary color
540 accent color 1
787 accent color 2

830 adjacent color
444 complementary color
702 accent color 1
598 accent color 2

832

611

835

596

833

834

180

80

832 adjacent color
611 complementary color
835 accent color 1
596 accent color 2

833 adjacent color
834 complementary color
180 accent color 1
80 accent color 2

368

385

686

426

575

261

277

307

368 adjacent color
385 complementary color
686 accent color 1
426 accent color 2

575 adjacent color
261 complementary color
277 accent color 1
307 accent color 2

hushed hue

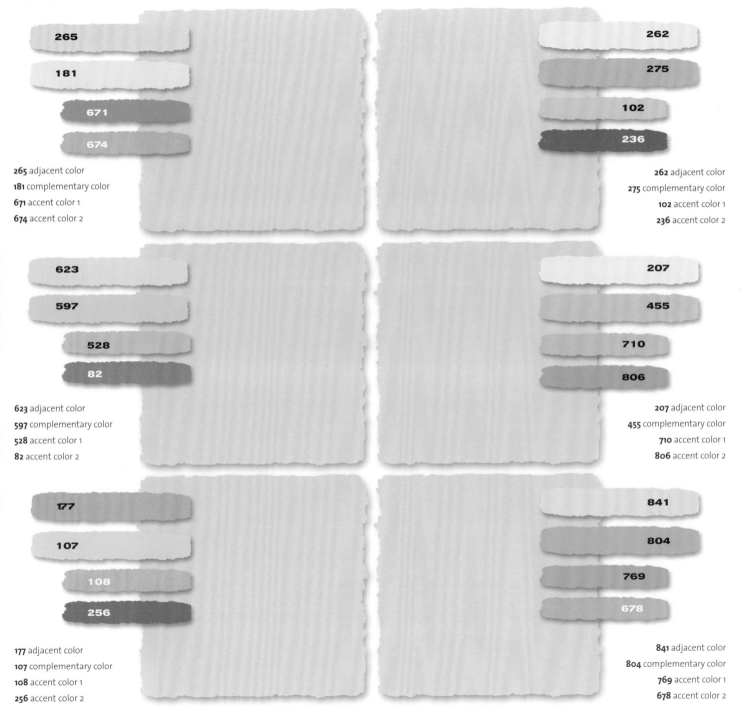

265

181

671

674

262

275

102

236

265 adjacent color
181 complementary color
671 accent color 1
674 accent color 2

262 adjacent color
275 complementary color
102 accent color 1
236 accent color 2

623

597

528

82

207

455

710

806

623 adjacent color
597 complementary color
528 accent color 1
82 accent color 2

207 adjacent color
455 complementary color
710 accent color 1
806 accent color 2

177

107

108

256

841

804

769

678

177 adjacent color
107 complementary color
108 accent color 1
256 accent color 2

841 adjacent color
804 complementary color
769 accent color 1
678 accent color 2

crisp morning air

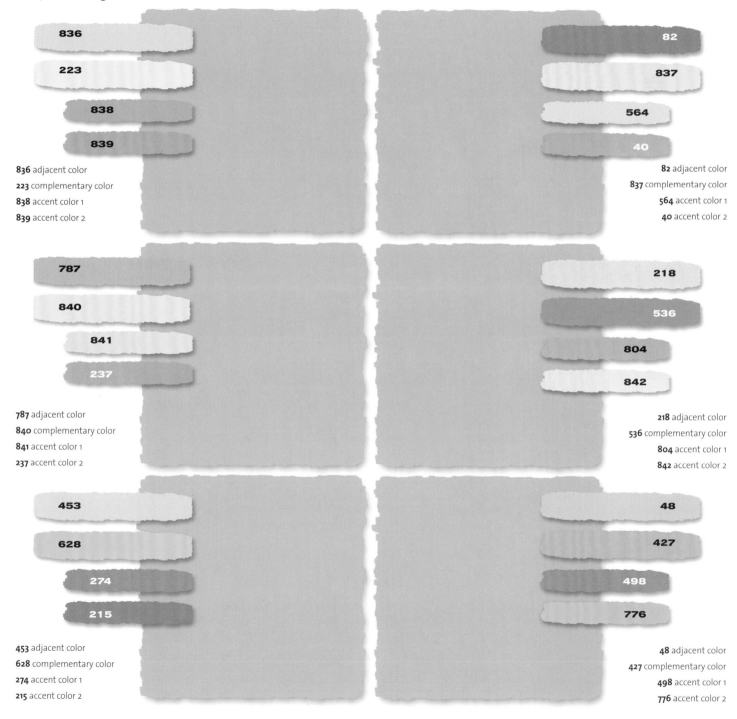

836

223

838

839

82

837

564

40

836 adjacent color
223 complementary color
838 accent color 1
839 accent color 2

82 adjacent color
837 complementary color
564 accent color 1
40 accent color 2

787

840

841

237

218

536

804

842

787 adjacent color
840 complementary color
841 accent color 1
237 accent color 2

218 adjacent color
536 complementary color
804 accent color 1
842 accent color 2

453

628

274

215

48

427

498

776

453 adjacent color
628 complementary color
274 accent color 1
215 accent color 2

48 adjacent color
427 complementary color
498 accent color 1
776 accent color 2

crisp morning air

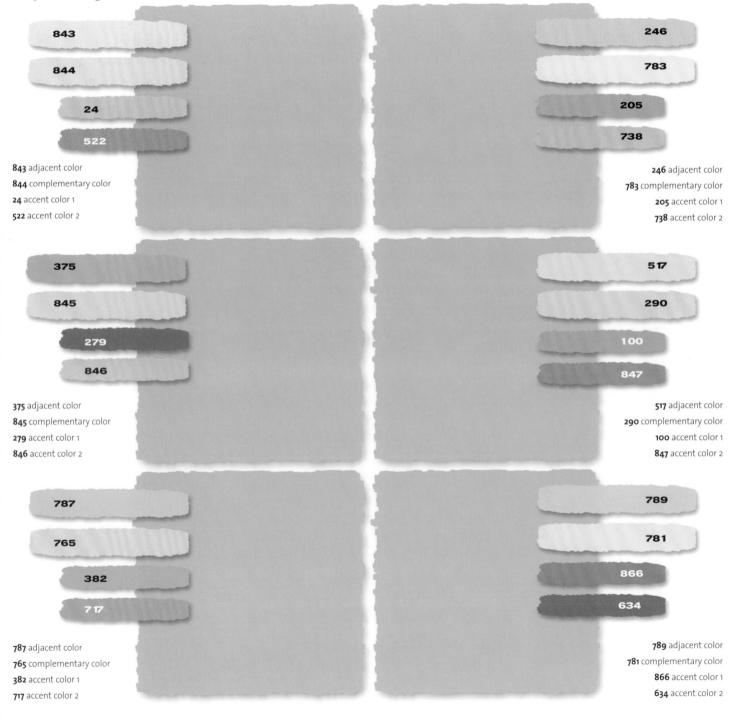

843

844

24

522

843 adjacent color
844 complementary color
24 accent color 1
522 accent color 2

246

783

205

738

246 adjacent color
783 complementary color
205 accent color 1
738 accent color 2

375

845

279

846

375 adjacent color
845 complementary color
279 accent color 1
846 accent color 2

517

290

100

847

517 adjacent color
290 complementary color
100 accent color 1
847 accent color 2

787

765

382

717

787 adjacent color
765 complementary color
382 accent color 1
717 accent color 2

789

781

866

634

789 adjacent color
781 complementary color
866 accent color 1
634 accent color 2

crisp morning air

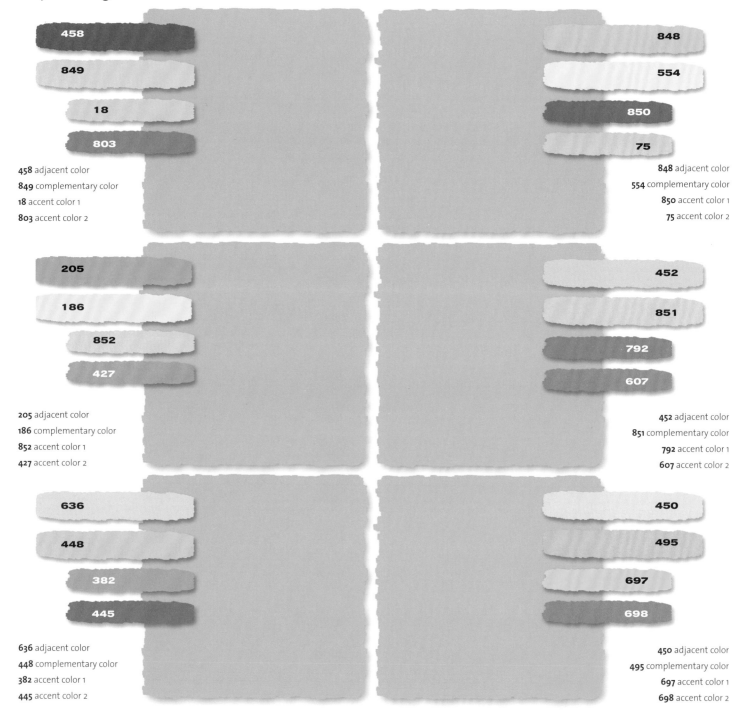

458

849

18

803

848

554

850

75

458 adjacent color
849 complementary color
18 accent color 1
803 accent color 2

848 adjacent color
554 complementary color
850 accent color 1
75 accent color 2

205

186

852

427

452

851

792

607

205 adjacent color
186 complementary color
852 accent color 1
427 accent color 2

452 adjacent color
851 complementary color
792 accent color 1
607 accent color 2

636

448

382

445

450

495

697

698

636 adjacent color
448 complementary color
382 accent color 1
445 accent color 2

450 adjacent color
495 complementary color
697 accent color 1
698 accent color 2

crisp morning air

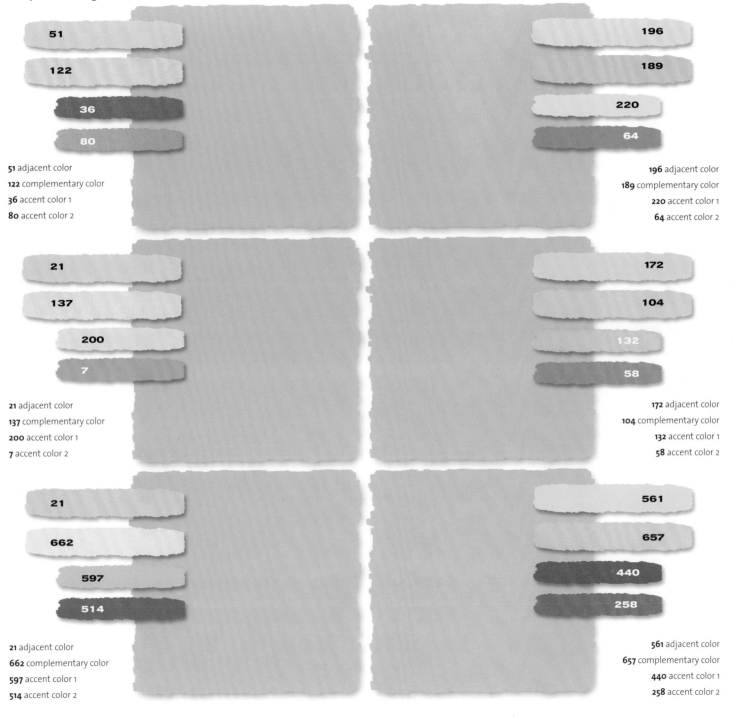

51
122
36
80

51 adjacent color
122 complementary color
36 accent color 1
80 accent color 2

196
189
220
64

196 adjacent color
189 complementary color
220 accent color 1
64 accent color 2

21
137
200
7

21 adjacent color
137 complementary color
200 accent color 1
7 accent color 2

172
104
132
58

172 adjacent color
104 complementary color
132 accent color 1
58 accent color 2

21
662
597
514

21 adjacent color
662 complementary color
597 accent color 1
514 accent color 2

561
657
440
258

561 adjacent color
657 complementary color
440 accent color 1
258 accent color 2

mint julep

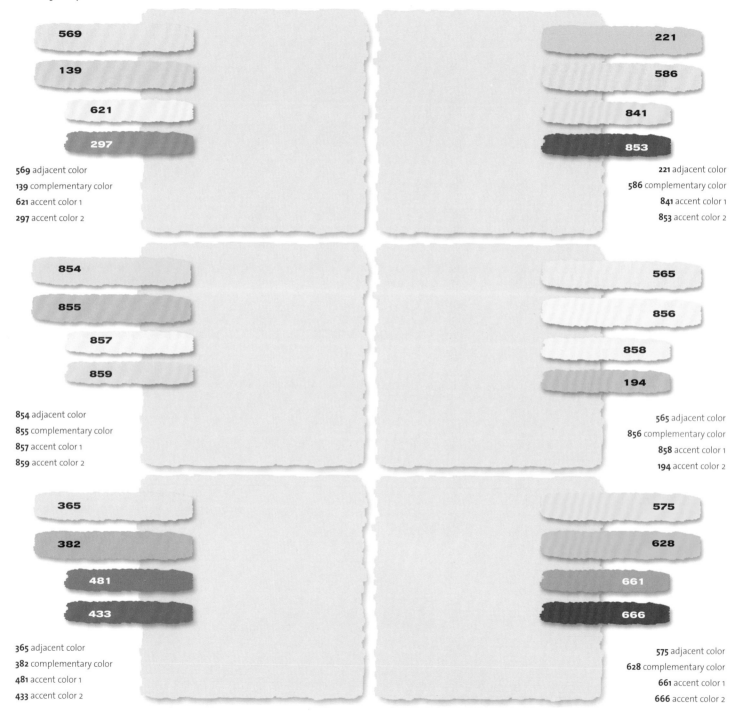

569

139

621

297

221

586

841

853

569 adjacent color
139 complementary color
621 accent color 1
297 accent color 2

221 adjacent color
586 complementary color
841 accent color 1
853 accent color 2

854

855

857

859

565

856

858

194

854 adjacent color
855 complementary color
857 accent color 1
859 accent color 2

565 adjacent color
856 complementary color
858 accent color 1
194 accent color 2

365

382

481

433

575

628

661

666

365 adjacent color
382 complementary color
481 accent color 1
433 accent color 2

575 adjacent color
628 complementary color
661 accent color 1
666 accent color 2

mint julep

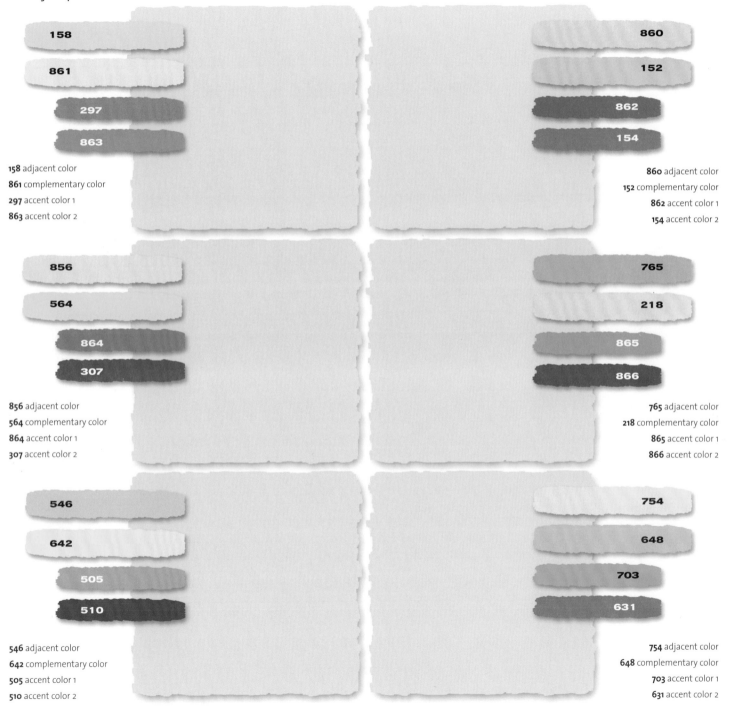

158
861
297
863

860
152
862
154

158 adjacent color
861 complementary color
297 accent color 1
863 accent color 2

860 adjacent color
152 complementary color
862 accent color 1
154 accent color 2

856
564
864
307

765
218
865
866

856 adjacent color
564 complementary color
864 accent color 1
307 accent color 2

765 adjacent color
218 complementary color
865 accent color 1
866 accent color 2

546
642
505
510

754
648
703
631

546 adjacent color
642 complementary color
505 accent color 1
510 accent color 2

754 adjacent color
648 complementary color
703 accent color 1
631 accent color 2

mint julep

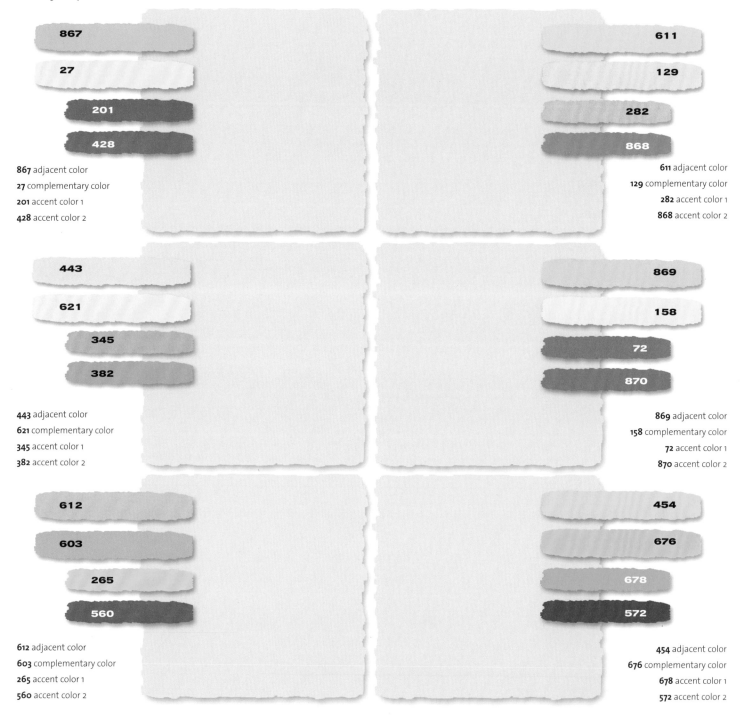

867

27

201

428

867 adjacent color
27 complementary color
201 accent color 1
428 accent color 2

611

129

282

868

611 adjacent color
129 complementary color
282 accent color 1
868 accent color 2

443

621

345

382

443 adjacent color
621 complementary color
345 accent color 1
382 accent color 2

869

158

72

870

869 adjacent color
158 complementary color
72 accent color 1
870 accent color 2

612

603

265

560

612 adjacent color
603 complementary color
265 accent color 1
560 accent color 2

454

676

678

572

454 adjacent color
676 complementary color
678 accent color 1
572 accent color 2

mint julep

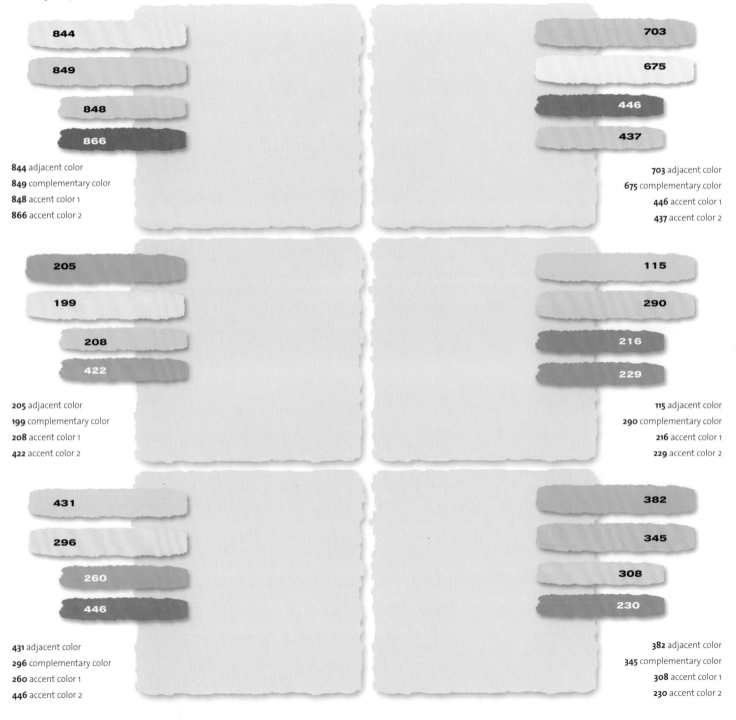

844

849

848

866

844 adjacent color
849 complementary color
848 accent color 1
866 accent color 2

703

675

446

437

703 adjacent color
675 complementary color
446 accent color 1
437 accent color 2

205

199

208

422

205 adjacent color
199 complementary color
208 accent color 1
422 accent color 2

115

290

216

229

115 adjacent color
290 complementary color
216 accent color 1
229 accent color 2

431

296

260

446

431 adjacent color
296 complementary color
260 accent color 1
446 accent color 2

382

345

308

230

382 adjacent color
345 complementary color
308 accent color 1
230 accent color 2

orange froth

383

419

395

679

479

399

438

693

383 adjacent color
419 complementary color
395 accent color 1
679 accent color 2

479 adjacent color
399 complementary color
438 accent color 1
693 accent color 2

674

601

643

644

719

796

800

792

674 adjacent color
601 complementary color
643 accent color 1
644 accent color 2

719 adjacent color
796 complementary color
800 accent color 1
792 accent color 2

642

703

340

178

714

534

566

644

642 adjacent color
703 complementary color
340 accent color 1
178 accent color 2

714 adjacent color
534 complementary color
566 accent color 1
644 accent color 2

orange froth

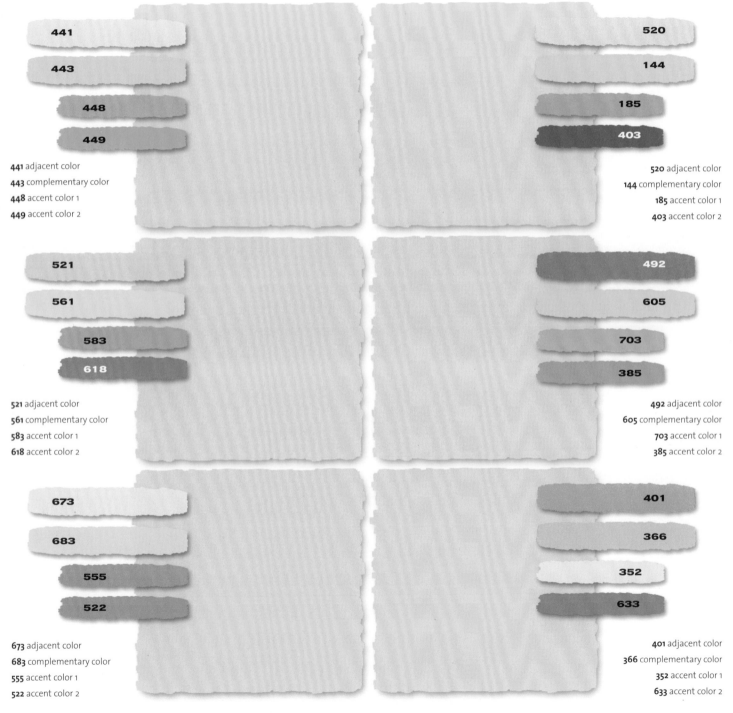

441

443

448

449

520

144

185

403

441 adjacent color
443 complementary color
448 accent color 1
449 accent color 2

520 adjacent color
144 complementary color
185 accent color 1
403 accent color 2

521

561

583

618

492

605

703

385

521 adjacent color
561 complementary color
583 accent color 1
618 accent color 2

492 adjacent color
605 complementary color
703 accent color 1
385 accent color 2

673

683

555

522

401

366

352

633

673 adjacent color
683 complementary color
555 accent color 1
522 accent color 2

401 adjacent color
366 complementary color
352 accent color 1
633 accent color 2

orange froth

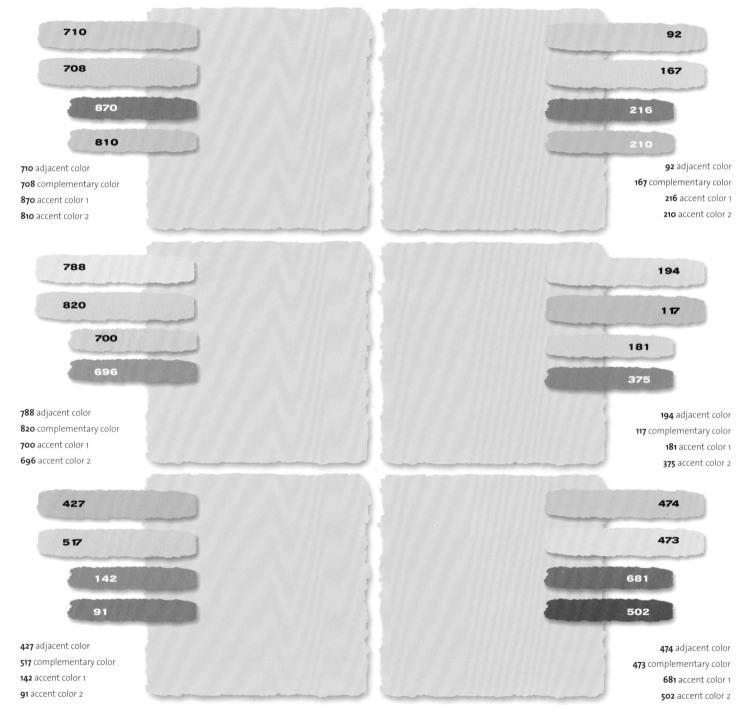

710

708

870

810

92

167

216

210

788

820

700

696

194

117

181

375

427

517

142

91

474

473

681

502

710 adjacent color
708 complementary color
870 accent color 1
810 accent color 2

92 adjacent color
167 complementary color
216 accent color 1
210 accent color 2

788 adjacent color
820 complementary color
700 accent color 1
696 accent color 2

194 adjacent color
117 complementary color
181 accent color 1
375 accent color 2

427 adjacent color
517 complementary color
142 accent color 1
91 accent color 2

474 adjacent color
473 complementary color
681 accent color 1
502 accent color 2

orange froth

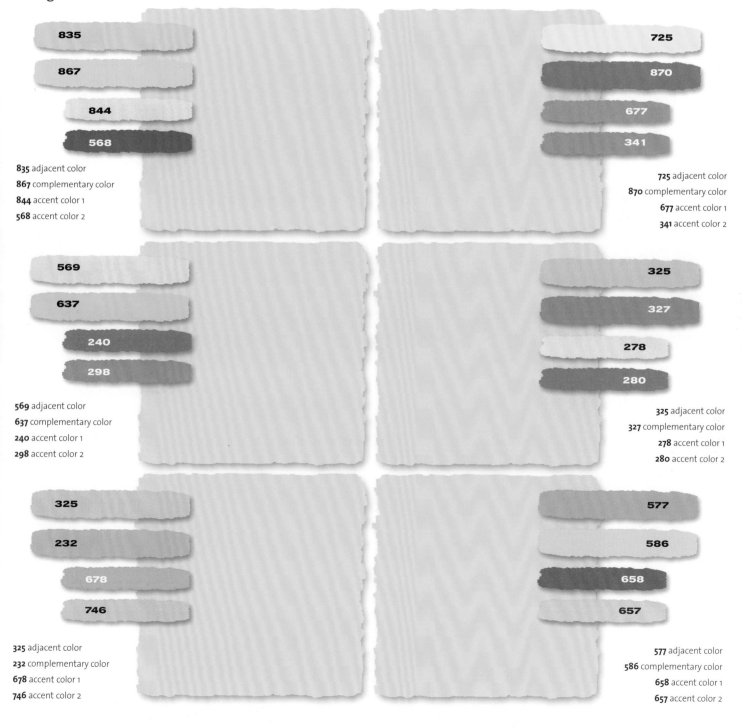

835

867

844

568

835 adjacent color
867 complementary color
844 accent color 1
568 accent color 2

725

870

677

341

725 adjacent color
870 complementary color
677 accent color 1
341 accent color 2

569

637

240

298

569 adjacent color
637 complementary color
240 accent color 1
298 accent color 2

325

327

278

280

325 adjacent color
327 complementary color
278 accent color 1
280 accent color 2

325

232

678

746

325 adjacent color
232 complementary color
678 accent color 1
746 accent color 2

577

586

658

657

577 adjacent color
586 complementary color
658 accent color 1
657 accent color 2

wishing well

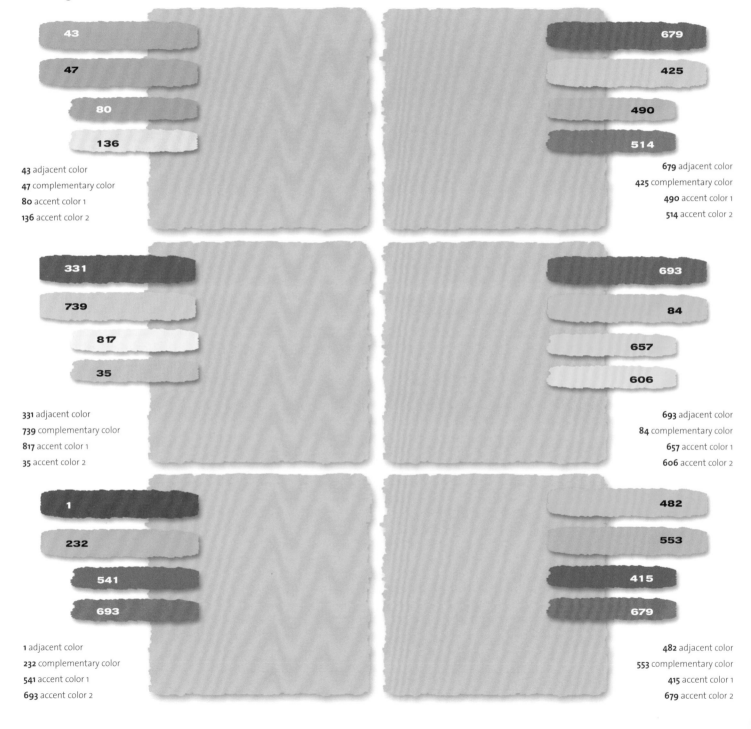

43
47
80
136

43 adjacent color
47 complementary color
80 accent color 1
136 accent color 2

679
425
490
514

679 adjacent color
425 complementary color
490 accent color 1
514 accent color 2

331
739
817
35

331 adjacent color
739 complementary color
817 accent color 1
35 accent color 2

693
84
657
606

693 adjacent color
84 complementary color
657 accent color 1
606 accent color 2

1
232
541
693

1 adjacent color
232 complementary color
541 accent color 1
693 accent color 2

482
553
415
679

482 adjacent color
553 complementary color
415 accent color 1
679 accent color 2

wishing well

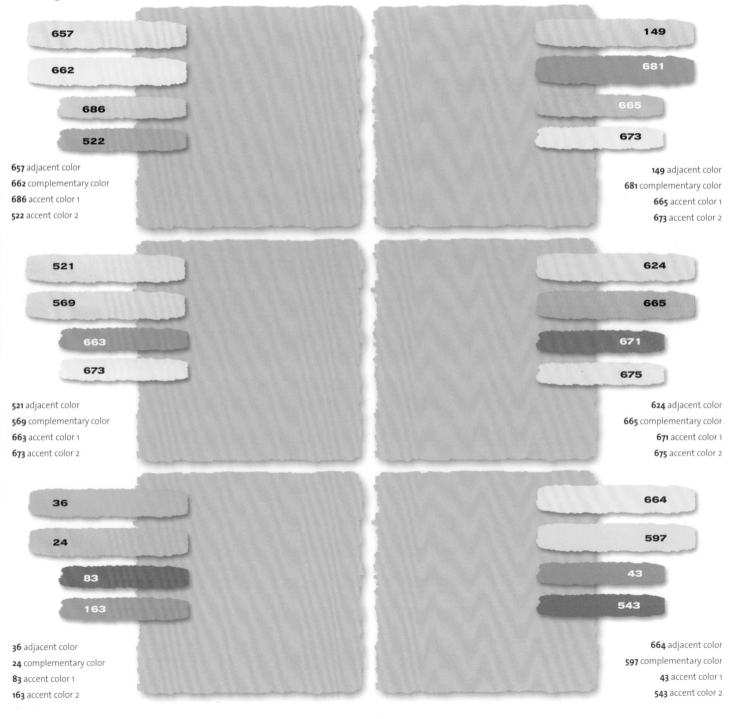

657

662

686

522

657 adjacent color
662 complementary color
686 accent color 1
522 accent color 2

149

681

665

673

149 adjacent color
681 complementary color
665 accent color 1
673 accent color 2

521

569

663

673

521 adjacent color
569 complementary color
663 accent color 1
673 accent color 2

624

665

671

675

624 adjacent color
665 complementary color
671 accent color 1
675 accent color 2

36

24

83

163

36 adjacent color
24 complementary color
83 accent color 1
163 accent color 2

664

597

43

543

664 adjacent color
597 complementary color
43 accent color 1
543 accent color 2

wishing well

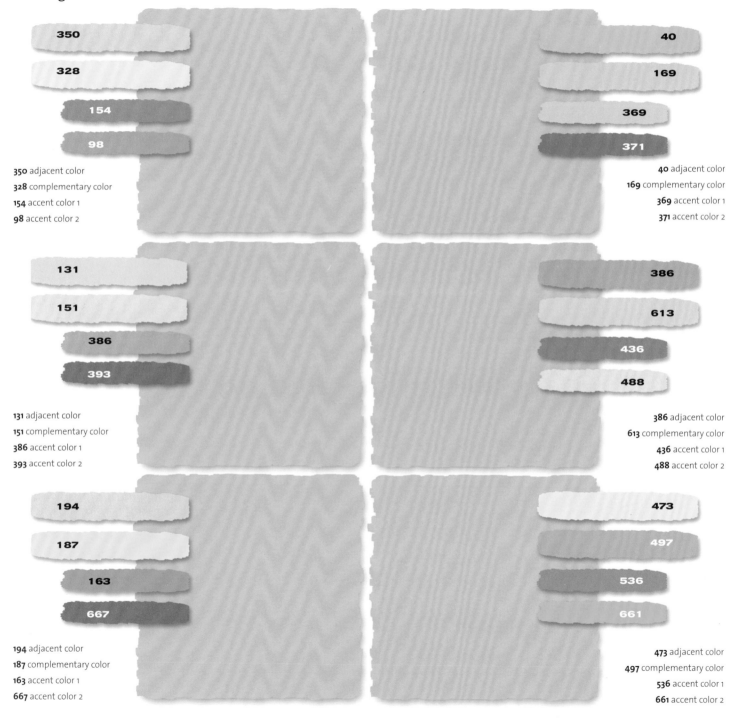

350

328

154

98

40

169

369

371

350 adjacent color
328 complementary color
154 accent color 1
98 accent color 2

40 adjacent color
169 complementary color
369 accent color 1
371 accent color 2

131

151

386

393

386

613

436

488

131 adjacent color
151 complementary color
386 accent color 1
393 accent color 2

386 adjacent color
613 complementary color
436 accent color 1
488 accent color 2

194

187

163

667

473

497

536

661

194 adjacent color
187 complementary color
163 accent color 1
667 accent color 2

473 adjacent color
497 complementary color
536 accent color 1
661 accent color 2

wishing well

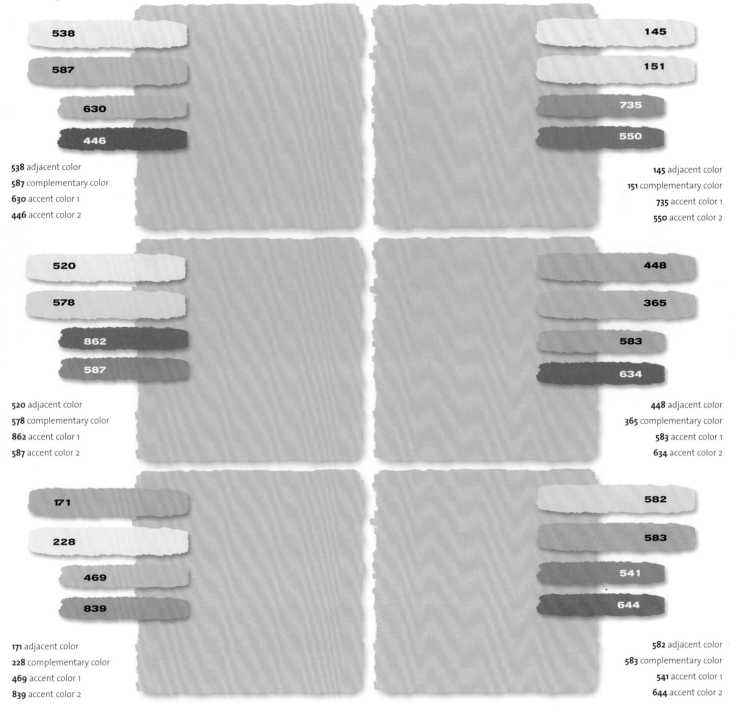

538
587
630
446

145
151
735
550

538 adjacent color
587 complementary color
630 accent color 1
446 accent color 2

145 adjacent color
151 complementary color
735 accent color 1
550 accent color 2

520
578
862
587

448
365
583
634

520 adjacent color
578 complementary color
862 accent color 1
587 accent color 2

448 adjacent color
365 complementary color
583 accent color 1
634 accent color 2

171
228
469
839

582
583
541
644

171 adjacent color
228 complementary color
469 accent color 1
839 accent color 2

582 adjacent color
583 complementary color
541 accent color 1
644 accent color 2

pine forest

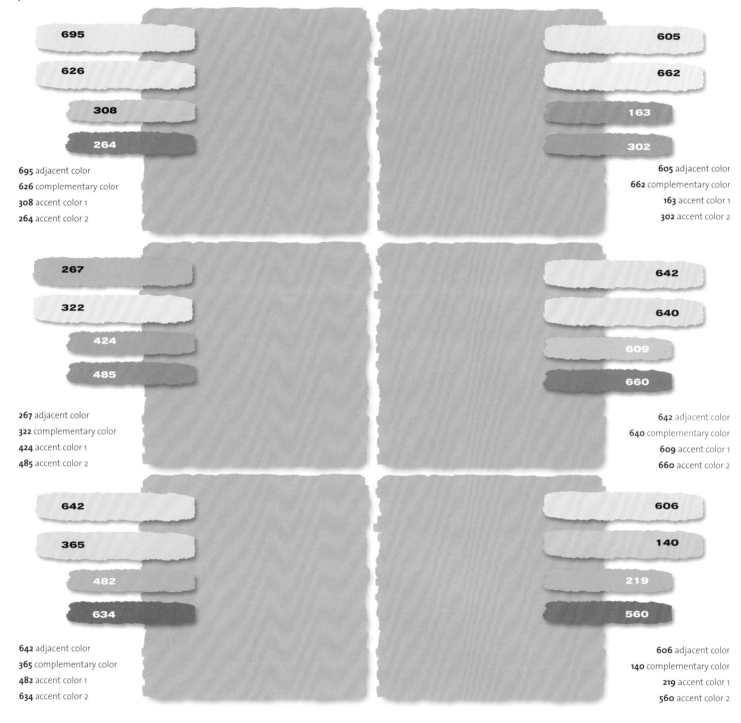

695

626

308

264

695 adjacent color
626 complementary color
308 accent color 1
264 accent color 2

605

662

163

302

605 adjacent color
662 complementary color
163 accent color 1
302 accent color 2

267

322

424

485

267 adjacent color
322 complementary color
424 accent color 1
485 accent color 2

642

640

609

660

642 adjacent color
640 complementary color
609 accent color 1
660 accent color 2

642

365

482

634

642 adjacent color
365 complementary color
482 accent color 1
634 accent color 2

606

140

219

560

606 adjacent color
140 complementary color
219 accent color 1
560 accent color 2

pine forest

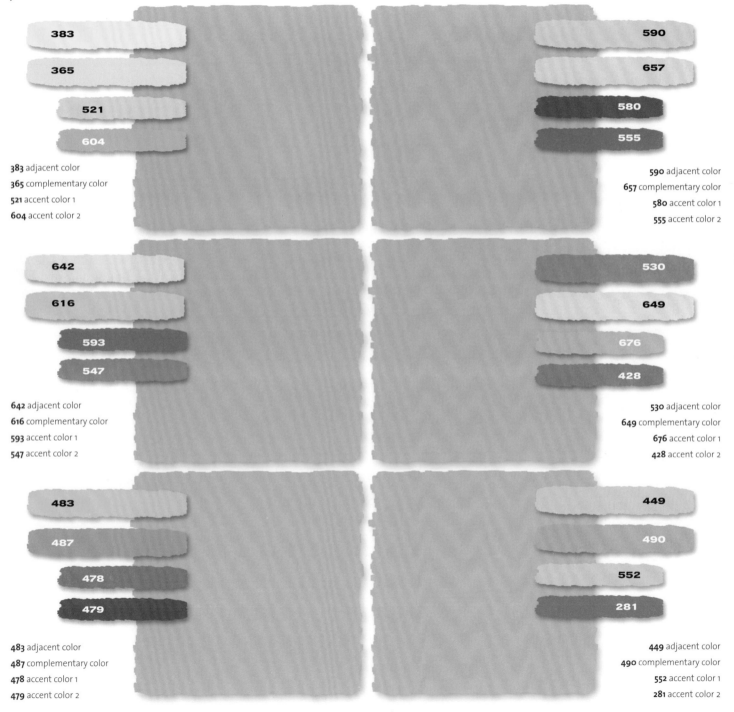

383
365
521
604

590
657
580
555

383 adjacent color
365 complementary color
521 accent color 1
604 accent color 2

590 adjacent color
657 complementary color
580 accent color 1
555 accent color 2

642
616
593
547

530
649
676
428

642 adjacent color
616 complementary color
593 accent color 1
547 accent color 2

530 adjacent color
649 complementary color
676 accent color 1
428 accent color 2

483
487
478
479

449
490
552
281

483 adjacent color
487 complementary color
478 accent color 1
479 accent color 2

449 adjacent color
490 complementary color
552 accent color 1
281 accent color 2

pine forest

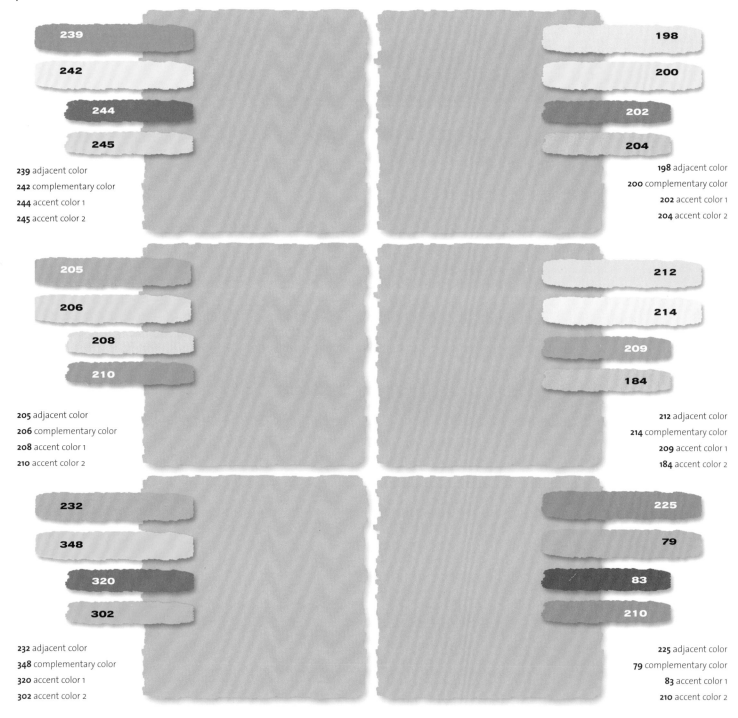

239

242

244

245

239 adjacent color
242 complementary color
244 accent color 1
245 accent color 2

198

200

202

204

198 adjacent color
200 complementary color
202 accent color 1
204 accent color 2

205

206

208

210

205 adjacent color
206 complementary color
208 accent color 1
210 accent color 2

212

214

209

184

212 adjacent color
214 complementary color
209 accent color 1
184 accent color 2

232

348

320

302

232 adjacent color
348 complementary color
320 accent color 1
302 accent color 2

225

79

83

210

225 adjacent color
79 complementary color
83 accent color 1
210 accent color 2

pine forest

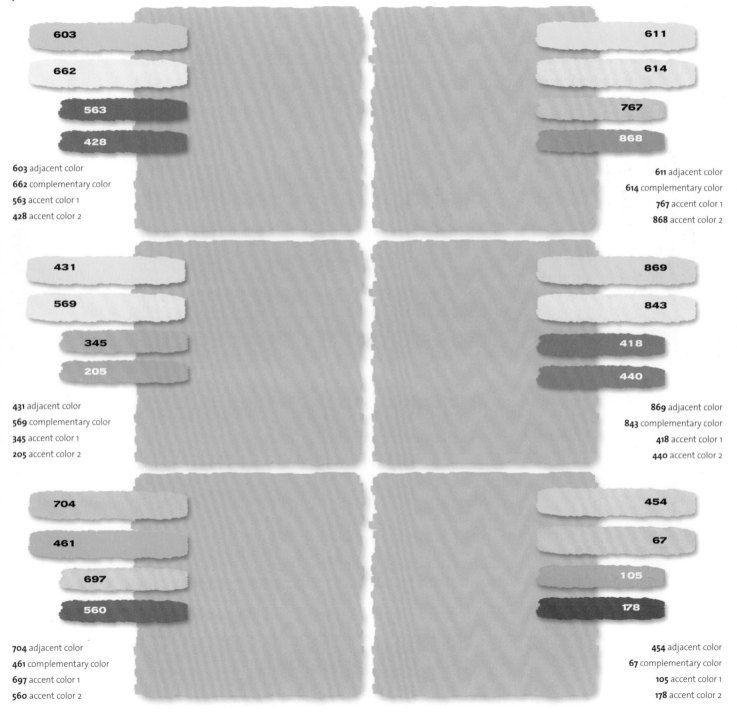

603
662
563
428

611
614
767
868

603 adjacent color
662 complementary color
563 accent color 1
428 accent color 2

611 adjacent color
614 complementary color
767 accent color 1
868 accent color 2

431
569
345
205

869
843
418
440

431 adjacent color
569 complementary color
345 accent color 1
205 accent color 2

869 adjacent color
843 complementary color
418 accent color 1
440 accent color 2

704
461
697
560

454
67
105
178

704 adjacent color
461 complementary color
697 accent color 1
560 accent color 2

454 adjacent color
67 complementary color
105 accent color 1
178 accent color 2

25	714
221	3

780	791
519	639

ABOVE Providing the perfect place to relax, this is a classic combination of red and white. The assuredness of these contrasts is underlined by the classic materials on offer: leather, glass, wood, stone, and terra-cotta.

RIGHT Blue, green, and yellow are a combination of colors often found in nature that can be used to create a relaxed, simple, and fresh kitchen that is a cheerful and social place to spend time in, and that has a timeless quality.

28	528
170	871

RIGHT The neutral color of the walls in combination with warm tan, with a hint of pink and lilac, generate an air of sophistication and calm in this bedroom.

28	26
158	871

LEFT A color scheme chosen to work with the view, the pink sofa is complementary to the blue sky while the gray walls provide the perfect backdrop to the sofa.

25	519
714	203

RIGHT The use of neutral textures and materials works well together with the strong focal point of the fireplace to enhance the sense of harmony and relaxation.

302	244
180	177

LEFT Orange can be a strong and intense color, but it has many guises. Here the soft orange of the furniture is fresh and inviting, the whole scheme is supported by accents of adjacent colors on the color wheel.

194	178
262	418

RIGHT Decorating a room in light green creates a relaxing space where you can stop and breathe. Being in the middle of the color spectrum, green works well in combination with most colors. Here the warmth of the wooden table prevents the room from becoming too cold and impersonal.

493	542
662	656

RIGHT White creates a fresh, clean atmosphere in a room, especially when contrasted with warm natural tones, such as the warm lighting above the kitchen cupboards, and the accents of strong color in the ornaments and flowers.

| 703 | 600 |
| 610 | 389 |

BELOW The subtle tones of the colors in this bathroom make for a clean, restful, calm space. The bright vibrant color on the blind brings a freshness to the room.

| 372 | 358 |
| 389 | 404 |

ABOVE Combining bright orange with more restrained tones helps it to retain its vitality, but prevents it from becoming overpowering.

205	666
670	677

RIGHT An array of complementary colors supplied by the cushions keep this room fresh and lively, making it a great space for entertaining.

492	592
661	776

BELOW Using bright accent colors against a neutral scheme makes this room a fresh, bright, and airy space.

600	313
662	205

RIGHT A cool neutral room can be given a fresh and light mood with clever use of these two complementary colors. Being opposite on the color wheel, red and green, when used together, add a vibrant energy.

color index

BM No. These refer to the numbering system in the Benjamin Moore Classic and Affinity ranges.

Swatch	Code	BM No.	CMYK	Swatch	Code	BM No.	CMYK	Swatch	Code	BM No.	CMYK
	1	1357	30c 71m 34y 34k		35	828	38c 10m 12y 1k		69	111	6c 55m 64y 1k
	2	1272	13c 56m 25y 3k		36	4	50m 42y		70	301	44m 82y
	3	1467	32c 24m 27y 4k		37	333	1c 13m 48y		71	716	31c 5m 17y
	4	1105	17c 51m 64y 6k		38	1676	49c 7m 18y 2k		72	259	23c 49m 82y 17k
	5	793	38c 1m 11y		39	1392	52c 59m 16y 20k		73	1021	34c 49m 54y 24k
	6	673	30c 3m 19y		40	1200	8c 49m 39y 1k		74	359	1c 11m 43y
	7	1372	48c 64m 20y 27k		41	835	37c 5m 14y 1k		75	381	12c 16m 39y 1k
	8	1196	22c 69m 69y 14k		42	701	28c 8m 21y 1k		76	1288	23c 80m 68y 14k
	9	1262	11c 22m 13y		43	1355	14c 59m 13y 3k		77	1347	3c 62m 4y
	10	1144	6c 31m 39y 1k		44	218	3c 11m 23y		78	1350	19c 84m 50y 6k
	11	1432	44c 18m 10y 2k		45	839	70c 22m 24y 13k		79	1517	26c 26m 41y 5k
	12	af710	45c 34m 38y 15k		46	1367	6c 19m 6y		80	1390	33c 38m 6y 2k
	13	af385	17c 24m 42y 3k		47	1544	32c 34m 38y 9k		81	1249	19c 28m 19y 2k
	14	47	14c 57m 49y 4k		48	626	37c 4m 33y 1k		82	1420	62c 34m 9y 6k
	15	1011	19c 28m 28y 2k		49	579	63c 50y		83	1203	21c 74m 66y 10k
	16	1411	30c 18m 12y 1k		50	1566	48c 28m 37y 12k		84	132	41m 60y
	17	414	10c 2m 30y		51	1606	42c 26m 28y 7k		85	211	3c 8m 22y
	18	1437	26c 11m 13y 1k		52	634	52c 15m 43y 8k		86	1296	34m 18y
	19	af285	14c 75m 64y 3k		53	1447	35c 37m 28y 9k		87	171	21c 48y
	20	343	32m 92y		54	1320	65m 43y		88	1342	16c 76m 43y 5k
	21	796	78c 8m 13y 1k		55	867	24c 5m 16y		89	af625	31c 54m 26y 16k
	22	1091	19c 55m 69y 9k		56	901	2c 11m 18y		90	af495	51c 19m 37y 9k
	23	339	1c 12m 47y		57	1496	38c 30m 45y 11k		91	1371	37c 60m 18y 16k
	24	396	10c 14m 65y 1k		58	1274	25c 77m 61y 22k		92	356	25m 81y
	25	af230	8c 65m 82y 1k		59	878	7c 12m 11y		93	1382	23c 22m 9y 1k
	26	1296	34m 18y		60	1276	4c 29m 12y		94	175	1c 48m 81y
	27	337	1c 7m 27y		61	872	10c 4m 10y		95	af240	25c 70m 85y 27k
	28	1520	12c 12m 20y		62	1370	25c 45m 10y 4k		96	af75	15c 8m 21y
	29	780	51c 12y		63	2	31m 23y		97	1559	39c 31m 38y 10k
	30	547	16c 1m 25y		64	180	28m 58y		98	af185	18c 35m 35y 4k
	31	1252	39c 53m 41y 26k		65	706	58c 25m 44y 18k		99	af255	2c 7m 9y
	32	1363	21c 59m 13y 5k		66	822	50c 14m 11y 2k		100	1377	25c 43m 12y 4k
	33	948	5c 12m 21y		67	194	8c 40m 61y 1k		101	1290	2c 28m 16y
	34	684	63c 20m 45y 15k		68	224	23c 49m 77y 16k		102	349	29m 79y

Swatch	Code	BM No.	CMYK	Swatch	Code	BM No.	CMYK	Swatch	Code	BM No.	CMYK
	103	691	60c 22m 42y 17k		137	248	10c 21m 38y 1k		171	1454	40c 38m 31y 11k
	104	357	1c 30m 90y		138	1437	26c 11m 13y 1k		172	1484	56c 44m 52y 43k
	105	119	5c 61m 75y 1k		139	401	11c 5m 40y		173	1513	9c 7m 16y
	106	315	41m 82y		140	1292	7c 50m 31y 1k		174	687	32c 8m 21y 1k
	107	1653	30c 2m 14y		141	245	31c 43m 56y 17k		175	48	24c 66m 56y 19k
	108	251	2c 45m 72y 14k		142	1440	52c 34m 24y 13k		176	1489	44c 42m 54y 26k
	109	1236	29c 53m 52y 23k		143	440	44c 26m 57y 15k		177	489	4c 35m 67y 26k
	110	283	1c 10m 33y		144	491	13c 9m 23y		178	1456	51c 49m 44y 35k
	111	35	22c 76m 74y 12k		145	204	4c 8m 20y		179	1563	27c 12m 22y 1k
	112	22	2c 14m 17y		146	435	18c 7m 23y		180	932	4c 5m 17y
	113	323	1c 8m 29y		147	715	20c 3m 14y		181	1646	21c 4m 14y
	114	1674	29c 3m 13y		148	510	40c 37m 57y 20k		182	941	11c 14m 26y
	115	625	29c 3m 25y		149	376	9c 25m 54y 1k		183	474	41c 29m 48y 13k
	116	1540	45c 46m 57y 34k		150	628	53c 17m 50y 11k		184	193	4c 31m 48y 1k
	117	377	10c 31m 68y 2k		151	1478	16c 8m 15y		185	244	27c 36m 50y 10k
	118	1679	83c 26m 28y 22k		152	1444	19c 17m 15y 1k		186	148	1c 12m 25y
	119	433	43c 26m 67y 19k		153	680	21c 1m 18y		187	8	1c 21m 17y
	120	1269	1c 26m 10y		154	1448	40c 43m 32y 15k		188	506	21c 12m 24y 1k
	121	1455	48c 43m 38y 24k		155	1622	55c 26m 30y 12k		189	1002	12c 15m 18y
	122	1492	12c 7m 15y		156	1588	54c 33m 39y 19k		190	1190	24c 72m 72y 17k
	123	1658	75c 21m 32y 14k		157	344	2c 8m 22y		191	675	46c 3m 26y 1k
	124	1280	20c 62m 39y 9k		158	393	6c 5m 29y		192	78	1c 16m 18y
	125	123	32m 49y		159	407	12c 2m 27y		193	1416	25c 7m 8y
	126	1476	40c 37m 45y 16k		160	596	23c 1m 19y		194	403	16c 11m 66y 2k
	127	723	43c 1m 19y		161	382	10c 26m 52y 2k		195	1504	40c 38m 55y 20k
	128	925	6c 6m 16y		162	518	43c 44m 64y 33k		196	1657	67c 15m 26y 7k
	129	232	7c 12m 20y		163	405	27c 22m 79y 10k		197	782	82c 1m 20y
	130	708	28c 6m 21y		164	719	62c 19m 33y 11k		198	415	12c 3m 38y
	131	1639	28c 6m 16y		165	859	19c 16m 22y 1k		199	930	3c 9m 27y
	132	332	1c 9m 35y		166	1458	17c 12m 15y		200	57	1c 14m 19y
	133	1490	46c 44m 56y 32k		167	865	15c 4m 14y		201	517	38c 44m 65y 28k
	134	425	35c 6m 59y 2k		168	1481	31c 18m 26y 2k		202	539	37c 29m 72y 18k
	135	1670	60c 17m 25y 8k		169	1095	12c 22m 33y 1k		203	348	21m 65y
	136	1240	9c 17m 14y		170	1449	41c 54m 43y 30k		204	131	35m 52y

color index

Swatch	Code	BM No.	CMYK	Swatch	Code	BM No.	CMYK	Swatch	Code	BM No.	CMYK
	205	412	34c 11m 75y 4k		239	802	70c 9m 19y 2k		273	1553	39c 38m 46y 16k
	206	305	22m 46y		240	1098	19c 44m 62y 9k		274	1677	62c 15m 22y 7k
	207	934	4c 7m 23y		241	929	3c 9m 23y		275	1412	42c 25m 15y 4k
	208	410	18c 4m 47y 1k		242	330	2c 6m 21y		276	1536	28c 24m 32y 4k
	209	1663	56c 12m 22y 4k		243	1000	41c 49m 59y 35k		277	808	49c 8m 14y 1k
	210	378	15c 40m 79y 6k		244	231	32c 49m 73y 30k		278	253	4c 11m 25y
	211	1583	21c 8m 18y		245	369	4c 20m 56y 1k		279	1427	63c 40m 24y 23k
	212	848	21c 1m 16y		246	411	21c 5m 56y 1k		280	1258	21c 44m 76y 13k
	213	1037	12c 17m 24y 1k		247	1555	15c 10m 18y		281	af590	50c 42m 31y 20k
	214	281	3c 7m 21y		248	885	3c 13m 10y		282	215	5c 27m 54y 1k
	215	1594	50c 32m 36y 15k		249	1012	25c 37m 38y 8k		283	360	1c 14m 55y
	216	677	71c 15m 42y 7k		250	1560	42c 35m 45y 16k		284	7	80m 86y
	217	1488	38c 34m 45y 13k		251	1013	31c 47m 49y 18k		285	1312	58m 29y
	218	409	15c 3m 36y		252	1015	33c 56m 57y 32k		286	28	5c 72m 70y 1k
	219	605	53c 33y		253	818	85c 28m 9y 7k		287	34	16c 75m 71y 5k
	220	358	1c 9m 36y		254	15	1c 18m 16y		288	336	26m 89y
	221	512	9c 12m 23y		255	138	38m 49y		289	322	37m 93y
	222	432	37c 19m 59y 9k		256	832	72c 37m 23y 26k		290	1303	30m 18y
	223	365	1c 9m 28y		257	345	1c 9m 28y		291	1233	18c 30m 28y 3k
	224	623	87c 24m 63y 22k		258	47	14c 57m 49y 4k		292	1316	21c 85m 69y 9k
	225	1649	60c 23m 29y 12k		259	125	47m 67y		293	1368	11c 26m 5y
	226	1516	20c 19m 31y 1k		260	419	42c 7m 88y 1k		294	41	18c 68m 64y 7k
	227	36	3c 22m 17y		261	481	32c 23m 47y 6k		295	317	11m 38y
	228	351	1c 8m 30y		262	352	1c 11m 42y		296	199	1c 21m 39y
	229	1518	31c 36m 53y 13k		263	408	13c 2m 33y		297	530	29c 29m 68y 12k
	230	1048	21c 48m 67y 12k		264	516	30c 40m 60y 16k		298	33	5c 67m 57y 1k
	231	1419	54c 26m 9y 4k		265	292	1c 25m 59y		299	1307	8c 84m 76y 1k
	232	431	34c 17m 53y 6k		266	103	4c 50m 55y 1k		300	1326	44m 13y
	233	162	2c 11m 25y		267	663	80c 43y		301	1364	26c 72m 27y 23k
	234	29	2c 18m 16y		268	1396	32c 28m 1y 1k		302	294	6c 46m 84y 1k
	235	326	16m 59y		269	690	52c 18m 37y 9k		303	271	15c 33m 52y 4k
	236	1435	65c 41m 30y 30k		270	1548	13c 10m 17y		304	280	21c 44m 76y 13k
	237	1216	11c 47m 47y 2k		271	526	12c 10m 31y		305	1386	54c 65m 23y 43k
	238	676	56c 5m 31y 1k		272	726	85c 14m 41y 4k		306	1398	51c 49m 3y 2k

Swatch	Code	BM No.	CMYK	Swatch	Code	BM No.	CMYK	Swatch	Code	BM No.	CMYK
	307	797	98c 25m 14y 13k		341	21	69m 75y		375	1424	41c 19m 12y 2k
	308	364	8c 31m 92y 1k		342	361	16m 64y		376	217	13c 48m 80y 4k
	309	1360	6c 24m 7y		343	765	37c 14y		377	1439	44c 25m 19y 5k
	310	68	1c 45m 48y		344	1272	13c 56m 25y 3k		378	900	3c 9m 17y
	311	783	95c 7m 23y 1k		345	228	15c 30m 47y 4k		379	1139	17c 51m 62y 6k
	312	196	18c 53m 79y 9k		346	840	76c 39m 29y 36k		380	1384	41c 43m 16y 9k
	313	77	16c 79m 84y 5k		347	247	7c 16m 30y		381	1566	48c 28m 37y 12k
	314	105	23c 69m 81y 15k		348	321	35m 90y		382	426	39c 9m 66y 3k
	315	396	10c 14m 65y 1k		349	19	51m 49y		383	389	7c 17m 46y 1k
	316	308	1c 50m 91y		350	1375	18c 25m 10y 1k		384	1225	27c 63m 64y 31k
	317	14	1c 74m 73y		351	747	72c 5m 30y 1k		385	542	29c 11m 45y 2k
	318	754	96c 11m 42y 2k		352	309	2c 9m 25y		386	1621	45c 19m 23y 5k
	319	46	6c 45m 35y 1k		353	1399	66c 59m 11y 13k		387	629	62c 23m 59y 24k
	320	831	63c 30m 19y 13k		354	742	98c 23m 53y 14k		388	290	1c 18m 45y
	321	536	22c 11m 41y 1k		355	229	18c 37m 57y 7k		389	238	35c 48m 66y 30k
	322	325	1c 12m 45y		356	1438	36c 19m 15y 2k		390	40	10c 59m 49y 2k
	323	76	4c 71m 77y 1k		357	1445	26c 22m 19y 1k		391	471	25c 12m 28y 1k
	324	1	21m 17y		358	337	1c 7m 27y		392	1301	23c 81m 76y 15k
	325	166	1c 35m 55y		359	1208	16c 52m 54y 5k		393	1257	26c 57m 42y 19k
	326	342	27m 82y		360	1383	35c 36m 15y 6k		394	1441	58c 40m 29y 23k
	327	488	37c 27m 60y 13k		361	461	51c 32m 53y 24k		395	1629	59c 31m 28y 16k
	328	260	3c 10m 25y		362	1470	46c 46m 49y 29k		396	1680	82c 38m 32y 42k
	329	756	97c 26m 47y 24k		363	1218	23c 66m 73y 16k		397	1154	14c 47m 52y 4k
	330	915	3c 11m 21y		364	1194	14c 55m 50y 4k		398	1404	36c 27m 8y 2k
	331	1372	48c 64m 20y 27k		365	437	23c 8m 28y 1k		399	444	37c 15m 38y 4k
	332	327	20m 71y		366	1619	27c 9m 15y		400	1232	37c 60m 58y 42k
	333	1358	39c 64m 46y 43k		367	1616	57c 42m 41y 32k		401	279	11c 40m 77y 3k
	334	1163	5c 18m 18y		368	1131	18c 48m 58y 8k		402	1400	69c 63m 13y 16k
	335	274	2c 14m 35y		369	717	43c 8m 23y 2k		403	475	46c 35m 55y 22k
	336	1391	41c 50m 9y 5k		370	633	45c 10m 35y 4k		404	210	13c 46m 76y 3k
	337	1405	47c 34m 8y 4k		371	1434	60c 34m 26y 17k		405	242	18c 23m 37y 2k
	338	1330	21c 84m 64y 10k		372	168	10c 62m 87y 2k		406	1648	48c 15m 22y 4k
	339	1339	1c 37m 10y		373	269	8c 17m 30y		407	529	21c 21m 54y 4k
	340	406	33c 24m 82y 15k		374	1472	25c 17m 22y 1k		408	804	95c 24m 20y 17k

color index

Swatch	Code	BM No.	CMYK	Swatch	Code	BM No.	CMYK	Swatch	Code	BM No.	CMYK
	409	af405	35c 27m 51y 10k		443	624	20c 1m 19y		477	af355	19c 51m 68y 9k
	410	af705	46c 36m 36y 16k		444	834	32c 3m 13y		478	af270	22c 60m 45y 13k
	411	af550	54c 27m 27y 11k		445	1581	54c 38m 46y 28k		479	af160	31c 50m 53y 22k
	412	af565	66c 47m 37y 45k		446	476	51c 41m 62y 37k		480	af170	42c 55m 57y 42k
	413	af560	61c 43m 41y 36k		447	1666	80c 36m 36y 43k		481	af355	19c 51m 68y 9k
	414	af645	50c 58m 40y 44k		448	494	26c 24m 46y 5k		482	af215	11c 47m 51y 2k
	415	af530	87c 31m 26y 30k		449	416	17c 5m 54y 1k		483	af595	32c 36m 18y 5k
	416	af630	40c 63m 31y 33k		450	421	14c 1m 26y		484	af545	41c 20m 22y 4k
	417	492	15c 13m 28y 1k		451	533	12c 5m 23y		485	af125	22c 41m 49y 9k
	418	1064	23c 56m 77y 20k		452	575	32c 24y		486	af635	43c 49m 33y 22k
	419	836	43c 7m 16y 1k		453	736	37c 18y		487	af155	34c 35m 41y 10k
	420	630	63c 30m 63y 41k		454	397	9c 16m 79y 2k		488	af85	8c 14m 23y
	421	1575	55c 39m 50y 32k		455	241	16c 22m 34y 2k		489	af245	16c 38m 40y 4k
	422	1524	27c 33m 48y 9k		456	239	10c 15m 25y		490	af615	22c 27m 16y 2k
	423	1547	52c 48m 54y 44k		457	423	22c 2m 38y		491	af585	40c 30m 22y 7k
	424	573	67c 8m 72y 2k		458	770	98c 23m 36y 14k		492	af105	31c 41m 54y 16k
	425	527	15c 14m 39y 1k		459	373	3c 10m 29y		493	af640	45c 47m 37y 24k
	426	543	34c 16m 58y 6k		460	980	43c 45m 53y 29k		494	af40	4c 8m 13y
	427	515	25c 31m 48y 7k		461	420	54c 11m 96y 3k		495	af345	9c 30m 50y 2k
	428	546	50c 25m 72y 27k		462	1430	29c 11m 8y 1k		496	af600	40c 41m 23y 11k
	429	679	77c 31m 45y 42k		463	1457	13c 10m 14y		497	af395	31c 30m 42y 8k
	430	225	6c 11m 21y		464	890	5c 6m 12y		498	af475	54c 29m 49y 21k
	431	583	28c 23y		465	868	23c 7m 15y		499	af305	3c 8m 21y
	432	823	59c 20m 13y 5k		466	1001	44c 51m 60y 40k		500	af280	16c 78m 78y 5k
	433	483	40c 36m 64y 23k		467	1510	31c 28m 44y 7k		501	af525	82c 23m 30y 16k
	434	385	21c 38m 81y 12k		468	1403	27c 17m 7y 1k		502	af165	32c 57m 66y 36k
	435	622	76c 13m 59y 5k		469	1591	24c 12m 19y 1k		503	af335	3c 21m 35y
	436	720	74c 26m 38y 25k		470	1221	17c 54m 60y 6k		504	af620	30c 30m 21y 4k
	437	528	16c 16m 43y 1k		471	1421	83c 53m 14y 17k		505	af675	36c 30m 29y 6k
	438	800	49c 2m 13y		472	1428	63c 51m 34y 44k		506	af295	25c 86m 69y 17k
	439	448	60c 38m 56y 41k		473	af330	1c 9m 29y		507	85	2c 12m 18y
	440	825	75c 35m 17y 21k		474	af205	6c 37m 39y 1k		508	477	14c 9m 27y
	441	935	8c 6m 17y		475	af570	47c 27m 22y 7k		509	1224	26c 60m 62y 25k
	442	858	15c 13m 19y		476	af460	45c 31m 49y 16k		510	1267	29c 70m 56y 45k

Swatch	Code	BM No.	CMYK
	511	1275	3c 20m 11y
	512	1369	14c 34m 5y 1k
	513	1264	20c 42m 27y 6k
	514	1426	58c 34m 19y 14k
	515	71	1c 20m 22y
	516	1352	4c 19m 9y
	517	1394	14c 11m 5y
	518	1379	43c 64m 27y 35k
	519	916	1c 15m 26y
	520	246	5c 10m 23y
	521	966	15c 20m 28y 1k
	522	384	20c 36m 73y 10k
	523	9	1c 27m 19y
	524	537	25c 18m 52y 4k
	525	1407	74c 60m 14y 19k
	526	1359	4c 17m 9y
	527	1212	2c 14m 16y
	528	1389	23c 27m 6y 1k
	529	1334	50m 24y
	530	1413	52c 38m 25y 15k
	531	1406	55c 42m 9y 6k
	532	1009	10c 16m 17y
	533	1338	2c 20m 10y
	534	1423	29c 14m 13y 1k
	535	1431	34c 13m 7y 1k
	536	1228	19c 49m 50y 8k
	537	1665	79c 27m 32y 24k
	538	960	10c 9m 16y
	539	1415	20c 8m 6y
	540	978	34c 38m 47y 13k
	541	1512	39c 42m 59y 24k
	542	1463	47c 52m 52y 41k
	543	1385	50c 52m 19y 20k
	544	1443	12c 11m 10y
	545	1093	7c 15m 22y
	546	799	39c 2m 12y
	547	1671	66c 23m 31y 15k
	548	230	26c 42m 64y 15k
	549	1633	31c 8m 18y 1k
	550	1462	48c 42m 42y 24k
	551	1149	4c 15m 21y
	552	1451	20c 14m 16y 1k
	553	696	36c 14m 30y 3k
	554	372	2c 7m 22y
	555	524	30c 35m 62y 14k
	556	441	52c 36m 65y 35k
	557	143	20m 37y
	558	428	7c 4m 25y
	559	522	20c 20m 39y 2k
	560	566	68c 20m 75y 17k
	561	1436	18c 6m 11y
	562	1366	7c 13m 8y
	563	999	37c 46m 53y 24k
	564	813	23c 1m 10y
	565	897	3c 7m 16y
	566	861	24c 23m 27y 2k
	567	236	26c 41m 59y 14k
	568	1235	27c 50m 51y 19k
	569	1388	17c 18m 6y
	570	911	3c 8m 17y
	571	1493	16c 11m 21y
	572	1442	61c 49m 44y 50k
	573	561	26c 3m 31y
	574	1380	13c 16m 7y
	575	375	5c 19m 43y 1k
	576	1141	25c 60m 70y 24k
	577	1244	28c 46m 34y 11k
	578	1401	17c 7m 7y
	579	1227	16c 42m 42y 5k
	580	1294	19c 69m 57y 8k
	581	1302	27c 71m 60y 33k
	582	936	9c 7m 18y
	583	1501	25c 19m 31y 2k
	584	1373	7c 12m 11y
	585	1499	13c 10m 18y
	586	722	35c 19y
	587	439	35c 19m 45y 6k
	588	1281	26c 71m 54y 21k
	589	697	43c 20m 37y 7k
	590	1494	25c 18m 29y 2k
	591	1660	24c 2m 13y
	592	417	25c 6m 68y 1k
	593	1538	39c 38m 47y 16k
	594	1331	2c 18m 11y
	595	1511	34c 36m 51y 14k
	596	1425	48c 24m 16y 5k
	597	806	30c 3m 11y
	598	838	59c 18m 20y 7k
	599	1090	15c 45m 54y 5k
	600	379	6c 10m 27y
	601	1565	41c 20m 29y 5k
	602	1265	27c 57m 39y 19k
	603	550	42c 3m 57y 1k
	604	619	40 1m 27y 1k
	605	554	16c 1m 29y
	606	480	28c 17m 40y 3k
	607	503	32c 31m 60y 12k
	608	127	2c 10m 20y
	609	807	34c 3m 11y
	610	514	18c 20m 35y 2k
	611	792	29c 1m 10y
	612	1634	45c 15m 25y 4k

color index

Swatch	Code	BM No.	CMYK	Swatch	Code	BM No.	CMYK	Swatch	Code	BM No.	CMYK
	613	1507	17c 12m 22y 1k		647	340	17c 62y		681	1217	18c 59m 63y 7k
	614	268	7c 12m 23y		648	1270	5c 36m 11y 1k		682	af540	21c 4m 11y
	615	1576	21c 10m 18y		649	1289	3c 20m 14y		683	1604	23c 12m 17y
	616	1521	16c 15m 23y 1k		650	203	10c 49m 87y 2k		684	272	17c 35m 56y 6k
	617	190	3c 8m 20y		651	154	48m 73y		685	1656	55c 8m 22y 2k
	618	1593	42c 24m 28y 6k		652	1311	38m 13y		686	362	22m 79y
	619	582	21c 1m 17y		653	1065	6c 12m 21y		687	1429	24c 10m 8y
	620	844	9c 3m 11y		654	81	41m 44y		688	1374	11c 18m 11y
	621	884	3c 11m 10y		655	1305	67m 54y		689	1151	8c 15m 22y
	622	584	36c 27y		656	1300	20c 81m 77y 9k		690	1245	33c 54m 47y 25k
	623	541	21c 7m 36y 1k		657	1192	3c 29m 22y 1k		691	1222	19c 58m 62y 9k
	624	220	5c 20m 36y 1k		658	1344	25c 83m 55y 17k		692	1402	22c 13m 7y
	625	718	50c 13m 27y 4k		659	1335	68m 42y		693	1202	17c 69m 64y 6k
	626	99	1c 16m 19y		660	1155	21c 59m 67y 12k		694	1256	14c 46m 29y 3k
	627	452	42c 19m 42y 7k		661	133	55m 77y		695	449	25c 5m 21y
	628	109	1c 39m 47y		662	346	1c 11m 39y		696	453	46c 26m 49y 14k
	629	766	47c 17y		663	27	2c 63m 57y		697	371	10c 31m 85y 2k
	630	1605	32c 17m 23y 2k		664	80	25m 25y		698	273	21c 39m 64y 11k
	631	1545	40c 40m 46y 17k		665	182	5c 50m 79y 1k		699	694	26c 8m 22y 1k
	632	725	71c 7m 32y 2k		666	1230	27c 60m 61y 28k		700	395	10c 8m 51y 1k
	633	1567	52c 32m 42y 19k		667	1223	23c 58m 63y 16k		701	277	6c 26m 57y 1k
	634	1554	43c 47m 56y 31k		668	1279	13c 56m 31y 3k		702	698	47c 21m 41y 10k
	635	af250	3c 15m 14y		669	1308	12c 83m 74y 2k		703	398	11c 22m 87y 3k
	636	603	28c 19y		670	147	51m 77y		704	1620	38c 14m 19y 2k
	637	363	1c 26m 86y		671	41	18c 68m 64y 7k		705	1422	22c 9m 11y
	638	586	64c 2m 52y 1k		672	1128	12c 26m 32y 1k		706	1150	7c 20m 23y
	639	350	1c 37m 90y		673	176	2c 11m 28y		707	1500	19c 15m 25y 1k
	640	65	1c 19m 22y		674	75	1c 56m 59y		708	1618	19c 6m 11y
	641	61	1c 45m 47y		675	380	7c 14m 32y		709	1047	17c 36m 51y 6k
	642	353	1c 16m 59y		676	222	12c 35m 56y 3k		710	216	7c 31m 64y 1k
	643	817	77c 18m 6y 3k		677	250	18c 40m 67y 8k		711	263	11c 21m 41y 1k
	644	42	26c 75m 66y 26k		678	126	3c 60m 79y 1k		712	478	17c 9m 32y 1k
	645	267	4c 8m 19y		679	1329	14c 85m 61y 3k		713	1205	6c 31m 30y 1k
	646	1378	39c 56m 20y 18k		680	1365	35c 69m 36y 40k		714	1211	27c 61m 63y 28k

Swatch	Code	BM No.	CMYK
	715	205	4c 11m 23y
	716	438	28c 13m 34y 2k
	717	391	15c 28m 75y 5k
	718	699	52c 27m 45y 17k
	719	1207	12c 41m 41y 3k
	720	1165	10c 29m 28y 1k
	721	1410	23c 12m 11y
	722	1242	16c 31m 23y 2k
	723	1452	28c 23m 19y 2k
	724	458	30c 11m 26y 1k
	725	142	16m 35y
	726	17	29m 25y
	727	464	22c 10m 23y 1k
	728	69	1c 59m 61y
	729	669	60c 31y
	730	115	1c 21m 32y
	731	940	10c 12m 22y
	732	794	44c 12y
	733	160	35m 59y
	734	544	39c 18m 66y 11k
	735	392	21c 33m 83y 11k
	736	599	60c 40y
	737	1136	5c 22m 26y 1k
	738	390	9c 23m 62y 2k
	739	436	22c 7m 25y
	740	278	8c 32m 71y 1k
	741	1069	14c 37m 48y 4k
	742	446	53c 29m 55y 23k
	743	429	21c 6m 31y
	744	674	38c 1m 22y 1k
	745	243	22c 27m 41y 4k
	746	404	17c 15m 79y 4k
	747	711	58c 16m 34y 8k
	748	165	1c 25m 43y
	749	387	2c 9m 30y
	750	1459	24c 16m 19y 1k
	751	434	51c 29m 77y 35k
	752	304	14m 36y
	753	866	21c 4m 14y
	754	334	16m 61y
	755	487	31c 21m 48y 6k
	756	424	26c 3m 43y 1k
	757	572	54c 3m 59y 1k
	758	556	32c 1m 51y
	759	324	10m 36y
	760	312	20m 50y
	761	299	31m 71y
	762	772	44c 14y
	763	202	3c 38m 69y 1k
	764	26	50m 47y
	765	23	1c 19m 21y
	766	92	1c 13m 19y
	767	208	5c 28m 51y 1k
	768	6	67m 64y
	769	383	15c 31m 60y 5k
	770	191	2c 15m 28y
	771	287	12c 43m 84y 3k
	772	64	1c 17m 19y
	773	3	38m 29y
	774	84	65m 73y
	775	354	21m 74y
	776	307	38m 73y
	777	1070	16c 43m 56y 5k
	778	157	20m 34y
	779	43	3c 21m 16y
	780	183	2c 8m 20y
	781	289	2c 12m 30y
	782	113	2c 11m 22y
	783	316	1c 9m 28y
	784	117	2c 38m 47y
	785	335	20m 74y
	786	291	1c 22m 54y
	787	557	39c 2m 64y 1k
	788	331	1c 8m 30y
	789	743	38c 16y
	790	597	27c 19y
	791	803	82c 16m 20y 6k
	792	600	74c 9m 54y 2k
	793	167	1c 46m 66y
	794	681	31c 3m 22y
	795	370	4c 25m 68y 1k
	796	666	31c 21y
	797	641	57c 12m 42y
	798	774	76c 8m 24y 2k
	799	647	52c 1m 33y
	800	500	22c 15m 36y 1k
	801	778	39c 12y
	802	1111	13c 43m 57y 3k
	803	1601	48c 32m 34y 14k
	804	418	33c 5m 77y 1k
	805	659	31c 20y
	806	427	47c 16m 80y 10k
	807	889	1c 19m 13y
	808	843	24c 2m 18y
	809	1297	1c 50m 30y
	810	399	11c 23m 97y 3k
	811	759	71c 28y
	812	891	3c 8m 14y
	813	873	12c 5m 11y
	814	1450	12c 10m 12y
	815	854	15c 3m 22y
	816	1072	6c 18m 24y

color index

Swatch	Code	BM No.	CMYK	Swatch	Code	BM No.	CMYK
	817	386	3c 7m 25y		851	513	3c 15m 27y 1k
	818	688	35c 9m 24y 1k		852	402	14c 6m 48y 1k
	819	1523	26c 28m 40y 5k		853	727	92c 22m 45y 13k
	820	875	21c 6m 13y		854	38	7c 36m 25y 1k
	821	1667	27c 4m 15y		855	764	29c 1m 12y
	822	388	3c 12m 38y		856	400	9c 5m 32y
	823	1418	39c 14m 8y 1k		857	880	6c 6m 9y
	824	1044	8c 17m 27y		858	967	6c 5m 12y
	825	1226	11c 30m 29y 2k		859	863	17c 8m 17y
	826	257	15c 32m 57y 5k		860	945	11c 13m 24y
	827	549	31c 1m 38y		861	617	23c 1m 19y
	828	1135	3c 14m 19y		862	979	40c 42m 52y 22k
	829	1417	30c 10m 7y 1k		863	621	62c 3m 44y 1k
	830	288	3c 8m 24y		864	545	43c 21m 67y 15k
	831	850	22c 1m 21y		865	773	64c 2m 19y
	832	877	6c 8m 11y		866	776	93c 24m 30y 20k
	833	1502	31c 27m 42y 7k		867	570	36c 1m 38y
	834	1395	22c 19m 3y		868	774	76c 8m 24y 2k
	835	52	4c 33m 26y 1k		869	820	31c 6m 9y
	836	645	27c 1m 20y		870	824	71c 27m 15y 14k
	837	1317	2c 17m 11y				
	838	591	54c 37y				
	839	523	26c 27m 50y 6k				
	840	50	2c 18m 17y				
	841	347	1c 14m 48y				
	842	394	7c 5m 37y				
	843	393	6c 5m 29y				
	844	374	4c 14m 36y				
	845	1261	8c 18m 13y				
	846	1354	6c 38m 6y 1k				
	847	1286	13c 69m 46y 3k				
	848	1597	27c 13m 18y 1k				
	849	402	14c 6m 48y 1k				
	850	468	51c 32m 54y 23k				